LAND-USE PLANNING

Environmental Resource Management Series

Consulting Editor

Donald R. Coates
State University of New York, Binghamton

In the same series:

Soils and the Environment
G. W. Olson

Field Guide to Soils and the Environment
G. W. Olson

Mineral Resources
John A. Wolfe

Geology and Society
Donald R. Coates

LAND-USE PLANNING: FROM GLOBAL TO LOCAL CHALLENGE

Julius Gy. Fabos

A Dowden & Culver book

Chapman and Hall
New York   London

First published in 1985 by
Chapman and Hall
29 West 35th Street, New York NY 10001

Published in Great Britain by
Chapman and Hall Ltd
11 New Fetter Lane, London EC4P 4EE

Printed in the United States of America

ISBN 0 412 25200 7 (cased edition)
ISBN 0 412 25210 4 (paperback edition)

Library of Congress Cataloging in Publication Data

Fabos, Julius Gy.
   Land use planning.
   "A Dowden & Culver book."
   Bibliography: p.
   Includes index.
   1. Land use—Planning. I. Title.
HD108.6.F32   1984   333.73'17   84-12076
ISBN 0-412-25200-7
ISBN 0-412-25210-4 (pbk.)

British Library Cataloguing in Publication Data

Fabos, Julius Gy.
   Land use planning.—(Environmental resource
   management).—(A Dowden & Culver book)
   1. Land use—United States—Planning
   I. Title   II. Series
   333.73'0973   HD205

   ISBN 0-412-25200-7
   ISBN 0-412-25210-4 Pbk

To my wife, Edith

ACKNOWLEDGMENTS

This book, nearly two decades in the making, would never have been written without the help of the agencies, groups and individuals who have given me both the opportunities to practice and help in formulating the ideas it explores. The experiences which have influenced this book can be divided into three categories. First, I have been fortunate enough to serve as a consultant for numerous planning activities ranging from large-scale, multistate projects to site planning and from public to private concerns. Second, I have been lucky to work at the University of Massachusetts with the Metropolitan Landscape Planning (METLAND) group, a stimulating research team which has contributed greatly to my work. This interdisciplinary group not only helped me to perpetuate a strong land-use ethic, but also involved me in significant innovations in land-use planning. Third, I have had the opportunity to test many of these ideas in my teaching through planning studios and through the synthesis of land-use planning trends and activities in planning theory courses.

While working as a consultant to several federal, state, regional, and local agencies, I came to realize that the current land-use planning literature, with its primary focus on local land-use control, fails to present accurately the practice of land-use decision making. The individuals and agencies who especially helped me to expand my views in this area were: Harry Schwartz, a former chief planner of the North Atlantic Regional Water Resource Study coordinated by the United States Corps of Engineers; Robert Ross, Chief Landscape Architect for the United States Department of Agriculture, Forest Service; Bernard Berger, former director of the Water Resources Research Center at the University of Massachusetts; Gerald Patten of the United States Department of Interior, National Park Service; Benjamin Isgur, formerly the State Conservationist of the United States Department of Agriculture, Soil Conservation Service in Massachusetts; several members of the planning staffs of the New England River Basin Commission and the Massachusetts Department of Environmental Management; numerous town planners and officials of the towns and cities of Amherst, Nantucket, Burlington, Greenfield and Springfield in Massachusetts, and Manchester in Connecticut; and Douglas Cox of Commonwealth Scientific and Industrial Research Organization together with planners of the Geelong Region, and the town of Bright in Victoria, Australia.

As a principal partner of Research Planning and Design Associates, Inc., and as a private consultant to real estate developers working on various projects, I have had to deal with those concerns of the private sector which have had an enormous impact on local land-use decisions. The individuals and corporations who have influenced me the most were Mark and Sol Lavitt of Lavitt Enterprises and several members of the Harford Realty Corporation for providing me with numerous land-use planning projects at various scales and locations.

Several of the assessment and computer-assisted planning techniques summarized in this book were developed by members and advisors of the landscape research team (METLAND) I established 14 years ago and have directed to date. The ideas of individual members during the course of the research have influenced my thinking throughout these years, and specific credit has already been given to those whose work appears within this book. Several of them commented on the initial outline and the manuscript, and their suggestions were included. My thanks go to Stephanie Caswell, Carl Carlozzi, Kimball Ferris, John Foster, Dorothy Grannis, Christopher Greene, Meir Gross, William Hendrix, Anthony Jackman, Spencer Joyner, Bruce MacDougall, Paul Shuldiner, Ross Whaley, and individuals who, during the years, have affected my thinking.

The third category of influence came from my teaching. The faculties and students of the Regional Planning and the Landscape Architecture programs at the University of Massachusetts have contributed significantly to my ideas. Several of these people have been acknowledged above. I extend my sincere thanks to the others.

Finally, I wish to acknowledge all those people who provided me with direct help during the writing and production of this book. Donald Coates as editor of this series gave me the impetus for the topic, has commented extensively on each draft, and provided me with continuous encouragement. I received other extensive reviews from Barrie Greenbie and Ervin Zube. Their constructive criticisms were most helpful. Daniel Bucko, Ellin Goetz, and Mark Jacobucci prepared the majority of the graphics, thus substantially improving this book. I wish to express a special note of gratitude to Helen Wise who edited this manuscript. Lastly and most importantly, this book is dedicated to my lovely wife Edith who has been my collaborator in every phase of its development from conception through its numerous drafts. The final responsibility for its content lies with me, but all of the people acknowledged shared in its creation.

CONTENTS

Acknowledgments   vii

List of Figures   xv

List of Tables   xvii

Introduction   xix

PART ONE: PAST AND CURRENT FORCES   1

Chapter 1   LAND-USE PLANNING ISSUES   3
             Land-Use Issues from Local to Global   5
             Common Characteristics of Land-Use Issues   7
             Types of Land-Use Issues   9
                 New Growth-Related Land-Use Issues   9
                 Issues Related to the Maintenance of Stable Population   12
                 Issues Related to Population Decline   13
                 Resource Utilization Related Issues   14
                 Preservation Issues   15
                 Reclamation Issues   16
                 Impact Issues   16
             Conclusions   18

Chapter 2   THE ROLE OF NATURAL SCIENCE IN
             LAND-USE PLANNING   19
             The Scientific Approach   20
             Historical Overview   21
             The State of Science   24
                 Land-Use and Management-Related Environmental Stresses   25
                 — Water and Land-Related Stresses   25

— *Atmospheric Pollution and Its Effects on Climate*   27

— *Human-Caused Stresses on Plants and Animal Life*   33

— *Synergistic Effects of Two or More Stresses*   34

The State of Science for Ecologically Sensitive
Land-Use Planning   34

— *Ecologically Compatible Land-Use Decisions*   34

State of Science for Communitywide Resource
Use and Management   36

State of Science to Measure and Assess Landscape Hazards   38

State of Science of Development Suitability Techniques   39

Conclusions   43

Chapter 3   **THE ROLE OF TECHNOLOGY**   44

Technologies with Incremental Changes   45

Technologies to Satisfy Needs   45

— *Resource Needs*   46

— *Building and Servicing Habitations*   46

Technologies to Mitigate Hazards   47

Technology to Improve Planning   48

Technologies with Contextual Changes   50

New Tools for Land-Use/Landscape Planning   53

Conclusions   56

Chapter 4   **VALUES AND ORGANIZATIONS**   58

Source of Values   59

Environmental/Cultural Sources   60

Science and Technology   61

The Articulators   62

Public Surveys   63

Value Changes in History   63

Origins of Opposing Values   64

Challenges to the Lockean Thesis   65

— *Preservation Movement*   66

— *Public Recreation*   68

— *Amelioration of Scenic Misfits*   68

— *Environmental Planning*   69

Evolution of Organizations   70

The Pyramid Organization   71

A Model for Change   73

Conclusions   76

Chapter 5   THE CULTURAL LANDSCAPE   78
             Monocultural Landscapes   78
             Importance of Diversity   79
             Monocultural Landscapes and Vulnerability   84
             Further Options   86

PART TWO: PLANNERS' RESPONSES   89

Chapter 6   EVOLUTION OF LAND-USE PLANNING   91
             The Changing Role of Land-Use Planners   92
                 Recent Utopians   93
                 Land-Use Planners as Catalysts for Learning and Action   95
             Disciplinary and Professional Planners   97
                 Disciplinary Planners   97
                 Professional Planners   98
             Public Vs. Private Planning   99
             The Planning Process   100
             Types of Planning   102
             Hierarchy of Planning   103

Chapter 7   LAND-USE PLANNING AT THE HIGHEST
             LEVELS OF GOVERNMENT   105
             Land-Use Planning at the Global Level   106
                 The Articulators of Global Issues   106
                 The Role of International Organizations and Institutions   107
                     — Population Growth, Maintenance, and Decline   108
                 Global Resource Utilization   109
                     — The International Preservation Movement   110
                     — International and Global Environmental Impact Issues   110
             Land-Use Planning at the National Level   110
                 Focus on Landscape Utilization   111
                 Focus on Land-Use Controls   114
             State and Multistate Level Land-Use Planning   116
                 Land-Use Policies to Accommodate Growth   116
                 Land-Use Policies Through Control   120
                 Toward Integrated Planning   121
             An Analysis   125

Chapter 8   LAND-USE PLANNING IN METROPOLITAN
             AND RURAL REGIONS   127
    Planning in Metropolitan Areas   128
        Multipurpose Planning   130
        Single-Purpose Planning   135
        The Landscape Approach   137
        The Landscape Approach as Part of Integrated Planning   139
    Rural Planning   143
        Single-Purpose Rural Planning   144
        Multipurpose Rural Planning   146
    An Analysis   148

Chapter 9   LAND-USE PLANNING AT THE LOCAL LEVEL   151
    Innovations in Physical Planning   152
        Physical Planning with a Focus on Needs   152
            — Innovations in Community Planning   153
            — Responses to Urban Decline   156
        Physical Planning with a Focus on Suitability   161
            — Suitability as the Basis of Community Planning   161
            — Suitability Assessment with a Focus on Resource
              Maintenance, Preservation, Resource Utilization,
              and Environmental Impact Issues   163
    Proliferation of Local Land-Use Controls   172
        Land-Use Controls with a Focus on Social Concerns   173
        Land-Use Controls with a Focus on Environmental Concerns   176
        Land-Use Controls with a Focus on Social and
            Environmental Concerns   176
    Moves Toward Integrated Local Land-Use Planning   179
    An Analysis   180

PART THREE: WHAT'S NEXT?   183

Chapter 10   FUTURE PROSPECTS IN LAND-USE PLANNING   185
    Challenge of Change   185
    Prospects on the Horizon   189
        Increased Availability of Research Findings   190
        Shift of Spatial Data from Maps to Electronic Formats   191
        New Tools for Land-Use Planners   192
        Technology Transfer   194

Integrative Approaches in Sight   195
    Interactive Land-Use Suitability Models   195
    New Integrative Procedures and Data Base Management Systems   202
The Future in Capsule   206

Bibliography   209

Index   219

LIST OF FIGURES

Figure   Page

 1. Doxiadis' Projected Ecumenopolis in 2100 A.D. — 10
 2. Benton MacKaye's Regional Approach for Boston Metropolis — 23
 3. Odum's Regional Ecosystem Compartment Model — 24
 4. Base Traffic Noise Levels Derived from Computer Simulation Model — 32
 5. Flood Hazard Assessment for a Portion of Wilmington, Massachusetts — 39
 6. Organic Versus Checkerboard Land-Use Patterns — 49
 7. Landsat 4 Advanced Satellite Image Using Thematic Mapper — 55
 8. Yosemite Valley — 67
 9. The Pyramid Organization — 71
10. The New Corporate Model — 75
11. LOGIN, The Local Government Information Network — 76
12. Natural and Cultural Landscape Continua — 80
13. The Megalopolis (after Gottman) — 81
14. Filarete's "Sforzinda," The Star-Shaped City — 92
15. Survey of a Township Under the Ordinance of 1785 — 112
16. Open Space Plan for the Commonwealth of Massachusetts, 1928 — 117
17. Wisconsin Heritage Trails Proposal — 118
18. The Island of Kauai — 119
19. Megalopolitan Development on Low-Quality Coastal Landscape — 124
20. Expansion of Boston, 1900–60 — 129
21. Boston Park System by Frederick Law Olmsted, Sr. — 131
22. Charles Eliot's Plan of the Boston Metropolitan Park System — 132
23. The Radial Corridor Plan, U.S. National Capital Region — 134
24. Metropolitanization of the Boston Region — 136
25. The Plan for the Valleys — 138
26. A Planning Procedure Illustrating a Landscape Approach — 141
27. Development Capabilities of the Boston Region — 142
28. Zoning Plan of Gros Morne National Park of Canada — 145
29. Connecticut River National Recreation Area — 147

Figure   **Page**

30. General Plan of Radburn   153

31. A Partial Site Plan for Radburn   155

32. Conceptual Plan for the New Town of Columbia, Maryland   156

33. Town Center of Columbia   157

34. Quincy Market in Boston   159

35. An Indoor-Outdoor Scene of Quincy Market in Boston   160

36. Riverside General Plan by Frederick Law Olmsted, Sr.   162

37. A Composite Site Assessment Map for Manchester, Connecticut   164

38. Synthesis of All Land-Use Suitabilities, Amelia Island, Florida   165

39. Composite Special-Value Resource Assessment for Burlington, Massachusetts   166

40. A Combined Composite Landscape Value of Hazards, Special-Value Resources
    and Development Suitability for Burlington, Massachusetts   167

41. Agricultural Productivity Assessment for Greenfield, Massachusetts   169

42. Visual Assessment of Nantucket, Massachusetts   170

43. Landscape Synthesis Map of Nantucket, Massachusetts   171

44. Evaluation of Two Extreme Alternatives   200

45. Proposed Development on the First 3,000 Acres on Areas Where Economic
    Losses for the Community are Minimized   201

46. Proposed Development on Areas Where Losses are Minimized While
    Agricultural Land is Preserved   203

LIST OF TABLES

Table	Page
1. Lyme Index for Water Pollutants	26
2. Water Quality Resource Value Rating for Selected Land Uses	28
3. Annual Space Heating and Process Emission for Selected Land Uses in Massachusetts	29
4. Land-Use Noise Levels	31
5. Ecological Compatibility Ratings	35
6. Source-Receiver Distances	40
7. Estimated Added Development Costs for Physical Factors	42
8. Hypothetical Search for Plan Alternatives	198

INTRODUCTION

Societies make continuous changes in the environment and many of these changes result from some kind of land-use planning. Hence land-use planning can be looked upon as both an all-inclusive process and as a collection of related activities.

During the past two decades, this latter approach has dominated the thinking of land-use planners with the great majority of the land-use planning books written by planners and published in recent years in the United States having focused on one aspect of planning, namely land-use control. Among the representative books on land-use planning which are read more frequently by planners are Fred Bosselman and David Callies's *The Quiet Revolution in Land Use Planning* (1971); Charles Haar's *Land Use Planning: A Casebook on the Use, Misue and Re-Use of Urban Land* (1971); Robert Healy's *Land Use and the States* (1976); and T. William Patterson's *Land Use Planning: Techniques of Implementation* (1979). All these books share a common theme: the description of legal devices used in controlling land uses. Furthermore, the great majority of devices and cases described in these books deal with land-use planning at the local level. Readers of these books may conclude that land-use planning is a highly specialized activity, which involves zoning, subdivision regulations, and other similar controls.

The underlying purpose of this book is to redefine land-use planning by presenting a more comprehensive, and perhaps a more accurate, description of relevant activities in the United States and other countries. Control has been a very important tool in American planning since the beginnings of the profession in the early twentieth century. Control, however, is primarily useful in dealing with those aspects of planning which aim to minimize future uncertainties based on past, often negative, experiences. Yet land-use planning, just like any other type of planning, can and should deal with positive opportunities of many kinds, an approach which calls for a different kind of thinking and often different tools and devices.

There are powerful reasons why control or the use of local regulation devices and state legislation have dominated recent planning literature, perhaps two of which stand out. First was the monumental failure during the 1950s of the physical planners who initiated insensitive, large-scale redevelopment projects in all major cities in the United States. Their work resulted in widespread public outrage well described in Jane Jacobs' classic *The Death and Life of Great American Cities* (1961). Clearly the land-use planners who directed bulldozers to poor neighborhoods to replace them with luxury complexes and towering office structures made unforgettable mistakes. A control-oriented approach inevitably arose to curb their unreasonable and insensitive dreams.

The second reason for the change in focus can be attributed to the large influx in the 1960s into planning of teachers and students from the legal profession and from political science. Hitherto, no one discipline had dominated land-use planning. It is interesting to note the distribution of disciplines and professionals who founded the planning profession during the period 1890–1930. Among the 16 distinguished pioneers whose biographies have been recently published by Donald Krueckeberg in the *American Planner* (1983), five, or about one-third, came into planning from law and political science; five came from physical planning backgrounds, of whom three were landscape architects and two were engineers; two were economists; one came from natural science (forestry); and three came from a liberal education without any disciplinary training.

The work and writing of these pioneers represent a much greater range of land-use planning approaches, procedures, tools, and devices than more recent practitioners with their control-oriented, legal approach. Currently we see a renewed interest not only in the pioneers but in the contribution of other disciplines to land-use planning. For instance, studio instruction is once again on the increase in planning schools (Lang, 1983).

This book is a response to the renaissance in land-use planning and to such other phenomena as the rapid increase in scientific knowledge; unprecedented technological advancements; major societal changes which are modifying the values and perceptions of people; and finally, and equally important, a profound reversal of previous migration patterns into city centers.

THE PLANNERS' CHANGING ROLE

Phenomena such as these provide land-use planners with a set of new opportunities and, perhaps, force them to redefine their role. Part one of this book examines the evolution of such trends and their present day implications, showing how planners, can no longer respond to a single problem with a single-purpose device, but rather with an awareness of a whole set of interrelated factors. The role emerging for the planner is one of a synthesizer of these ever-changing forces, capable of making informed decisions.

In the first place, it is the land-use planner's role to help to define the issues for the short, and especially the long, run. In dealing with long-term issues, such as a potential decline of a development a few decades hence, the planner may be able to pave the way for less costly future change without incurring extra cost for the initial planned use. For example, during the baby boom we built schools and colleges to satisfy rapidly growing demand. As the population growth rate has declined in recent years many schools and colleges have had to be closed. Land-use planners using demographic forecasts could have foreseen such occurrences. Using such information combined with creative thinking, planners could have envisioned a more flexible use, to change a school easily into offices, retirement homes, light industry, or recreational facilities, just to name a few.

In terms of scientific advancement, the planner's role is to interpret the results of rapidly increasing and available knowledge for land-use planning. Advancement in the understanding of ecological principles helps land-use planners to achieve a better "fit" between environment and use. More accurate measurements of pollutants can help in planning strategies to reduce environmental stresses. Scientific knowledge can aid in finding and asssesing critical resources, determining development suitability for any kind of land use, and can even improve planning from data gathering through plan implementation. With scientific knowledge having more than doubled during the past decade, and expected to double again within the next 5 years, planners must search continuously for relevant information.

Technological changes are proving to be similarly rapid and momentous. As society in general has begun to choose to accept certain new technologies, reject others, and accept several with modifications, so land-use planners are making similar choices in those technological areas which clearly affect land-use planning. Technology is also providing planners with tools, such as computer graphic technology, capable of drastically changing the mode of previous land-use planning practices.

In order to deal with changing societal values, planners ought to understand the reasons why the various segments of our pluralistic society hold particular values. In place of the advocacy approach which grew out of the turbulent years of the 1960s, the planner's role is defined in this study more as that of a mediator among the opposing views. By simulating the various consequences of plans based on differing views, planners can aid not only in resolving conflict, but also in selecting more viable options.

With regard to international organizational changes, planners need to understand the contextual changes which have occurred in the United States since the 1950s when the new corporate, horizontal mode of organization started to replace the hierarchical mode. Most planners have, in the past, supported the hierarchical mode, with many advocating increased state and Federal governmental regulation and more power vested in regional agencies, thereby reducing the power of decision making at local levels. Current forces are clearly moving planning in the opposite direction, to less centralized and increasingly more local planning. These positive, welcome, and most helpful changes are described in Chapter 4.

Land-use planning and land management, which was carried out in the past by increasingly hierarchical and centralized organizations, have created the environment in which we live. The results are seemingly endless mono-cultural urbanscapes and monocultural ruralscapes. The question raised in the final chapter of part one is how these monocultural landscapes may affect our economic, social, ecological, and aesthetic well-being.

PLANNERS' RESPONSES TO FORCES

Planning is an activity, an ongoing process. Just as historical forces have been unfolding, so have decision makers' and planners' responses changed accordingly over time. In part two, this fascinating evolution is described together with a discussion of the whole spectrum of land-use planning activities from global concerns to local actions and site planning.

This evolution has already changed the role, the type, and the number of planners. Conflicts between the public and private interest have been sharpened. Recently, a new breed of planners trained in mathematics, operations research, statistics and computer technology, has appeared on the horizon, bringing high technology with its sophisticated modeling techniques into the decision-making arena. Equally important, and reflecting a trend to redistribute decision making in industries and government to lower levels, is the increased interest of planners in local decision making.

An analysis of all the changes indicates that land-use planning of the future will be more localized yet significantly more complex than previous utopian approaches. It also will be able to respond to the larger environmental context. As planners adopt high technology, and become part of an information network, they will be able to evaluate greater numbers of alternatives against many more pertinent criteria than they are able to do today. They also will be able to respond to a greater number of public concerns, and in fact make the planning process more democratic. They also will have the ability to simulate the consequences of actions not only in the context of their primary, local impact, but also their impact on contribution on the region, the state, the nation, and beyond. To illustrate the above forecast, several innovative land-use planning cases at each level of planning are reviewed.

Since the theme of the book encompasses land-use planning from global to local concerns, three chapters focus on current land-use planning activities from the highest levels of government to site planning at the local level. This review shows that during the past two decades, planning in both the United States and other countries has become increasingly creative and innovative, contrary to the impression received from current land-use planning literature with its emphasis on control. It also takes issue with some other writers, who claim that the United States does not have a land-use policy.

The examination in Chapter 7 of land-use planning at the highest levels of government presents a whole range of activities. It also demonstrates clearly that the United States from its very beginnings has had a national land-use policy. This policy has not been accepted as valid by many planners, especially those advocates of control. Before hastening to advocate European techniques, themselves the response to different conditions, it is useful to understand the historical rationale for American land-use policy. The accompanying case studies illustrate the wide range of policy planning activities at the national multistate, and state levels.

In the United States, land-use planning innovations also have been plentiful at the substate level, namely in metropolitan area type planning and rural planning. While land-use controls once again have been very important in planning at this level, a closer examination of such land-use planning activities clearly reveals a great diversity in approaches and the involvement of many disciplinary planners, ranging from landscape architects to policy planners. Land-use planning at the local level has been clearly dominated by local land-use controls. This is the reason why, perhaps, the land-use planning literature is saturated with the description of legal devices. To redress the balance, in Chapter 9, several very important innovations in physical planning are described.

While land-use planners can learn much from recent and current planning, it is always fascinating to speculate about the near future. This speculation is especially fascinating at this particular time because never before has a society been exposed to such numerous and significant changes. Yet at the same time, and for the same reason, forecasting the future is more difficult. Thus part three of this book attempts to describe the future more in terms of the trends which have had the most profound impact on recent planning.

PART ONE
PAST AND CURRENT FORCES

CHAPTER 1

LAND-USE PLANNING ISSUES

From the planners' perspective, a land-use planning issue represents a point in question on a matter that is in dispute. It therefore follows that if no problem exists, there is no need for planning. Conversely, the necessity for planning arises from the "problems" raised by planning issues. However, a creative planner may see an opportunity or opportunities in every supposed problem. The next logical consideration seems to be the nature or origin of land-use issues. Where can one discover land-use planning issues? Does one go to find them in planning school, read books on land-use planning, or review public documents? Probably these are all good sources for land-use planning issues, but such issues may be even closer to us than we at first suspect.

We have only to consider some of the current events with which we are bombarded in the United States and elsewhere by news media almost every day. Thousands of Mexican people illegally enter the Southwest United States each year. This new population needs to be housed and serviced. Chrysler Corporation has been bailed out twice from bankruptcy by the Federal government. In spite of this, some experts forecast major and continuous decline of the U.S. auto industry. The Federal government has preserved in Alaska another 100 million acres, an area some twenty times larger than the Commonwealth of Massachusetts. This legislation is at the same time pleasing to conservationists and infuriating to industrialists who are claiming that they have lost access to potentially rich mineral and energy resources. New Jersey, Delaware, and parts of New York State and Pennsylvania have reported major water shortages and have instituted emergency measures to deal with the shortages. Residents of the Love Canal area of Niagara Falls have become fearful of serious effects on their health from the dumping of hazardous waste on the site of their homes during the Second World War. This tragic controversy has raised hazardous waste to the level of a national land-use issue almost overnight.

The examples just given may appear to be current, but they also have been continual problems to land-use planners for decades and some of them for centuries. For instance, immigration, both legal and illegal, has been with us since the Pilgrim Fathers arrived at Plymouth Rock. The land-use implication of declining industries has been a problem in the United States at least since the turn of the century, which marked the start of out-migration from some industrial regions, especially the Northeast United States. The bailing out of sunset industries such as the auto industry by public subsidies has been questioned by economists and public representatives. Preservation of highly valued land in the United States dates back to 1864, when the spectacular Yosemite Valley and Mariposa Big Tree Groves, with gorgeous and monumental redwoods, were placed permanently under public ownership. A water shortage problem also has been with us since population began to concentrate in urban areas. Hazardous waste also has been a problem ever since the start of the Industrial Revolution. Its importance was not understood, however, by most land-use planners until the Love Canal controversy raised the hazardous waste issue to the "threshold" level. Hazardous waste now has become another land-use planning issue in every region of the United States. In 1980, Federal legislators started to draft legislation to deal with this problem, and no doubt it will soon become an issue for planners around the globe.

The preceding observations form the thesis of this chapter. Indeed, they show that land-use planning issues are highly complex and demand the expertise of many disciplines. Some of the examples already discussed, such as immigration, do not appear to be land-use issues at first consideration. But with a little effort one can discover, for example, the enormous land-use implication of housing and servicing large new populations in such places as California. These issues also imply that land-use planning is not limited to localities or regions, but often has national or even global implications.

To understand land-use issues more fully, three propositions are put forward in this chapter. First, land-use planners should plan land-use conversion and land-use changes at all levels ranging from global to site level. If issues are occurring at all levels, planning solutions to deal with those issues should follow suit. Secondly, land-use issues have some characteristics in common, regardless of their scope. Thirdly, land-use issues constitute many kinds or types. Consequently, each of the different types of issues may warrant specialized knowledge and specific approaches. In the remainder of this chapter, each of these propositions is discussed in greater detail.

LAND-USE ISSUES FROM LOCAL TO GLOBAL

What makes one land-use issue merely local and others regional, national, or global? Why, for instance, in most American communities are subdivision regulations local issues, while water pollution is handled by the Federal government? The answers to these questions are many and highly complex. Three factors, however, seem to be most important in determining the level at which a land-use issue is addressed. Of primary significance is the number of people and the locality or localities a land-use issue may affect. Second is the magnitude or the potential cumulative effects which may result from a land-use issue. Third is the threshold effect, which can create a national or international issue from a local event.

Often the *significance of* any land-use issue in terms of its potential effects on numbers of people may be immeasurable in objective terms. For instance, we know precisely how many people would lose their jobs and in what localities if Chrysler Corporation was to close down, but many secondary impacts, such as the effects on the national economy and local business, are highly speculative. In the case of Chrysler, experts do not agree as to whether it deserves national assistance or not. The Carter administration obviously considered it a national issue. In the case of entry into the United States by legal and illegal immigrants from Mexico, both countries have held the opinion for years that the problem requires attention at the highest levels of their respective governments. Traditionally decisions on national parks have been made by the Federal government with the awareness that although not every American will visit each national park, by placing such unique and spectacular landscapes as Yosemite Valley or parts of Alaska in permanent preservation, all Americans will have an opportunity to benefit from them if they so desire. Hence, national parks are perceived as nationally significant.

Land-use issues found to be significant at national or international levels are never solely the concern of the Federal government. Indeed, all such issues are pertinent at the state, regional, and local levels. Mexican immigration, for instance, will affect the land-use policies of California and will result in many site-specific decisions within many communities in both the public and private sectors.

The *magnitude*, or the potential *cumulative effects* of land-use activities is another factor in determining the level at which a land-use issue must be handled. Issues relating to water supply and water quality provide good examples. Water supply in a sparsely populated area is, most often, a local issue. However, over a period of time, as population grows demand for water increases. In areas such as the North Atlantic Megalopolis development has spread over 60,000 square miles with high concentration in and around cities.

By the late nineteenth century, Charles Eliot, a well-known landscape architect, warned city officials in Boston that they should secure at least a river basin for water supply for the growing metropolitan population (Newton, 1971, p. 324). The decision makers, however, did not perceive the significance of this need until the 1920s, when they were forced to seek a remedy in Western Massachusetts in the impoundment of the Quabbin Reservoir, some 80 miles (130 kilometers) from Boston to satisfy the water supply needs of the region (Fabos, 1979, p, 86). Ever since the late 1930s, the Boston metropolitan region has been receiving the majority of its water supply from Quabbin. Population growth and increased per capita use have spurred demands for increasing the water supply. Periods of drought highlight this problem.

Similarly, the magnitude of water pollution problems has increased in industrial regions in the United States and all over the world since the beginning of industrialization. When few industries and municipalities disposed of small amounts of waste in rivers it was possible to obtain drinking water from the same river. As populations increased upstream, pollutants accumulated with increased concentrations carried downstream. By the mid-1960s, the Johnson administration perceived water pollution as a national disaster. In response to these concerns, the Federal government has addressed both water supply and quality issues at the national, regional, and local levels. On water clean-up alone, the U.S. Federal government spent 150 billion dollars during the 1970s. Some planners claim that the water clean-up has been the single most expensive public work to date. In comparing it with the construction of the U.S. interstate highway system, it has been 50 percent more costly.

Finally, the effects of land use may reach a *threshold* which often triggers an awareness of related issues. This phenomenon is very similar to the water supply and quality issues already discussed. Prior to threshold events, the effects of certain land uses became apparent rather slowly. Although planners or decision makers may recognize the potential seriousness of certain problems, "threshold" occurs when the effects are dramatically emphasized by catastrophic events of one kind or another. One local event may give the impetus for regional, national, or even global concern.

The history of land-use planning is filled with threshold events. Most flood protection devices such as flood walls and levees are built soon after flood disasters. In the case of air pollution, the incrementally accumulating levels of pollutants in the air over London in the winter of 1952 contributed to one of the most disastrous episodes of smog, to which approximately 4,000 deaths were attributed (Stern, 1973, pp. 127–137). A current example of a threshold event is the Love Canal area controversy in Niagara Falls, New York, which triggered a new awareness of the long-term problems of hazardous waste as a major land-use issue. Indeed, it became a national concern overnight.

In summary, these three factors seem to be the major determinants of the levels at which land-use issues are perceived. When the effects of land uses impinge on other areas and when their significance and magnitudes are greater, land-use issues necessitate solutions at a higher, rather than the local level of planning.

COMMON CHARACTERISTICS OF LAND-USE ISSUES

Land-use issues may be local or regional, simple or complex, yet they all have common characteristics. Four are discussed here, namely: all land-use issues present or generate one or more uncertainties; each can be perceived as both a problem and an opportunity; all land-use issues have a supply and a demand aspect; and finally, all issues can be dealt with in one of two ways, either systematically or conceptually. These four characteristics are discussed to provide the reader with some fundamental understanding of the planning process, which is discussed in greater detail in the second section.

The reason why land-use issues are articulated is because someone perceives some future uncertainty. The *raison d'etre* of any government and many institutions is to help to make our future more certain or, in other words, to decrease any possible uncertainties. When we buy auto, life, or health insurance or when the government establishes national parks or builds dikes and levees for flood control, these are all designed to make the future more certain or minimize possible uncertainties by these actions. This human need for greater certainty provides the compelling reason for all planning, regardless of whether it responds to a land-use, economic, or social issue.

Each land-use issue can be perceived as both a problem and an opportunity. The word "issue" does not carry the negative connotations of the word "problem." This distinction is essential, especially because the majority of contemporary planners perceive land-use issues primarily as problems. That mentality helps to limit the scope of planning. Planners who perceive issues only as problems tend to be more control-oriented, and more likely to become the creators of regulations and increased bureaucracy. On the other hand, planners who look on an issue not only as a problem but also as an opportunity are more likely to offer a creative approach in dealing with it. I cannot think of any land-use issue which would not present some opportunity, even if the issue is as problematic as the failure of the Chrysler Corporation. Clearly there are infinite numbers of other potential uses for its huge industrial complexes. The people who would be dismissed could be retrained to do a great variety of other work. In fact, land-use planning history is filled with case studies which testify to the success of creative approaches to the attitude which links problems with opportunities, ranging from converting San Francisco's cannery to creating a viable shopping center to using a former granite mining pit as a swimming lake on Vinal Haven Island in Maine.

Land-use planning issues have another common characteristic: each has a supply and demand aspect. Analogous to economic issues but in place of dollars, the supply side of a land-use issue is the natural and cultural resource base. The most common issue is *how* and to *what degree* one modifies the existing natural and cultural resources by solving a problem or by achieving any number of human objectives, which are the *demand* on the natural/cultural resource base. It is essential that land-use planners understand this characteristic. Without such comprehension of land-use issues, a planner may have a very limited approach. For example, transportation planners in the greater Boston area during the 1960s ignored the natural resource base of the expanding northern metropolitan region of Boston by building two six-lane belt ways only 10 miles apart, and thus creating enormous growth pressures on the area in between. The planners assumed that 80 percent of the area was developable. However, about 40 percent of this region was wetland, hardly suitable for development (Boyce, Day, and McDonald, 1970, p. 199; Fabos, 1973, Chapter II). Yet, wetlands are just one of several natural constraints which limit the development options of a region. If in this instance the supply aspect had been considered, the erroneous assumption that 80 percent of the region in question was developable would not have been made.

Finally, all land-use issues can be dealt with in one of two ways, either systematically or conceptually. The application of a systematic approach often requires larger amounts of data, and an analysis and assessment of a great many factors or parameters. The process can result in an infinite number of alternatives, which are then evaluated against a well-developed set of criteria. The conceptual approach is often based on intuition and only some of the seemingly significant factors. A planner, who is often a visionary person, may consider only a few options and select a plan by using personal judgment. It is useful to understand at the outset that these two possible approaches do exist. Without this understanding, a planner may select an unnecessary, overly complex, highly systematic approach for a simple problem, which could be solved easily by a creative planner using a conceptual approach. Land-use planners are guilty of increasing planning complexity unnecessarily, especially because the data manipulation capability of computers provides contemporary planners with a great temptation to apply increasingly complex problem-solving approaches to simple problems.

TYPES OF LAND-USE ISSUES

Land-use issues, like social, political, and economic questions, are varied yet interrelated. In the previous section the common characteristics of land-use issues are discussed; in this section the differences are highlighted. The reason for classifying land-use issues into different types is to indicate the need for specialized knowledge and disciplinary input. A land-use planner can be a generalist, just like a family doctor, who is a general practitioner. A land-use planner who is a generalist may perform well regardless of the type of land-use issue. There is, however, a need for highly specialized knowledge or expertise to deal with the great majority of land-use issues.

To illustrate the range of land-use issues, seven types are discussed here. These issues are: (1) new growth-related; (2) planning for maintenance of stable populations; (3) decline-related; (4) resource exploitation/utilization; (5) preservation; (6) reclamation; and (7) environmental, economic, and social impact related. Without discussing these types in detail, one can already make some inferences. For example, it is obvious that all new growth will have some environmental, economic, and social impacts, thus types (1) and (7) are interrelated. But this also implies that a new growth-related issue may require a different set of planning tasks from a preservation planning or reclamation project. To illuminate the differences, each of these seven types are further discussed.

New Growth-Related Land-Use Issues

Of the seven types of land-use issues identified, probably the new growth-related issue is the greatest concern to land-use planners. Affluence resulting from the Industrial Revolution during the 19th century (Galbraith, 1958), but more especially increased food production combined with better medical care, created a population explosion. While this unprecedented growth has subsided in the developed countries in recent years, *The Global 2000 Report to the President of the U.S.* (Barney, 1980) forecast growth of the world population from 4 billion in 1975 to 6.35 billion in 2000, an increase of more than 50 percent. The Greek urban theorist Constantine Doxiadis predicted some years ago that within a hundred years the total population of the earth would be in the order of 20 to 30 billion (Doxiadis, 1966). He predicted that by then the expanding megalopolitan regions such as the North Atlantic Region of the United States will be the dominating growth pattern and that they will all be interconnected in total universal settlement, or what he calls an ecumenic city or ecumenopolis. (The spatial configuration of this prediction can be seen in Figure 1.)

Translating population growth into land conversion at the national level, the United States alone has developed about three million acres of rural land per year since the 1950s. Most development in the first 25 years after the Second World War occurred around large cities. However, since the 1970s, the growth in metropolitan area development has been less uniform. The 1980 census report on population trends in metropolitan areas revealed that half of the 40 largest metropolitan areas had either lost population or their growth was insignificant. The census also found significant growth in many small rural communities, far from metropolitan areas. Analysts speculate that people started to move away from metropolitan regions for a variety of reasons, including a decrease in job opportunities and a desire to live in a safer and healthier environment. This new population trend has modified the new growth-related land-use issues by decreasing earlier pressures in at least half of the major metropolitan regions. However, one-third of the 40 largest regions still grew between 23 and 62 percent over the decade 1970–80. Growth pressure may decrease or change its location, but it will continue to be an issue until zero population growth replaces present trends.

New growth-related land-use issues at the global and national levels are the concern of governments and the United Nations and its numerous

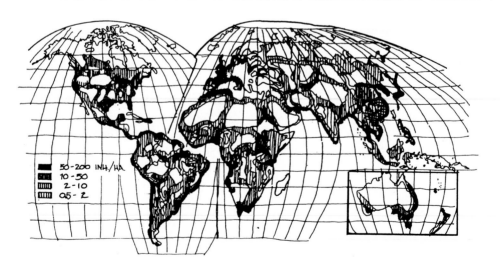

FIGURE 1 *Ecumenopolis in 2100 A. D. (C.O.F. Research Project, Athens Center of Ekistics).*

agencies. At the metropolitan and local levels, the land conversion or development issues are handled by both the public and the private sector. The
most fundamental land-use planning issue is to determine a growth policy,
that is: the degree to which the government should control the new growth.
The second order of issues that land-use planners face is the determination of
the changes in land uses. These include at least four concerns: first, how to
find the right land-use fit between the natural and cultural requirements. For
example, should we develop highly productive agricultural land or should we
instead channel developments away from such a valuable national resource?
In regard to cultural requirements, the land-use fit issue may take the form
of a concern for providing new commercial areas to service the new population. The choices for land-use planners may range from the possibility of
increase in the commercial uses in existing areas to the building of new
shopping centers.

Secondly, the land-use planner must be concerned about the interrela-
tionship of housing, commercial, industrial, and recreational uses. The
separation of uses started during the baroque era, when residential areas were
first set off from other uses. The evolution of land-use separation is
described eloquently by the historian Lewis Mumford (1961, p. 344) and the
adoption of the baroque practice of use separation is superbly illustrated by
Sigfried Giedion (1967, p. 147), citing the examples of the Circus and Royal
Crescent, those elegant 17th-century residential developments in Bath,
England. As safety and health-related problems increased during the Industrial Revolution, so did the concern for zoning. Starting in New York City
during the early part of this century, zoning rapidly became a land-use issue
all over America (Toll, 1969). In recent years, many planners believe that we
have zoned too extensively, and that in light of increased energy costs, the
working, living, shopping, and recreational environments need to be in closer
proximity to each other. Some planners are even advocating increasingly
mixed uses.

Thirdly, the land-use density is a significant concern of planners. Questions raised involve density limits and how they affect privacy. Other concerns relate to cost and flexibility. Higher densities require the construction
of more masonry materials, such as building from concrete and brick instead
of wood and thus involve higher costs and less flexibility. But the infrastructure — the roads, water/sewer lines and so on — needed to service higher
density areas is less extensive than in dispersed suburbs.

Finally, the flow of movement from one use to another and the volume
of the flow are significant issues. The movement of people, vehicles, and
supplies on the surface and underground are all complex land-use planning
issues. The issue of what constitutes an ideal size for a city or community
has often been debated by planners. At the turn of the century, many

advocated a limit to growth. Ebenezer Howard, for instance, believed that the size of a community should not exceed 30,000 (Howard, 1965).

Issues Related to the Maintenance of Stable Population

Will land-use issues disappear at zero population growth? The answer is that they may decrease but certainly they will not disappear. Planners face at least four common land-use issues in an area of stable population. Land uses continue to change at zero or even at negative growth. For example, industries may require new facilities in order to adapt to new technology and transportation, while old industrial buildings may be recycled for other uses. The nature of industry also can change. For example, the industrial base of the Boston metropolitan region has undergone significant changes since the Second World War. The shift of industry toward high technology has continued throughout the 1970s, a decade when growth was close to zero.

Secondly, conversion of land from rural to urban use in areas of no growth also occurs when demand for larger houses or more or new services increases. For example, when people's income or standard of living increases, demand for more space also increases. Changing lifestyles likewise contribute to new forms of development. From the 1960s onward a change from family-sized households to a greater number of individual householders has increased demands for various types of multifamily housing. This phenomenon is a very significant agent for change. While the U.S. population is expected to grow only 10 to 15 million over the decade, between 30 and 40 million people are expected to require new housing. The new lifestyle is a major contributor to this demand.

The third land-use issue in areas of stable population is the development of the natural resource base needed to maintain the existing population. This includes energy, food, water, or any other resource essential to the continuous functioning of a community. For example, since oil prices started to rise at the time of the first Arab oil embargo in 1973, the use of fuel wood has increased from an insignificant amount of 2K wood use during the 1960s, to one million cords per annum in Massachusetts by the late 1970s. If this demand for wood were increased to 3 to 4 million cords, it would significantly affect land-use patterns throughout the entire state. Similarly, in response to increased energy costs, food production has increased in New England during the same period. The extended use of those two natural resources could change the forest covered landscape of Massachusetts to a more open landscape.

Finally, the waste disposal issue is a continual concern in any area of concentrated population. It remains an issue with or without new growth.

The most ubiquitous by-products of urban areas are solid and liquid wastes. Both require large areas for disposal. Another waste product takes the form of gaseous atmospheric pollutants. These, too, often affect land-use planning. The fourth by-product of population concentration is visual degradation. For example, outdoor advertising or deterioration of various kinds both affect the visual quality of our environment.

Issues Related to Population Decline

Just as the medical profession is frequently concerned with treating the dying, so are land-use planners confronted with declining cities or regions. Population decline is often a regional phenomenon. Prominent examples come readily to mind. The decay of mining and heavy industry in South Wales has changed the land uses of an entire region. Redevelopment efforts in U.S. city centers in the 1950s attempted to arrest their rapid degeneration. Rural migration to the prairies of the Midwest in the nineteenth century left hundreds of northeastern communities without an economic base. On an even smaller scale, colleges have been going bankrupt since the mid 1970s as the college-age population has declined.

The land-use issues created by decline are evident. They include strategies for slowing down the inevitable process of decline and for finding new uses for the abandoned structures both to decrease financial losses and to provide job opportunities for the remaining population. Planning for decline does not have to be a negative exercise, however. Indeed, a creative planner can find infinite numbers of opportunities, especially when the problems are analyzed in the larger context. For example, a declining farm or farming town in a New England setting could very well provide opportunities for recreation farming for urbanites who have been removed from such experiences for generations. The surrounding larger landscape may provide such people with several additional recreational amenities.

Population decline has often been the consequence of external forces. The declining communities, regions, or sometimes even nations, have been helpless to mitigate these forces. This pattern will continue and probably intensify in developed countries, where population growth has slowed significantly. There are powerful reasons for advocating zero population growth and in some cases even population reduction. If present population trends continue, the world is expected to be "more crowded, more polluted, less stable ecologically, and more vulnerable to disruption than the world we live in now. Serious stresses involving population resources and environment are clearly visible ahead," wrote Gerald Barney in *The Global 2000 Report to the President of the U.S.* (1980, p. 1).

China, the most populous nation in the world, has taken steps in recent years to reverse her population trend, not only by slowing population growth but also through formulating a national policy to reduce her population of one billion to some 700 million within the next half century or so. The land area of China is slightly smaller than that of the United States but has to support almost five times the population. Chinese leaders share Barney's opinion and decided to do something about the problem at the national level. In light of these developments, issues related to population decline may become widespread during the decades ahead.

Resource Utilization Related Issues

The exploitation of natural resources has been among the most heated issues in decades. The construction of the Alaskan pipeline, for instance, was stalled by environmentalists for over a decade. Without the 1973 oil embargo or similar drastic events, the debate would have continued for many years. The large-scale deforestation and farming of the huge jungles of the Amazon river basin in Brazil have increased siltation and flooding and threatened air and water quality. The potential exploitation of oil shale and coal resources in such western states as Colorado, Utah, Wyoming, and Montana has stimulated consideration of other monumental land-use issues. Water is a potential problem in an area deficient in supplies to meet the demands of generating energy, mining, and transportation. The disposal of the overburden from mining operations and processed oil shale presents another enormous problem.

According to experts, the water resource issue is expected to parallel the energy issue in significance during the decades ahead. For land-use planners, water use has been a vital land-use issue for decades. The water use of the Colorado River, for instance, has been contested by a half dozen western states for almost a century. The Colorado River has been the major lifeline for millions of people. Agricultural products of this region are vital to the national supply. Similar issues, though lesser in magnitude, present themselves even in the water rich eastern United States. The manmade Quabbin reservoir in Western Massachusetts was built during the 1930s to provide water for Boston, located 80 miles to the east. By the 1970s, the Quabbin had reached its limits. Alternatives to augment the reservoir by lifting water from the nearby Connecticut and Millers Rivers have been debated. Regardless of what alternatives are adopted, they will affect not only land use in Western Massachusetts, but also downstream in Connecticut where water already diverted to the east will not be available.

Resource utilization is not only a regional but often also a local issue. Local water supply, sand, and gravel, trap rock and other so-called renewable and nonrenewable resources present both problems and opportunities for land-use planners. The nature of these resource issues is very different from the other land-use issues discussed earlier.

Preservation Issues

Preservation in terms of land-use planning refers to making something last or maintaining it as is. Indeed, preservation is just as important a land-use decision as development. Preservation decisions can be classified into two basic types, the first being the preservation of nature. The preservation of game for hunting, for instance, can be traced back many centuries. But the current meaning of preservation of *nature* is different. This phenomenon of preservation started in the United States with the national park movement. The preservation of unique scenes of superlative quality and areas of scientific value was initiated by visionary planners such as Frederick Law Olmsted during the nineteenth century. Olmsted and his contemporaries believed that the monumental beauty of American virgin lands...[should be] preserved from human desecration (Fabos, Milde, and Weinmayr, 1968, p. 42). Since the 1870s, the United States government has followed suit, preserving many of the nation's unique landscapes (Ise, 1967). The preservation of over 100 million acres of Alaska's spectacular landscape is the most recent addition to the National Park system, while proposals for other areas in the United States and other countries around the world are many.

Preservation of natural areas has also been a concern at the local level. For example, the preservation of local wetlands in New England has been a "promising citizen response to the problem of landscape change and environmental deterioration" which gave the impetus for wetland legislation and the establishment of conservation commissions from 1957 on (Scheffey, 1969). This movement has spread throughout the United States, initiating local preservation not only of wetlands, but also of scenic rivers, roads, and other unique areas.

The second type of preservation issue deals with our cultural heritage. It includes historical sites such as battlefields, trails, and structures. Their significance may be national, statewide, or local. Preservation of cultural areas often raises two land-use concerns. One is the conservation of the site or the structure itself. The second is how to treat the surrounding areas, since historical sites are usually part of a built-up or populated area. For instance, what is the effect of a conventional Mobil gas station next to the birthplace of a president? In other words the compatibility of the neighboring land uses and their effect on the cultural heritage is an added consideration.

Reclamation Issues

In the past, reclamation was most often defined in planning terms as an act to change a previously useless area such as a wetland into productive land. The current meaning of the term reclamation emphasizes some sort of correction or change of a land use from an undesirable or less desirable to a more desirable or appropriate one. The interpretations of what constitutes desirable or appropriate are broad, and land-use planners will surely struggle to better define them in the future.

Land-use planners are primarily concerned with two types of reclamation issues. The first type stresses correction and is based on the premise that certain "incorrect" land uses or land-management practices must be changed in order to make the area more useful. Reclamation work at Boston's Revere Beach was one of the early expressions of this concern. Charles Eliot, its planner, convinced Boston's Trustees of Public Reservations during the 1890s to acquire this valuable beach, which was already built up with a row of private cottages. He proposed to change it into a major public recreational area, perceiving that it was too valuable and important a resource so close to Boston to be used only by relatively few people (Newton, 1971, p. 327). Probably the most common reclamation issue has been found in central commercial areas of cities and towns, where the incremental growth of the automobile has made hazardous and unpleasant conditions for shoppers. This issue gave impetus to the creation of pedestrian malls through the closing off of parts of streets in central business districts.

The second type of reclamation issue is the result of inevitable resource uses, such as surface mining. Mining activities, while essential, can destroy or impair the original surface of large landscapes. The question is: what other uses, if any, can be allocated to such areas? These issues are ideally considered together with resource utilization issues.

Impact Issues

For a long time many land-use planners attempted to avoid impact issues. The decade of the 1960s, however, illuminated these issues so much that environmental, social, and economic impacts have often become the central issues for much land-use planning. This trend is hardly unexpected since each of the previous six types of land-use issues does generate some kinds of impact both positive and negative. By separating the impact-related issues from the others, land-use planners are now able to ask the more specific questions which are needed before specific answers can be obtained.

There are at least two basic ways in which land-use planners can deal with impacts. One is a response to impacts which have been generated by one of the six types of land-use planning discussed above. Another way is to try to prevent potential impacts by estimating or forecasting the consequences which would result from any land-use decision.

Until recently, the first approach has dominated land-use planning. Concerns for potential impacts were limited or nonexistent. The results of such planning have often been dramatic and harmful to people, property, and the environment. For example, flood walls, dikes, and levees have often been erected after floods have destroyed property and even killed people. The social, economic, and environmental impacts of flooding can be enormous. It is estimated that the annual losses to property alone from floods rose to nearly $2 billion by the 1970s in the United States — even though over $9 billion had been spent since 1936 on public works aimed at controlling floodwaters (Fabos, 1979). Most of the flood hazards have resulted from development of flood plains, that is, from earlier land-use decisions. Similarly, air pollution, noise pollution, and large-scale erosion of soils are among the many disruptive impacts on people and the environment.

Past disasters have provided ample studies for land-use planners. They also have given the impetus for preventive planning through proper use of the land. The objective of contemporary land-use planners is to find ways to reduce or eliminate potentially negative impacts by sensible land-use decisions. The question remains as to whether land-use planning can achieve this objective. Such threats of disruption to existing communities as floods, noise, and air pollution can certainly be reduced if not eliminated by land-use planning.

Nevertheless, however extensive an impact assessment is carried out prior to the making of land-use decisions, two issues will provide enormous challenges to planners in the future. The first is the synergistic impact of several factors to produce a significantly greater hazard than the combined effects estimated by planners. For example, the possibility of a flood may be greatly reduced by not building on flood plains. However, the combined effects of development above the existing flood levels and large-scale deforestation for firewood may extend the existing flood plains further than it is possible to predict with current methods.

The second issue deals with situations for which land-use planners do not have a solution: for example, car accidents, potential hazards from nuclear power generators, or dangerous accumulations of carbon dioxide from the burning of coal. Regardless of how well land-use planners respond to these issues, the risk of accidents or hazards cannot be eliminated. The issue thus remains: how much risk are we, the society at large, willing to take by driving cars, building nuclear power plants or burning coal?

CONCLUSIONS

Land-use planning issues are many and extremely complex, ranging from global to local levels. While they exhibit some common characteristics, there are greater differences than similarities among the seven types discussed in this chapter. Furthermore, it has been shown that the number of land-use planning issues has increased over time, and that they have emerged from three sources. First, greater scientific knowledge has illuminated certain consequences of land uses. For example, our ability to measure water pollutants and their consequences on human, animal, and plant life has made water quality a significant and ubiquitous issue. Secondly, numerous references have been made to the role of technology. Indeed, land-use planning has frequently relied on technological devices ranging from flood walls, a protective device, to solar panels, which can provide a new energy source. Thirdly, the values of society as a whole and of its individual members have also greatly stimulated the proliferation of land-use planning issues. Articulators of environmental and social problems, such as the Love Canal hazardous waste issue, can significantly affect our perception. They can be powerful influences in creating new land-use issues.

These three forces will continue to be dominant in the future, most likely creating in their turn additional land-use issues. In short, the role of scientists, the inventors of new technologies, the public at large, and special interest groups will continue. These factors collectively have changed the role of the land-use planner from a problem solver to a catalyst, or a facilitator. The challenge for present day and future land-use planners is to incorporate these three factors — the scientific and technological knowledge and the values of the public — in the planning process. The major task confronting the planner is to help in sorting out the pros and cons of land-use issues by illuminating the possible consequences and articulating a vision of the future which is beyond the imaginative capacity of the average person.

To give a better understanding of the three forces, each of them is examined in greater detail in the following three chapters. Land-use planners need to understand these forces fully to become effective and useful.

CHAPTER 2

THE ROLE OF NATURAL SCIENCE
IN LAND-USE PLANNING

Natural science is a fundamental source for an understanding of our environment, which is modified continuously by land-use activities. However, the utility of natural science for planning is of very recent origin. Most helpful scientific knowledge accrued only during this century. Before the rise of empirical science, human intuition, incidental knowledge gained by observation, and various myths guided land-use decisions. During recent decades, advances in natural science have been enormous. While they have begun to influence land-use decisions, most findings in natural science have not yet been incorporated into land-use planning.

Natural science is especially valuable because it explains the degree to which the environment can supply us with needed resources, and it provides planners with the understanding of the limits, or the carrying capacity, of the globe and various parts of it. In Chapter 1, reference was made to the natural environment as one aspect of the supply side of land-use planning. The understanding of the resource base is essential for each of the seven land-use types discussed previously. Natural science is an aid to determining the quantity, the quality, the location, and the distribution of the natural resource base, and the environmental effects or impacts of the various land uses. For these reasons, the importance of natural science will grow in the future.

This discussion of the role of natural science in land-use planning is divided into three parts. The first part describes the approach used by scientists in their investigations. It is followed by a brief historical overview focusing on some of the pioneering scientists who made a special effort in aiding the land-use planning process. Finally, the last and major portion of this chapter is a discussion of how current scientific knowledge can aid us in our understanding of environmental stresses from global to local levels and in the selection of land uses compatible with the environment.

THE SCIENTIFIC APPROACH

Before planners can decide on the usefulness of scientific findings, it is essential that they understand the process scientists use in their work and their claims to its validity. Scientific investigation commonly consists of five basic steps starting with intuition, followed by hypothesis, theory, and the formulation of principles in this order, with some scientific findings being considered as the law of nature when they gain general acceptance.

Just like the planning and design process, scientific investigation starts with *intuition*. For example, when botanists observed the succession of plant communities in many parts of the world, they inferred that succession of plant and animal communities, as a natural phenomenon, may be universal. This intuition was the first step in their investigation, just as when planners identify a planning issue.

The next step for the scientist is the formulation of a *hypothesis*, that is: a proposition or set of propositions as a possible explanation for the occurrence of a natural phenomenon such as the universality of the succession of plant and animal communities. To test this hypothesis, scientists set up a procedure, an experiment, in this case to observe the succession of plant and animal communities in several parts of the world under different climatic and environmental conditions.

After completion of the experiment, the scientist may conclude that the hypothesis was either true or false. Other scientists will continue the investigation, and when several scientists find a similar pattern and predictability of succession in plant and animal communities, this proposition is accepted by the scientific community as a *theory*.

Over the years, many more scientists all over the world will continue to challenge the theory of succession of communities. When after repeated investigations no one can dispute this finding, the scientific community accepts the results and refers to it as a scientific *principle*. In the case of the principle relating to the succession of communities, botanists and ecologists have described the universality of succession as "a universal tendency toward ecological community succession which is an orderly, progressive sequence of communities which replace each other at a given place" (Cain, 1968, p. 14).

This scientific finding, together with many others, has great relevance to land-use planning. For example, when changing land uses, such as the building of transmission lines, result in the clearing of large areas of the native vegetation, the principle relating to the succession of communities is useful to planners for an understanding of the degree and speed of regeneration possible in different regions and climatic zones.

At present, hundreds of useful scientific principles are available for application to the land-use planning process. For example, in ecology alone, Cain (1968) described 17 principles relating to the structure of plant communities, 15 relating to the function of communities, and 11 principles of conservation. Similarly, geology, soil science, and climatology among other natural sciences, have developed many pertinent principles for land-use planning. But the question that remains is how to incorporate them into the land-use planning process to enable planners to make better, more sensitive decisions. The following brief historical overview describes some earlier attempts of scientists to make their findings more useful for planning.

HISTORICAL OVERVIEW

One of the significant 19th-century innovations in natural science was the attention paid to the interaction between natural phenomena and human activities. George Perkins Marsh's seminal volume, *Man and Nature*, appeared in 1865 (Marsh, second printing, 1967). In this book, Marsh, a philologist, undertook in effect to summarize the scientific understanding of land-use impacts on the environment as it existed in his day, for the first time raising questions about the "uncertainties" resulting from the expanding use of the natural environment by rapidly growing industrial societies. Since this most influential book was published over a hundred years ago, scientists and land-use planners have made extensive attempts to increase the understanding of Marsh's hypothesis. This effort has taken at least three forms.

Numerous scientists have followed the example of Marsh by warning planners and society at large about the impact of human use on the environment. Several of them actually became land-use planners. Planners also have turned to scientists to get their input in land-use planning. Finally, scientists and planners have collaborated in formal attempts at planning. The two most influential groups of scientists in land-use planning have been biologists and earth scientists.

Among the biological scientists turned planners, Geddes and MacKaye were prominent pioneers. Sir Patrick Geddes (1854–1932) was a Scottish biologist-cum-sociologist. Alerted by his scientific training to the issues of interaction between human beings and natural surroundings, Geddes pioneered many efforts aimed at resolving environmental conflicts. Among his many contributions were the development of refined landscape survey techniques and the proposal of a classification system for natural resources. His theory of planning, worked out over many years, was based on "geotechnics" — a means of restoring the earth and its resources through modern scientific methods (Stalley, 1972).

Geddes had a trans-Atlantic counterpart in the American forester Benton MacKaye. Working in the Boston area, MacKay developed one of the earliest regional approaches to the planning of a modern metropolitan region (Figure 2). Based on a careful assessment of the entire metropolitan landscape, he identified several categories of land that were especially valuable or fragile and as such should be protected from development. These areas, which included topographic ridges, steep slopes, canyons, river flood plains, swamps, lakes, and shorelines, would act, MacKaye argued, as natural "levees" controlling the "metropolitan invasion" (MacKaye, second printing, 1962, pp. 168–200).

While both Geddes and MacKaye were trained scientists, their approach to land-use planning was highly theoretical. The recent advancement of biological research produced a new generation of very influential scientists. An example is Pierre Dansereau, (1966, pp. 459–460), who described 27 "ecological laws" of our time. Several of these ecological laws have special applicability to land-use planning or the relation of man to the environment, including the Law of Tolerance and the Law of Irreversibility. Another distinguished theorist of ecologically based planning has been Eugene Odum. He has formulated an elegant model of land-use allocation based on ecological principles (Odum, 1969, pp. 262–270). This model classifies all land into one of four "compartments" depending on its function in the regional ecosystem (Figure 3).

Equally important are the geological consequences of land use, which have always been the concern of earth scientists. Many of the familiar environmental problems that have always plagued people — flooding, erosion, and siltation, for example — continue to be severe to the present day. In addition, new problems are occurring that had little or no reportable precedent before the turn of the century, such as encroachment of seawater in coastal freshwater aquifers and the collapse of land caused by the withdrawal of water and other fluids. Earth scientists have increased their understanding of the effects of these land-use problems and interpreted their findings in books useful for planners. Among these are: *Environmental Geology* (Flawn, 1970), which relates earth science to land-use planning and resource management; *Environmental Geomorphology and Landscape Conservation* addresses the geological consequences of urban land uses (Coates, 1973); Leopold's elegant statement on hydrology, water supply, and water use (Leopold, 1974). These represent only a small sampling of an enormous effort on the part of the scientific community which both explains the natural phenomena but more importantly measures the effects of human activities on the biological system and the geosystem. The remaining portion of this chapter deals with a more detailed analysis of the state-of-the-art of the application of natural science to the making of land-use allocation

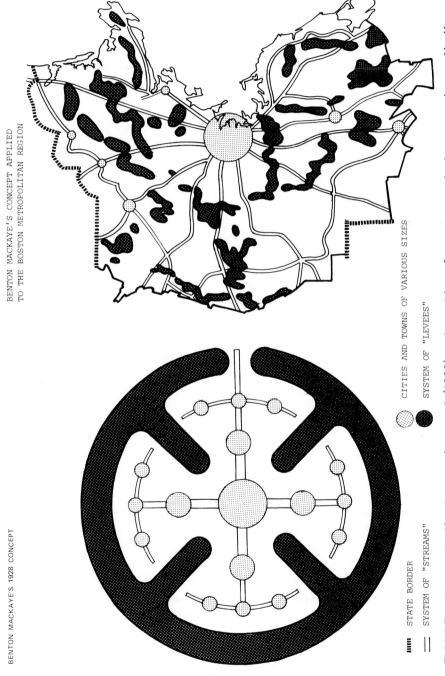

BENTON MACKAYE'S CONCEPT APPLIED
TO THE BOSTON METROPOLITAN REGION

BENTON MACKAYE'S 1928 CONCEPT

STATE BORDER

SYSTEM OF "STREAMS"

CITIES AND TOWNS OF VARIOUS SIZES

SYSTEM OF "LEVEES"

FIGURE 2 *Benton MacKaye's regional approach (1928) to the problem of open space and urban encroachment. MacKaye believed that what he described as "systems of levees," such as natural wetland systems, could control the metropolitan "invasion" ("flow").*

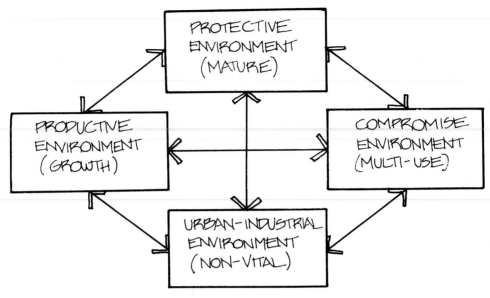

FIGURE 3 *Odum's regional ecosystem compartment model.*

decisions which are compatible with ecological and environmental principles and to the understanding of environmental stress.

THE STATE OF SCIENCE

Since George Perkins Marsh voiced his concerns in the mid-1860s over the rapid modification of the earth's surface by industrial societies, scientists have developed increasingly more pervasive theories of how human actions and land uses may affect not only a site or an area, but the larger environment. For instance, scientists have taught us: how the elimination of a coastal wetland can reduce the food supply to ocean life; how the large-scale burning of coal in the Midwest of the United States can produce acid rain which can damage and even eliminate all aquatic life in lakes in the Adirondacks, New England, and Eastern Canada; how the cumulative effects of land uses have polluted the Great Lakes in the United States and the Mediterranean Sea, which is surrounded by parts of three continents; how air pollution has affected humans, and animal and plant life, especially in areas where population concentrations combine with unfavorable climatic conditions; and how the quality and quantity of many local groundwater supplies have been impaired by inappropriate land uses in their aquifer recharge areas. The listing of such impacts could continue almost indefinitely, but even the limited examples already supplied point to two kinds of findings. Scientists have demonstrated that the various land uses have a measurable effect on the immediate environment, but more importantly the accumulated effects of land-use activities also contribute to regional and often global environmental changes.

Land-use planners need to understand how each individual land use may contribute to contextual changes of the larger environment and to the more immediate areas. The state of science must be interpreted continuously for application to planning, if we wish to minimize future uncertainties and to maintain or improve the quality of life for this and future generations. In summarizing the state of science, the large environmental and site-related findings are separated, though it should be realized that the two are often interrelated.

Land Use and Management-Related Environmental Stresses

The post-industrial era has produced major, cumulative environmental stresses on water, land, air, climate, and plant and animal life. The scientific evidence for these effects is conclusive, and has found — and will find increasingly — application in many countries in legislation and land-use management decisions.

Water and Land-Related Stresses

To scientists, water has been one of the most important indicators of environmental quality (Thomas, 1972). As water is collected in rivers, lakes, or in the ocean, the pollutants are often dispersed uniformly, making chemical analysis easy. Water quality assessment, until the 1970s, consisted of measuring and classifying the quality of water bodies. The classes represented degrees of estimated environmental stresses (Pettyjohn, 1972; Council on Environmental Quality, 1972, p. 11; Detwyler, 1971, pp. 195–324). Using sophisticated analytical techniques, scientists have been able to measure increasing numbers of pollutants more accurately. Current procedures measure at least 10 pollutants; namely, pathogens, phosphates, nitrates, pesticides, oil, lead, various industrial chemicals, sediments, radioactivity, and heat (Fabos and Caswell, 1977, p. 69).

In addition to identifying at least 10 harmful pollutants, scientists have measured and/or estimated the effects of these pollutants on the public health, and its environmental consequences, often referred to in the literature as "ecohealth." Two additional characteristics of harmful pollutants also have been studied. The first is the amount of time a pollutant without treatment may take in affecting the environment. Sediments in water, for instance, settle relatively fast, while radioactivity, most industrial wastes, and lead stay in the environment for a long time. Second, scientists have studied how resistant to treatment the various pollutants are. For example, pathogens, which are very harmful to public health, are relatively easy to treat, while lead, very harmful to public and ecohealth, stays in the system for a very long time defying treatment. Recently, planners have attempted to interpret these complex scientific findings to aid land-use decisions. The effects of these characteristics are estimated in the Water Pollution Indices, developed by the landscape planning research team at the University of Massachusetts, which indicates the relative behavior of these 10 pollutants against the four criteria described above, namely: public health, ecohealth, time, and treatment resistance (Table 1).

Scientists also have developed a good understanding of the hydrologic cycle (Hjelmfelt and Cassidy, 1975, p. 5) and by using an index such as the Water Pollution Indices (Table 1), planners can estimate how the various

TABLE 1. *Water pollution indices.*

Pollutant	Degree*				Pollution Index**
Pathogens	10.0	1.1	7.8	1.1	5.0
Phosphates	1.1	8.9	7.8	7.8	6.4
Nitrates/ites	7.8	8.9	7.8	7.8	8.1
Pesticides	10.0	8.9	8.9	10.0	9.5
Oil, Gasoline	1.1	6.7	7.8	2.0	4.4
Lead	10.0	8.9	10.0	10.0	9.7
Industrials	10.0	8.9	10.0	10.0	9.7
Sediments	2.3	2.3	2.3	1.1	2.0
Radioactivity	10.0	6.7	10.0	10.0	9.2
Heat	0.0	8.9	7.8	7.8	6.1
Public Health					
Ecohealth					
Time					
Treatment Resistance					

*The *degree* of pollution is estimated by interpretation of water pollution research results. "10" represents the highest degree of pollution for each of the four pollution characteristics (criteria), while "0" represents absence of effect.

**The pollution index represents the average of the four estimates, assuming that each of the four characteristics has equal weight. This assumption, however, is not substantiated by water pollution researchers.

land-use types actually affect water quality. Water, as it moves down through the topsoil and subsoils, carries many dissolved chemicals and various particles. Much of these end up in water bodies, affecting all aquatic life and the usefulness of water for human consumption. Current measurement techniques have enabled scientists to make inferences of water pollution from use and surface characteristics of the land (Fabos and Caswell, 1977, pp. 70–71). These can also be used to estimate the degree of stress and potential stress by simulating future land uses (Table 2).

The analysis of Table 2 shows that golf courses and tilled agricultural lands are among the land uses which create the greatest water pollution. It should be noted, however, that while these estimates are useful in showing the relative degree and type of pollution created by various land uses, they are based on several assumptions which may be often incorrect in specific instances. For instance, certain crops on tilled land require extensive pest controls while others can be produced without application of any pesticides. The numbers used here reflect an average application and traditional management practices.

Other major water and land-related stresses include, among others, irrigation, surface mining, agricultural soil loss, and desertification. Irrigation has had deleterious effects on large areas of Australia (England, 1973, pp. 217–236), and other semi-desert areas by raising the water table, which increases the salinity of soils. Scientists have also measured the acidity, erosion, and biological effects of surface mining (U.S. Department of Agriculture, 1973, pp. 414–434). Mining covers millions of acres of land in the United States alone, and its effects are far-reaching. Agricultural soil loss, for instance, is measured by tons per acre per year. Scientists have monitored soil losses resulting from various soil-slope conditions and land-use management practices (Leopold, 1956, pp. 639–647). Desertification or the increase in the size of deserts is taking millions of acres of land out of use yearly.

Atmospheric Pollution and Its Effects on Climate

Everyone on earth is a contributor, both directly and indirectly, to increasing atmospheric pollution. Scientists have measured, with ever increasing accuracy, the various kinds of air pollutants and identified the sources of air pollution, and the geographical aspects of the problem (Detwyler, 1971, pp. 77–174) and from all this research they have developed theories.

Climatologists have advanced two opposing theories. According to the first, the growing carbon dioxide content of the atmosphere will raise the earth's temperature through the so-called greenhouse effect. The second major theory suggests that the earth will grow cooler as the increasing air pollution makes its surface more reflective (Bryson, 1971, pp. 167).

TABLE 2. *Water quality resource value ratings for selected land uses.*[1]

The Estimated Degree of Pollution of Each Pollutant Generated by Land Uses, Ranging from a 100 Unit (the highest) to "0"

Land-Use Types	Pathogens	Phosphates	Nitrate/ites	Pesticides	Oil, Gasoline	Lead[2]	Industrials	Sediments	Radioactivity	Heat	Degree of Water Pollution[3] — the adjusted numbers are based on Pollution Indices	Water Quality Resource Value Rating where:[4] 100 is highest 0 is lowest
Golf Course	11.5	64.0	84.0	95.0	4.6	10.7	0	0	0	0	26.69	0
Agriculture-Tilled Land	0	64.0	84.0	95.0	0	0	0	16.4	0	0	25.94	4
Divided Highways	0	0	0	84.6	42.0	97.0	0	16.4	0	0	24.00	11
Housing (10–20 Du/acre)	44.5	13.7	0	10.5	28.1	70.0	0	0	0	0	16.68	38
Detached Housing	11.5	0	0	0	4.6	70.0	0	0	0	0	8.61	68
Abandoned Fields	0	13.7	19.3	21.9	0	0	0	4.8	0	0	5.97	79
Gravel Pit	0	0	0	0	4.6	10.7	0	16.4	0	0	3.17	89
Forests	0	0	0	10.5	0	0	0	0	0	0	1.05	96
Water Bodies	0	0	0	0	0	0	0	0	0	0	0	100

[1] Based on METLAND research at the University of Massachusetts. For more detail, see Fabos and Caswell 1977, Research Bulletin 637 of the Massachusetts Agriculture Experiment Station.

[2] With the increased use of lead-free gasoline during the past decade, lead pollution has decreased significantly, hence these estimates may not represent the lead pollution during the 1980s.

[3] For the purpose of this study, each of the pollutants received equal weight, hence the *degree of water pollution* was calculated by adding up all the numbers assigned for each pollutant, divided by the number of pollutants that is 10.

[4] The *water quality resource value* was further adjusted by the Pollution Indices shown in Table 1. While this number is surely not an accurate representation of pollution generated by land use, it shows the relative significance and magnitude of each land use as potential contributor to water pollution. Hence this table is useful for land-use planning and evaluation of existing and proposed land uses.

While scientists offer conflicting theories on our effects on global air pollution and its possible consequences in climatic terms, empirical data on the impact of regional air pollution on people, fauna within urban regions, and on property are plentiful and more convincing (Hor, 1972; Stern, 1973; Fabos and Caswell, 1977, pp. 139–153). Evidence linking metropolitanwide air pollution to human illness and death is conclusive. Environmental pollutants such as carbon monoxide, oxides of sulphur and nitrogen, and photochemical oxidants are direct or contributing causes of nearly a dozen chronic diseases such as allergic asthma, cancer, and emphysema. Industrialized cities and regions have experienced dramatic rises in mortality or illness. One of the most tragic episodes occurred in London in 1952, where approximately 4,000 deaths were linked to air pollution (Stern, 1973).

In response to the London smog and a later, similar episode in Pittsburgh, Pennsylvania, governments have increased research efforts into measuring air pollution and studying its effects. Scientists today are able to monitor air pollution through mathematical modeling, estimating the pollution generated by space heating, industrial processing, and transportation activities with ratings similar to those devised for water quality resources (Table 2). A generalized estimate of selected land uses in Massachusetts is based on detailed information such as: the number of households using oil or gas or other fuel for space heating; the amount they use; and the quality of the fuel, for example, the level of sulfur in the fuel (Table 3).

TABLE 3. *Annual space heating and process emission estimates for selected land uses in Massachusetts (in lbs./year-acre).* *

Land-Use Types	Annual Space Heat Emissions**	Annual Process Emissions***	Total Emissions
Low Density Housing	14.1	2.7	16.8
High Density Housing	386.0	74.0	460.0
Commercial	4,440.0	1,250.0	5,690.0
Industrial	440.0	4,860.0	5,300.0

*Source, METLAND Research, of the University of Massachusetts, Fabos and Caswell, 1977, Research Bulletin 637 of the Massachusetts Agricultural Experiment Station. The emission estimates are calculated for sulphur dioxide (SO_2).

**Space heat emissions estimates include all fuel (oil, gas, coal, etc.), inventoried by Walden Research Corporation for the Massachusetts Bureau of Air Quality Control.

***Process emissions result from fuel consumed for other than space heating (i.e., other non-space heating combustion emissions plus incineration emissions, mobile source emissions, and process losses).

Scientists can model these data together with climatic information including temperatures, wind directions, and speed, and several other pertinent factors. As a result, they can draw spatial contour maps of air pollution concentrations. Scientists and air pollution engineers also have developed various devices to control or decrease the different kinds of air pollution generated by the various land uses. This scientific modeling also has helped the land-use planners. By understanding the cause-effect relationships of land uses and climatic conditions, planners can use these modeling techniques in land-use allocation to minimize air pollution hazards.

Another atmospheric pollution concern to scientists and land-use planners is noise pollution. Unlike air pollution, noise pollution has not produced dramatic episodes of death and widespread illness. Nonetheless, scientists have proved that excessive urban noise has been harmful to people in several ways. Scientists note three common biological effects of noise. First, it affects the auditory system: prolonged exposure to noise can result in significant and permanent hearing loss (Glorig, 1975). Second, at extreme levels, noise can cause physiological effects on other parts of the human organism such as the digestive tract. Finally, noise is associated with psychological disorders and stress.

Noise pollution in developed countries, while ignored by the majority of land-use planners, is nevertheless very significant in its overall effect. Scientists estimate that currently over 40 million people in the United States (or over 20 percent of the population) are exposed on a regular basis to outdoor noise conditions that are potentially hazardous to their hearing (U.S. Environmental Protection Agency, 1972). Measurements also indicate that the level of urban noise has steadily increased during the decade. While much noise pollution must be corrected by technical devices, sensitive land-use planning could also reduce the noise level in many areas.

In responding to noise pollution, scientists have measured the level of noise generated by many land uses under different environmental conditions. Published research data on these measurements have become increasingly available during the past two decades, with the result that planners began to make inferences on land use and related noise levels during the 1970s, much in the same way as they have started to take into account air and water quality.

Average noise level estimates can be calculated for all major land-use categories (Table 4). The noise generated by highway traffic can also be shown as a function of the density of vehicles per mile and the average speed of the vehicles (Figure 4). These estimates represent an adjusted decibel level of noise. Decibel levels are measured using a logarithmic scale, which means that the apparent noise level of 40 decibels is 10 times as loud as that of 20 decibels.

TABLE 4. *Land-use noise levels.*

Noise Levels in dB(A)**	Land-Use Type
45	Clustered Residential Land, Low Density Urban Residential, Low Density
50	Urban Residential, Moderate Density Drive-in Theatre Golf Course
55	Townhouses; Rowhouses Garden Apartments Institutional Urban Park Alpine Ski Area Tennis Courts, Facilities (5+ acres)
60	Light Industry
65	Athletic Field and Stadium Playground Swimming Pool, Facilities, and Parking (5+ acres) Shopping Centers, and Parking
70	Commercial Amusement Park Fairgrounds Highway (strip) Commercial Development Dumps
75	Racetrack Urban Core Commercial Railyard Truck or Bus Terminal Heavy Industry
80	Sand and Gravel Pit, Quarry Other Mining
90	Airports

*Obtained from the METLAND Landscape Plannning Research, Fabos and Caswell, 1977, Research Bulletin 637 of the Massachusetts Experiment Station.

**The dB(A) is a symbol for "decibel A" and is the unit of noise measure given by an A-weighted sound level meter. Unlike the standard decibel (dB), the decibel-A unit approximates the way in which people actually perceive sound or noise.

Land-use noise levels are assigned on the basis of results of an outdoor noise environment measurement survey undertaken by the State of California. Although the noise produced by a noise environment varies greatly over a 24-hour period, this survey statistically reduced the time-varying noise output of each measured land-use environment to a single noise level in units of dB(A).

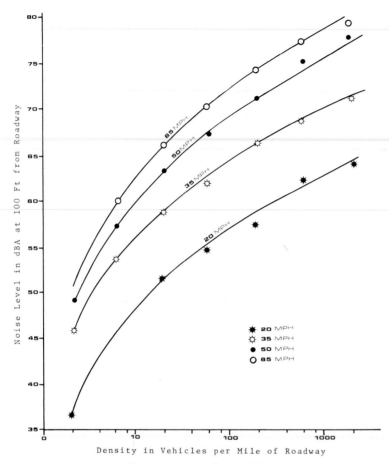

FIGURE 4 *Base traffic noise levels derived from computer simulation model. (It is assumed that: (1) the highway is level and at grade, (2) the road surface is in average condition, and (3) the traffic is freely flowing and comprised only of passenger vehicles.) Obtained from the METLAND Landscape Planning Research, Fabos and Caswell, 1977, Research Bulletin 637 of the Massachusetts Experiment Station.*

Later in this chapter the assessment of manmade hazards is discussed, e.g. in assessing manmade hazards, land-use planning and design approaches may be used to decrease noise levels (Table 6). For example the land-use noise levels shown in Table 4 and the traffic noise levels shown in Figure 4 can be reduced at various degrees by creating barriers or buffer zones as shown in Table 6. These studies together show the importance of interdisciplinary activities among scientists and land-use planners.

Human-Caused Stresses on Plants and Animal Life

The effects of people on plants and animal life is less direct than their effects on water, land, air, and climate. The cumulative effects of many land uses and land management practices, however, create three types of effects pertinent to land-use planning. First, in the words of Detwyler, we are experiencing "ecological explosions [which] have resulted from the introduction by man of foreign plants, animals, or diseases into new environments" (Detwyler, 1971, p. 447). This ecological explosion refers to the enormous increase in numbers of some kinds of living organisms — it may be an infectious virus like influenza or a fungus like that of the potato disease which created famine in Ireland and was the reason for large-scale emigration of her people during the late nineteenth century.

The second kind of human-caused stress on plants is the large-scale destruction of vegetation by man. The changes we have induced in native vegetation, especially since the early days of colonization, range from simple modification through severe degradation to complete destruction and replacement. All these changes in plant cover are accompanied by changes in the environment within and adjacent to the affected vegetation. These stresses are a result of three kinds of activities: large-scale modification of (1) *surface vegetation*, such as the massive timber harvesting of the jungles of the huge Amazon River Basin; the widespread damage to forest and agricultural areas caused by air pollution; (2) *defoliation* of vegetation by insects, fungi, or chemicals, such as was the case in Vietnam during the war, and (3) scientists have studied the *large-scale destruction and extinction of animals by man.*

One of their most important findings has been a widespread, perhaps worldwide, decline among many species of carnivorous birds, primarily because of an equally widespread use of insecticides such as DDT. It is estimated that one percent of our higher animals have become extinct since 1600 and nearly 3 percent are now in danger.

The human-caused stresses on plant and animal life have been extensively researched by scientists all over the world. The focus of their concern has been large-scale land conversion for housing, industrial, commercial, and recreation uses, mining, and food production. Land-use planners must be concerned with the effects of these activities, because any of the resulting environmental stresses can create uncertainty and often irreversible damage which may be not only more costly to repair, but also may limit the options of this and future generations.

Synergistic Effects of Two or More Stresses

Scientists and land-use planners have been interested not only in the individual effects of a given land-use on land and water, air and climate, or plant and animal life, but also how they interact and how two or more stresses may have a greater effect than the sum of their parts. For example, massive erosion and mud slides in drier climates such as California may be significantly more severe where air pollution and other modifiers of vegetation have reduced the ground cover.

Individual scientific findings are often extremely useful but each must also be analyzed in the context of the many potential effects of a land use or land uses.

The State of Science for Ecologically Sensitive Land-Use Planning

In terms of site-level decisions, science can aid land-use planners in at least four areas. Current findings can help in making ecologically compatible land-use decisions, in managing the vital natural resource base of the community and the region, in reducing natural and human-caused hazards, and finally in selecting suitable areas for development. Scientific knowledge is extensive in each of these four areas. The aim of this review is to provide readers with a mere summary.

Ecologically Compatible Land-Use Decisions

In the historical overview of this chapter, some of the current conceptual ecological models were mentioned. Those models have been further developed to aid land-use planners in making more acceptable decisions at the site level. One of the most promising pieces of ecological/land-use research has been the adaptation and further development of Odum's regional ecosystem model (Figure 3) to site-level decisions (Hendrix, 1977). How can the ecological "carrying capacity" of an area be maintained? Or, in other words, how is it possible to determine the sort and amount of development that is conducive to maintaining an optimal degree of ecological stability and productivity? If a value is to be put on minimizing the unnecessary degradation of the environment, then its "carrying capacity" — its ability to accommodate human activities without being irreparably damaged — must be identified and respected.

The Hendrix procedure has attempted to provide answers to this question by the development of a three-step procedure. First, each land-use type (for instance, in Massachusetts planners have distinguished 124 different land uses) was placed into one of five ecological compartments. This classification was based on measurements of the biological production/respiration ratio. To give an example, the biological production of a cornfield is much higher than its respiration, providing a surplus for man and animal consumption, while the respiration of an urban land use is higher than its biological production.

The second step of this ecological procedure is to measure two types of potential of each homogenous site. The first type is the biological potential. For example, highly productive agricultural land will reach its production potential as cornfields but when it is used for housing, its biological use potential is not utilized. The second type of potential that ecologists are concerned with is the denudation potential. By estimating the erodibility of the various soil types and the water run-off potential, which can be calculated from the steepness of the slope of the land, the ecologist can determine how fragile or resilient a site or an area can be.

Using thse two steps, Hendrix developed an ecological compatibility rating (Table 5). Under "substrata potential" Hendrix estimates the intrinsic productive capacity of each homogenous land area and the degree of its

TABLE 5. *Ecological compatibility ratings.***

| | Land-Use Function | | | | |
	Protection	Production (Agricultural)	Production (Natural)	Compromise	Urban
A. Protection	+3*	−2	−1	−2	−3
B. High Production (Agri. and Nat.)	0	+3	+2	−3	−3
C. Production (Agri. and Nat.)	0	+2	+2	−2	−2
D. High Production (Agri.)	0	+3	−1	−3	−3
E. High Production (Nat.)	0	−1	−3	−2	−2
F. Production (Agri.)	0	+1	−1	−1	−1
G. Production (Nat.)	0	−1	+1	−1	−1
H. Non-Production	0	−1	−1	+3	+3

Notes:
   *The ratings reflect the following "compatibility" estimates:

+3 = very appropriate	−1 = slightly inappropriate
+2 = moderately appropriate	−2 = moderately inappropriate
+1 = slightly appropriate	−3 = very inappropriate
0 = neutral	

**Obtained from the METLAND Landscape Planning Research, Research Bulletin 653 of the Massachusetts Experiment Station.

denudation or erodibility potential. The current general land-use categories are identified under land-use functions. The degree of compatibility is expressed on a scale from (+3) to (−3). A (+3) means the greatest compatibility between the land and its present use while a (−3) suggests the greatest degree of incompatibility. For example, the ecological substrata potential of class A is protection. This class often means a climax landscape on a fragile hillside or high on the steep slopes of a mountain. When this land is preserved in this protection class, the ecological compatibility is the highest, that is (+3). If this fragile hillside were developed for housing or other urban use the erosion or the denudation resulting from the increased run-off would be very negative from the ecological point of view. Hence urban use of this substrata potential class would receive a (−3) rating.

By employing this procedure, land-use planners can assess the degree to which any proposed land-use conversion would violate ecological principles. This research, though useful, does not assess the potential effects of a land use on its adjacent areas. For example, a land-use planner using the Hendrix procedure could find that a housing development on a lake site property was compatible, or a right ecological fit. But he could not estimate by this method the effects of the development on possible induced eutrophication of the lake. Ecologists are busy developing a better understanding of the transactions or the flow of minerals and energy among the various land units and uses. We can conclude that while the current state of ecological understanding is useful, it is somewhat limited.

State of Science for Communitywide Resource Use and Management

The history of land conversion from rural to urban uses is replete with instances of unnecessary degradation and obliteration of valuable local resources. The effects of this short-sighted land-use policy have been felt in both monetary and energy terms. To make better land-use decisions, planners need to assess the relative quantity, quality, and distribution of those landscape resources useful in maintaining the continuous needs of a community. The most common critical landscape resources are surface water and groundwater, land productivity for agriculture, and other biomass production including timber and firewood, wildlife, and various earth resources such as rock, sand, and gravel. Scientists, including hydrologists, geologists, soil scientists, biologists, and others have developed methods to measure the quantity, quality, and distribution of these and several other valuable resources.

The assessment of surface water potential or the location of a site which can be impounded requires a relatively complex procedure. Scientists and engineers need to assess the cause/effect relationships of several significant physical parameters, including the amount and quality of water available, topography, surficial and bedrock geology, erosion characteristics, evaporation rates, seismic hazards, and slope stability. Of course, it is critical that the scientific procedure needs to be complemented by several nonphysical factors of concern to land-use planners, such as projected need, cost, and political acceptance.

In measuring and assessing groundwater supply potentials, scientists have developed four basic procedures ranging from least costly but less accurate, to most costly and most accurate. These are: remote-sensing techniques, surficial geologic techniques, on-site geophysical interpretive techniques, and on-site subsurface techniques respectively. Water quality assessment can be done by making inferences from surficial characteristics and land uses. However, a more accurate assessment of water quality is made by laboratory testing of sample water obtained by on-site subsurface drilling.

Land productivity assessment for agriculture is among the most highly developed procedures. Over the past 70 to 80 years, soil scientists have developed, tested, and refined a body of accurate techniques for the classification and assessment of soils. The soil scientists' measurements include a variety of soil characteristics. Among the ratings that they regularly assign is an estimate of the "capability" of the soil to support agricultural production. In the United States, scientists use eight capability classes, ranging from most productive to least productive. These classes are based on such parameters as slope, moisture-holding capability, erosion characteristics, texture, structure, and drainage characteristics. Soil capability is also the basis for the assessment of forest productivity and other land-based biomass production.

In assessing wildlife, the science of wildlife biology provides detailed information on most pertinent species. Wildlife biologists have ascertained, for example, that the most important characteristics of good wildlife habitat are climate, soil productivity, and vegetation conditions.

Assessment techniques for the various types of earth resources have been developed by geologists. They usually include a three-level approach: first, a general survey using surficial geologic information or remote-sensing data, followed by site-specific seismic tests to better ascertain the quantity, and finally, a site-specific sampling of core borings to verify quantity, distribution, and quality.

It is evident, even from this brief summary, that the ability of science to measure or assess critical resources is extensive, thereby also suggesting that scientists in these disciplines can be useful allies of land-use planners.

State of Science to Measure and
Assess Landscape Hazards

Environmental circumstances have caused significant harm to people and property. These "landscape hazards" can be grouped into two categories. In the first category are the hazards caused by natural phenomena that are harmful only when exacerbated by human activity, the most important examples being flooding, landslides, and earthquakes. The second category includes hazards generated by human action, such as air pollution and noise pollution. Although scientists have provided us with increasingly accurate measurements and assessment of these hazards, the resulting damage has increased significantly during this century (Kates and Snead, 1969).

Among the natural hazards, flooding has generated the greatest volume of research effort since it has been the most ubiquitous and damaging. The changing water level of streams has been recorded continuously over many decades in older developed areas by gaging stations located at regular intervals. For each gaging station, the hydrologist can construct relatively accurate hydrographs, which describe the amount of water flow (called "discharge") at that point (Leopold, 1974, pp. 37–57). From these water level measurements and from topographic maps of a given landscape, flood plain contour lines of a given recorded flood can be delineated. The accuracy of these flood contour lines is directly dependent upon the number of gaging stations, the length of the period for which these records have been kept, and the accuracy of topographic maps and land-use/land-cover survey maps. With detailed and accurate data, hydrologists can forecast flood probability lines with a high degree of accuracy. They also have developed several computerized mathematical models which not only measure the flood probability of a given landscape, but can also simulate the extent of future, larger flood plains which often result from increased urbanization (Fabos, Caswell, 1977, p. 129), (Figure 5).

Scientists also have researched landslides, which are also known as "mass wasting," earthquakes, and other seismic risks. These efforts are useful for the development of land-use planning norms such as excluding developments from those slopes that are 15 percent or steeper, and avoiding development on or near known geologic faultlines.

The human-caused hazards, namely air and noise pollution and their effects on the environment and people have been discussed earlier. In addition to their contribution to the investigation of those large-scale stresses, scientists have studied the impact of these hazards on local, site-specific areas. For example, both air and noise pollution studies at the local level are designed to estimate the effects of various land uses on the air quality or noise levels of adjacent land uses. They assess, for instance, the

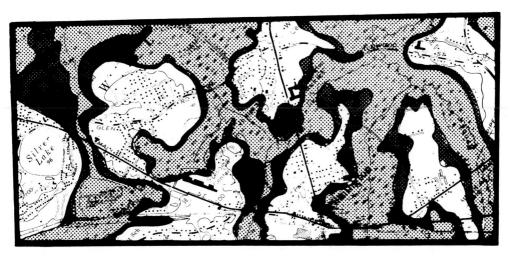

FIGURE 5 *A comparison of the flood hazard assessment results when applied to a community subject to heavy metropolitan growth pressures from 1952 (ligher tone) to 1971 (darker tone). This process was applied to Wilmington, Massachusetts, in 1952 and 1971. An assessment of flood plain extent and land-use types during this 20-year period indicates the correlation of increased surface impermeability and increased flood plain size. In addition as flood plain size grew, land uses that were free from flood hazard in 1952 became subject to that hazard probability by 1971, indicating the dynamic nature of the flood plain. To show this apparent flood plain change clearly, the figure represents only a small portion of the town of Wilmington. The assessment process was developed by Dr. Donald Doehring and Susan Cole, environmental geologists of the University of Massachusetts landscape research group. The process evaluates the effects of urbanization on increasing the flood hazard over the 20-year period. It also identifies those areas in which maximum economic flood loss occurs.*

effects of a heavily traveled highway on nearby housing. Such estimates of air and noise pollution are being designed to provide planners and designers with standards for the location and size of buffer strips between various land uses. For example, empirical data is available on noise attenuation by transmission path types, useful for determining the width and type of buffer strips to attenuate noise to a desired level (Table 6).

State of Science of Development
Suitability Techniques

Land-use characteristics or attributes make one area more suitable for development than others. Scientists in recent years have begun to study pertinent physical and local or topoclimatic characteristics. Using the find-

TABLE 6. *Source-receiver distances.*

Source-receiver distances required to produce prescribed amounts of attenuation for eight alternative transmission path types (in feet), where dBA = frequency-weighted decibles and h_1 = that height of a barrier that is actually interrupting the sound traveling from a source to a receiver.

Total Attenuation in dBA; re 0.0002 microbar	Distance Only	Transmission Path Type						
		Agricultural Land or Grass	Reverting Field	Forest	Very Dense Forest	Barrier $h_1 = 5'$	Barrier $h_1 = 10'$	Barrier $h_1 = 15'$
5	100	80	70	60	50	0	.0	0
10	250	150	120	90	80	100	0	0
15	700	300	200	150	130	250	100	0
20	1600	600	300	250	200	700	250	100
25	2600	1000	500	350	300	1600	700	250
30	3800	1700	750	600	450	2600	1600	700
35	5000	2500	1000	800	600	3800	2600	1600
40	6500	3500	1300	1000	800	5000	3800	2600

Source: This table was adapted from the work of Stephanie Caswell, resource specialist of the University of Massachusetts landscape research group.

ings of scientists, land-use planners can reduce the cost of development and increase the livability of a given area.

In determining the physical development suitability, scientists can provide accurate measurements of depth to water table and soil drainage characteristics; bedrock characteristics, including the depth to bedrock from surface and the hardness of rock types; percent of slopes or topographic steepness; the quality of topsoil to support vegetative growth; and soil-bearing capacity (sandy soils, for instance, can support heavier structures than peat soils in marshy areas). These measurements combined with cost estimates on overcoming limitations for development provide planners with good estimates of the degree of physical suitability (Fabos and Caswell, 1977, p. 203). These findings may be shown for a temperate climatic region or a New England type landscape where basements are commonly built, since a small (2 to 3 feet) extension of the foundation provides the basement walls of a house (Table 7). It should be noted that creative design could overcome much of these physical constraints now expressed in added development costs. Obviously, cost may also change with new technology. The role of technology on this and other land-use planning issues is discussed in the following chapter.

Finally, information on topoclimatic or local climatic and microclimatic characteristics has become essential, especially in recent years when energy supplies have been less certain and costs have fluctuated. In addition, land-use planners need to understand climatic factors to improve the comfort of people through planning. Scientists have studied several pertinent topoclimatic characteristics important for land-use planning, including: orientation to the sun — a building's orientation, for instance, and the degree of slope determines the amount of solar receipt of sites, which can vary up to almost 50 percent (Fabos and Caswell, 1977, p. 222); orientation to winds (exposure to prevailing winter winds increases heat costs and decreases comfort, and exposure to summer winds moderates heat and increases comfort); topographic features (these may shield winds or channel their direction); vegetation, which can protect development from winter winds; and water bodies (large lakes or oceans can have a climatic influence for several miles inland).

Although scientific measurement of each of these parameters has been ample, only the measurement of solar receipt is sufficiently developed for land-use planning. Other findings are useful only as guidelines or as providing a basis for land-use planning norms.

TABLE 7. *Estimated added development costs for physical factors.*

Factors and Dimensions	Estimated Added Development Costs
Depth to Bedrock:	
0 –2'	$20,000
2 –5'	5,000
5' +	200*
Depth to Water Table:**	
0 –3'	$5,000
3 –5'	1,400
5' +	0
Drainage:**	
Poorly to Very Poorly Drained	$5,000
Mod. Well-Drained with Hardpan	1,400
Otherwise	0
Slope:	
15% +	$*****
8-15%	1,300
0-8%	0
Topsoil:	
Poor (0-4")	$1,500
Fair (4-6")	600
Good (6" +)	0
Bearing Capacity:	
Plastic and Non-Plastic; Silts and Clays; Peat; Muck	$1,500
Otherwise	0

*Depths of bedrock well below 5 feet would incur no additional costs to development. However, since very deep bedrock cannot be ascertained from soil typings, a minimum cost of $200, which is applicable for less deep bedrock conditions, is assumed.

**It should be noted that high water table and poor drainage conditions often occur simultaneously, and that the same correction techniques and costs are usually involved. As will be seen, the METLAND assessment technique recognizes this fact. However, the two factors are shown separately here because they can in certain instances occur independently of each other.

Source: METLAND Landscape Planning Research, Fabos and Caswell, 1977, Research Bulletin 637 of the Massachusetts Experiment Station.

CONCLUSIONS

This brief summary on the role of the natural sciences in land-use planning has documented the great utility of many past and current scientific works. The dissemination of scientific findings has profound influence on our understanding of the major environmental stresses as well as efforts in land-use decisions at the local level. It has been shown that the body of pertinent scientific knowledge is enormously large, yet it is also clear that in some areas of investigation science is at present more of an art.

This review also indicates that much of the empirical data and scientific findings have already had an effect on land-use decisions. However, many of them have not yet reached the land-use planning community. This latter deficiency suggests that not only do we need more scientific knowledge but we must also develop better links between scientists and planners. The major function of planners is that of a catalyst for learning and action. It means that planners must incorporate the pertinent research results of scientists and should interact with them regularly. In the absence of such an interaction, we certainly increase environmental risks. In the words of Barney, (1980, p. 1): "If present trends continue, the world in 2000 will be more crowded, more polluted, less stable, ecologically and more vulnerable to disruption than the world we live in now." The contribution of natural science to judicious land-use planning offers the possibility of improvement on this forecast.

CHAPTER 3

THE ROLE OF TECHNOLOGY

Presently only 3 percent of the population of the United States provides food for the remaining 97 percent and there is plenty to spare for exports. We have twice as many university students and approximately as many Federal employees, (including a small peacetime army), as farmers. Only 300 years ago, food production involved over 80 percent of the population of the advanced countries of the time. Even today in developing countries in Africa, the agricultural labor force is over 70 percent of the population (Heady, 1976, p. 110). Advancements in science and especially in technology were responsible for this unprecedented change, freeing the remainder of the population for industry and service.

In recent decades, automation has significantly reduced the industrial labor force to below 25 percent of the total population. Available technology will certainly further reduce the need, probably to the level of farm workers before the end of this century.

The land-use implications of past technological changes were enormous. They gave rise to large metropolitan and industrial regions and immense agricultural landscapes based on monocultural food production. Current changes may equal or even surpass the effects of industrial technologies. But even if this forecast is only partly accurate, planners should examine carefully the role of technology in land-use planning.

Technology has influenced land-use decisions in two ways. Most often society has turned to technology to help satisfy one of our human needs or to solve a problem. Each of these many technological advancements results in *incremental changes*, many of which affect land uses. For example, off-shore drilling technologies have resulted in numerous oil spills, with consequent effects on many forms of life, and they have also been the cause of large coastal developments. In responding to these undesirable effects, inventors have advanced further technologies such as specialized ships to clean up oil spills in the ocean. Secondly, some earlier technological advancements such as the invention of railroads, electric power, automobiles and more recently, the development of two fundamental and interactive technologies — computers and integrated circuits — have produced major changes. The effects of these kinds of technologies are many times more powerful because they create new opportunities of great significance and many incalculable consequences. They result in what is described in this book as *contextual changes*.

TECHNOLOGIES WITH INCREMENTAL CHANGES

Whenever a human need exists, there are, most often, three basic options available for meeting it. We may decide to conserve a resource, or in some cases, to forego it completely. Secondly, we can look for new or alternative resources elsewhere. In the case of satisfying our energy need, we may, for instance, obtain firewood in place of increasingly scarce oil to heat our houses. Thirdly, we may turn to technology. For example, a technological invention may produce a more efficient oil-burning furnace which would also reduce air pollution.

Technological solutions have been sought throughout human history, but they have been especially plentiful since the start of the Industrial Revolution. Land-use planning is affected by at least three types of incremental technologies, each resulting in some change. First, we have increased our needs for some resources to build and maintain our habitations. Second, we have turned to technology to mitigate hazards resulting from earlier, often unwise, land-use decisions. Finally, we have used technology to improve planning.

Technologies to Satisfy Needs

Many thousands of technological developments have been advanced over the centuries in response to human needs. The great majority of these occurred after the contextual changes at the dawn of the Industrial Revolution, which unleashed all the nonrenewable energy sources — first coal, then oil, gas and finally uranium for nuclear energy. In spite of these enormous changes, the pattern of land use did not change until this century. Urban centralization, which was evident during the Middle Ages and the Renaissance, has continued into this century.

Technological developments have provided the necessary resource base for the ever-growing urban concentrations, and the housing and servicing of these mammoth populations.

Resource Needs

Parallel developments have occurred in all resource uses including food production, water developments, and mineral and energy use for industry. Technological advancements in agriculture have been steady since the beginings of mechanization in the mid-19th century. Cultivating and harvesting machines have grown bigger, more diversified, and more efficient. These technologies have been primarily responsible for the reduction of the agricultural labor force to 3 percent of the U.S. population by the 1970s.

The invention of the tomato-picking machine is a good illustration of the effects of technology on food production. When this machine was introduced in California in the mid-1960s, it changed tomato growing within a few years from low-acreage units to farms of over 500 acres each, eliminating the need for thousands of farm workers, while shifting production elsewhere in the state.

In water resource development, the supply of water from local rivers shifted initially to small impoundments, or manmade lakes, and by the early part of this century to reservoirs of ever-increasing capacity (Legget, 1973, Ch. 4). The Boston Metropolitan Region, for example, acquired a watershed of over 100 square miles in area, razed four towns and impounded the Quabbin Reservoir 80 miles from Boston to supply the growing metropolis with water. This project used the technology of the 1930s. Current water projects being developed for the dry West are many times larger. The beautiful Hoover Dam at Lake Mead in northwest Arizona and southeast Nevada is an impressive technological achievement.

The technologies for mining, energy development, and industrialization have made similar changes in terms of increased mechanization, centralization, and overall growth. Developed countries have built large industrial regions; current mining machines can scoop up hundreds of cubic feet with one bite; and large power plants are scattered as imposing monuments within growing regions of developed countries, all interconnected with transmission lines which are increasing in size. All these technologies bolstered supplies to the masses who moved to metropolises, which in turn grew into megalopolitan regions by the mid-20th century (Gottman, 1961).

Building and Servicing Habitations

The inventions of serial production of prefabricated iron, the use of cast iron columns, and the elevator, among other technological developments, enabled engineers and architects to build large industrial structures, high-rise office buildings in Chicago, and the Eiffel Tower in Paris by the late nineteenth century (Giedion, 1967). By the mid-twentieth century, skyscrapers, completed or under construction, and culminating in such monumental buildings as New York City's World Trade Center, dominated all the major cities of the world. Technologies had to be developed not only for the construction of the visible above ground portions, but also for the secure foundations of buildings of this magnitude, employing methods such as, in Boston, the hammering of large steel pipes through soft clay and filling them up with concrete, or the invention of a floating foundation used for a large millhouse in Georgetown, Guyana (Legget, 1973). These increasingly large structures enabled greater concentration and centralization of industrial powers and urban regions.

The technological advancements for major public transportation systems during the past 300 years complemented the other technologies. The railroads, the streetcars, and buses have all helped to perpetuate the further concentration and centralization of cities and the imperial power of developed countries. The first nonconforming technology to reverse this pattern was the automobile. Since this individualized transportation has had a major, profound effect, it is discussed later in this chapter under technologies with contextual changes.

Technologies to Mitigate Hazards

At the same time technology began to make possible the large-scale exploitation of natural resources and the creation of centralized urban settlements, it also caused monumental problems by harming both people and the environment. These hazards have been introduced into the previous chapter under the consideration of natural hazards, including flooding, landslides, and earthquakes, and manmade hazards in the form of water, air, and noise pollution. It was shown that science has indeed a very important role to play not only in assessing the problems, but also in their mitigation. In addition to science, at least three other plausible ways exist for dealing with natural or manmade hazards. First, we may accept increased risks to people and to the environment by doing nothing or not enough. Possible consequences under this scenario are greater flood damage, greater incidence of cancer or respiratory illnesses, and disruption of valuable ecosystems such as wetlands. In other words, we understand these consequences and we accept them. Second, we may place our settlements in safer areas, or employ land-use planning as a device for mitigating hazards. Finally, we can use technological devices to lessen harm. Among the four approaches (science, risk-taking, land-use planning, and technological devices) probably the risk-taking and the use of technology are the most prevalent. For this reason, some of the pertinent technological devices are reviewed here.

When Leonardo da Vinci proposed to change the city of Florence into an "ideal city," he devised a chessboard street pattern, but the most striking feature of his plan was the canalization of the meandering River Arno (Giedion, 1967, p. 53). Like the majority of contemporary engineers, Leonardo da Vinci looked as an inventor for a technological device to solve flooding problems. Ever since, the most frequently used flood devices have been structural. Improving on the technology, engineers have built thousands of miles of flood walls and levees. In many areas, dredging operations are continuous. The technology of building construction has been advanced to withstand periodic flooding. Engineers have also developed earthquake-resistant structures and have built large retaining walls to avoid landslides. Earthquake-prone Japan has employed these technologies most extensively. For instance, some of her hillsides are filled with huge concrete dams to protect against the floods of mud which often follow earthquakes.

Technological solutions have also been sought to mitigate manmade hazards. The proliferation of water treatment plants, especially since the 1970s, has improved water quality all over the United States. As mentioned earlier, this technical device has been one of the most expensive public works in this country, requiring the expenditure of over 140 billion dollars over a decade. Industrial air pollution is being reduced by specially designed scrubbers and other mechanical devices, while automobile exhaust is being reduced by catalytic converters. Aviation industries are developing quieter engines and huge walls are being erected along highways in urban areas to reduce traffic noise.

These are only a few examples of technologies designed to mitigate hazards, each of which has had effects on land-use planning. While the technological approach has been increasingly questioned by the public in recent years, it will, however, continue to be important in reducing natural and manmade hazards.

Technology to Improve Planning

The colonization of much of the world by European civilization dates back only four centuries. European domination of the rest of the world was aided by technology developed to survey and map the world, by the systemization of data collection, and by the development of deductive and inductive reasoning. By the 16th century, Mercator, the Flemish cartographer and geographer, was able to map the whole known world.

Contemporaneously with Mercator's improvement of navigation came advances in techniques for surveying the land. Initially, surveying of the Americas was limited to the coastal settlements of the colonists. By the early 19th century, however, this survey technology was used to open up the virgin lands of the New World. For example, the early settlements of the American East Coast in the period prior to independence were developed without this survey technology. The surveying of the rest of the country was based on the 1785 ordinance of rectangular survey, which subdivided this enormous land area into townships of 6 miles by 6 miles which were further subdivided into square mile grids. As one flies over the United States, Canada, Australia, New Zealand, or any other recently subdivided parts of the world, one can see the land-use impact of this survey technology. J. B. Jackson, the noted landscape historian, often refers to this as the landscape of the engineers. Indeed, this surveying created the ubiquitous "checker-board" landscape. The earlier organic land use has been replaced by this newer mechanical subdivision (Figure 6). City planning was also based on similar grid patterns.

Technological improvements on this early survey technique were slow to come during the 19th century. All land-use development required a detailed site survey during this period. However, by the late 19th century, map-making and more sophisticated cartographic techniques were advanced, and these maps became available for land-use planners. One of the earliest recorded uses of such survey maps was reported by Charles Eliot, a distin-

FIGURE 6 *Organic versus checkerboard land-use patterns.*

guished landscape architect and land-use planner, during the late 19th century. When Eliot was selecting the site for a college or a parkway, he analyzed the available maps of the United States Geologic Survey for topography, vegetation, and streams. His use of these maps, with roads depicted in "black, streams in blue, and 20-feet contours in red" is significant in its own right for it illustrates the mapmaking technology of his time (Eliot, 1902).

The next advance in land survey techniques was achieved by a series of developments in photography and remote sensing. Seeking to capture a "bird's eye view" of the earth, photographers ascended in balloons as early as 1858 to take pictures of scenes. In 1903, an enthusiast actually strapped an extremely light camera to the breast of a pigeon and succeeded in developing bird's eye views of a castle (Ford, 1979, p. xi). Aerial photography and technology to interpret air photos, such as the widely used stereoscope, have been used ever since in making increasingly more accurate survey maps all over the world. For example, the regular updating of the United States Geologic Survey maps is done from aerial photos. This technology has also helped in the preparation of topographic maps, flood surveys, and detailed land-use maps. For instance, a detailed map describing 124 types of land uses (MacConnell and Garvin, 1956) for the entire state of Massachusetts was completed by the mid-1950s. These maps, together with improved printing techniques, have aided not only the land-use planning effort, but also the explanation of the spatial attributes of plans and the rationale behind them.

More recently, the use of scale models and of specialized lenses to photograph them, combined with video or regular filming technology, have enabled land-use planners to simulate the appearance, the visual qualities, and the sequential characteristics of new developments. Indeed, the incremental development of survey, photo, and printing technologies have changed planning significantly since Eliot's use of crude maps less than a century ago.

TECHNOLOGIES WITH CONTEXTUAL CHANGES

Assuming that the leaders of the great powers of this earth have enough sense not to blow each other into oblivion fighting over liquid fossil fuels or other scarce resources, the following scenes forecast by David Sleeper (1980), may become commonplace in the next decade or so:

> In Vermont in a white clapboard house directly across from the village green, a woman begins the workday by scanning the videotext edition of the *Wall Street Journal*. Then she sifts through her mail, all of which was posted electronically the evening before and stored

in her computer's memory. The small computer in her office performs a multitude of functions: telephone, typewriter, copier, calculator, file cabinet, and mailbox. A colleague from Atlanta calls and reminds her of a teleconference that afternoon with the West Coast office.

In the eastern Pacific Ocean, a huge ship lowers a hydraulic scoop to the ocean floor 15,000 feet below. Thousands of baseball-sized nodules — rich in manganese, nickel, copper, cobalt, and iron — are lifted from the seabed and go directly into the ship's processing section which separates the minerals.

A salesman in New York City unplugs his EV (electric vehicle) and begins his daily rounds. The EV is constructed largely of light, highly durable plastics and has a zinc-chloride battery system that gives it a range of more than 200 miles. The cost of the electricity needed to power the vehicle is roughly equivalent to gasoline that sells for 50 cents a gallon [in 1980 dollar value].

Off the coast of Oregon, a string of wave-energy devices called "Dam-Atolls" provides electric power for 40,000 people. Each device is 250 feet in diameter at its widest and has a 60-foot-deep-central core all far below the water. Vanes at the top of the Dam-Atoll direct wave energy downward into the core where a whirlpool is formed which spins a turbine wheel, the only moving part in the entire unit.

In Cambridge, Massachusetts, a small firm made up largely of microbiologists specializes in developing microorganisms that recycle waste products and control pollution. Using the latest research techniques involving recombinant DNA, the firm produces microbes which clean up oil spills, reduce odors at chemical factories, and transform garbage (including plastic) into clean-burning fuels.

Each scenario features a highly advanced technology, or an activity such as microbiological research, which is dependent on it. Each of these technologies may have as profound an impact on people's lives as the railroad, telephone, electricity, and development of fossil fuel has had during the past three centuries. Historically, this period is similar to the pre-industrial era in that the major technological innovations were developed during the late baroque period, and these major advancements have been developed at the end of the industrial era.

Probably the most significant aspects of these new technologies are the promised abilities to shift from exhaustible fossil fuels to renewable resources, and to mine oceanic resources that will supply the present population and accommodate future growth. The effects of these technologies on land use may be greater than the technologies of the industrial era. It was pointed out earlier that the land-use pattern was not altered by the Industrial

Revolution, which affected the size of cities only, and not their pattern. The pre-industrial city which attained a population of about half a million or more has become 10 million or larger in this century. This new wave of high technologies, however, is expected to reverse the forces of centralization toward decentralization.

In a way, decentralization started with the automobile, although it made no real impact for several decades. Only after the Second World War were cities of the United States affected by the rapidly growing numbers of vehicles for individualized transportation. The automobile permitted people to move into suburbia with plenty of land around them. It freed them from dependency on public transportation. This newly acquired freedom of rapid movement over long distances has been the most powerful agent of change in urban growth patterns. The majority of land-use planners have fought it, since it has threatened planning designed to preserve the status quo. These planners have believed that they would be able to stop the ever-increasing out migration from the central cities into surrounding areas through land-use, social, and economic planning. The recent census data have proved that this out-migration is more significant than most planners would have thought. The 1970s appears to be the first decade ever in which people began to move back to small towns in rural areas.

What are people willing to pay for this individualized travel mode, for this freedom of movement? Will doubling, tripling, or quadrupling of current gasoline prices make people revert to pre-automobile centralization? Increases in energy costs may slow down migration in some areas but in light of the new high technologies, this will be, if anything, only temporary. To be convinced to the contrary, skeptics may wish to analyze human behavior in central European countries such as Romania and Hungary. I have encountered several people in these countries who were willing to spend from 40 to 50 percent of their disposable income for that freedom of movement, for their cars, while good, highly subsidized public transportation has been available to them in such capitals as Budapest and in all communist countries.

With this in mind, the scenario above by Sleeper on the woman in Vermont who is expected to do her work aided by an interactive electronic computer and conduct her business through teleconferences sounds plausible. Alvin Toffler's forecast of the coming electronic cottage idea described in his book *The Third Wave* (1980), is also more believable than a reversion to centralization. Adapting to this high technology will not be easy. It is always simpler to make an incremental than a contextual change. Nonetheless, it will provide one of the greatest challenges to land-use planners during the coming decades. The high technologies will influence all land-use issues discussed in the first chapter, but they will especially require planning for decline and for a new type of growth in presently rural areas. For example, Roger Starr, a planner, proposed to deal with the urban decline of New York City years ago by suggesting a reduction in her population, reclamation of decayed areas for open space, and attempts to make it a more livable city (Starr, 1976).

Another, and probably the most important, effect of the coming high technologies is that they will free the world from dependence on nonrenewable energy resources. While it is expected that several of the new technologies will be centralized, it is also evident that numerous new energy technologies such as several solar devices will decentralize and diversify much in the way of energy production. Both these scenarios will require new kinds of land-use planning.

Finally, the small-scale "appropriate technologies," championed by the late E. F. Schumacher and others, may have similar effects on natural resource use and the reduction of environmental impacts, but they actually represent the other side of the coin. For instance, with known high technologies, it is possible to see how books, newspapers, and mail could all become paperless or at least how the currently heavy use of paper could be reduced. How could this change affect resource use? Considering that a single issue of the Sunday New York Times presently consumes 62,860 trees, such a change could have tremendous impacts on the forest product industry (Sleeper, 1980). This example suggests that these high technologies, if properly used, have great potential for protecting the environment, conserving energy and other resources, and reversing the abuses caused by industrialization over the past three centuries. We should also be aware that these, like any other form of technology, will have many unforeseen, undesirable, consequences. Technological choices can be deceptive. Wide use of any new technology should be extensively debated, and in some instances, the wise decision may be not to adopt it. We have a good precedent for such debate in the case of SST flights. Our concern to protect the ozone layer of the outer atmosphere and save ourselves from the repeated sonic booms were reasonable criteria for banning the commercial application of this supersonic airplane.

New Tools for Land-Use/Landscape Planning

We can be certain that high technologies will dramatically change land uses during the coming decade. The question remains: will we be able to solve the problems of tomorrow with the tools of yesterday? We probably could not and we will not need to do so. The same high technology which is causing the highly industrialized world to become paperless will also eliminate the need for traditional mapmaking and printing of reports for land-use plans. It will more likely help to make planning more responsive to human needs and will aid planners in becoming more of a catalyst for learning and action. This assertion is not made on forecasts of future technology but rather on technology which is already available and is now being adopted by land-use planners. The new tools of land-use/landscape planning are being developed from three fundamental and interactive technologies — remote sensing, computers, and integrated circuits.

Remote sensing as a tool for planners is not new. However, there are two major developments in remote-sensing technology which are recent, contextual developments. First is the invention of the "multispectral scanner" or "multiband reconnaissance," as it is known, consisting of a number of camera units, each with a different combination of film and filter, which can provide separate images of the same area of the ground. It extends much beyond the visible spectrum into the ultra-violet range of the electromagnetic spectrum; into heat detection by specially designed scanners, circumventing many of the temporal or atmospheric conditions that impede most other kinds of remote sensing; and into radar technology which can record images through all but the heaviest rain (Parker and Wolff, 1973). These powerful devices have been scanning the earth continuously from satellites. In the United States alone, four satellites with ever-increasing capabilities and accuracy have gone into orbit since 1972, the date of the launching of the first so-called *Landsat* satellite (National Aeronautics and Space Administration, 1980). The French space agency, *Centre National d'Etudes Spatiales* (CNES), is now developing its own high resolution earth resource satellite to be launched in early 1984 (CNES 1978). Satellites with multispectral scanners are also being developed by Japan, Germany, and several other countries.

The second major development of this new remote-sensing technology is the ability to record data and store it electronically. Radiance received by individual detectors is converted into digital values. The received signals of Landsat 4, the fourth satellite in the series, is designed to record each 30 meter by 30 meter area in the form of pixel or picture elements, and is capable of identifying 256 different values (Figure 7). In place of visual inspection of earlier photographic information and generalization of homogenous areas into land-use and cover types, the electronic and numerical data processing open up enormous use potentials. Traditional mapping is being replaced by pertinent land-use data made available electronically and ready for numerical and quantitative data manipulation.

The two other fundamental technologies to complement the development in remote sensing are the interactive technologies of the computers and integrated circuits. The computer has been an important land-use planning tool since the early 1960s. In that decade, two powerful groups of planners emerged, the transportation engineers and water resource planners.

FIGURE 7 *Landsat 4 advanced satellite image using thematic mapper. The 30 X 30 meter pixel size provides land-use planners with sufficient information for planning at the substate and even at the community levels. (Source: Eros Data Center, Sioux Falls, S.D.)*

Both groups can attribute their influence to the availability of relatively high-speed, large-capacity computers. The transportation engineers have been able to analyze economic, social, and cultural characteristics of metropolitan regions and make forecasts of future economic development, population, and growth based on trend projections. They have used this information to determine highway location, size, and capacity and to successfully implement their recommendations. In turn, these highways have been the major pattern setters of land use and decentralization. As it was pointed out earlier, automobile technology and human desires for freedom of movement complemented this kind of transportation planning. It is safe to say that transportation planners, aided by computers, have become the most effective planners of recent decades (Boyce, Day, and McDonald, 1970). At the same time, water resource engineers advanced mathematical models, using multi-objective planning, made possible only by advances in computer technology (Dee, Baker, Drobney, Whitman, and Fahringer, 1973).

The integrated circuits, or "chips" as they are called, have the potential to make these new tools of land-use/landscape planning ubiquitous. A recent article in *Newsweek* featured a story under the title "And Man Created The Chip" (Sheils, 1980). It is this "chip" which has already made enormous impacts on our lives. We are now at the dawn of the era of the smart machine — an "information age" that will irrevocably change all land-use planning. Nowadays, all land-use planners should be able to work with computers. As machines become smarter, less computational knowledge is required of planners. As the power of computers — their ability to perform more tasks more quickly — has increased, their interactive capability has also emerged. It is now possible to train a planner of average abilities in a short course to use this powerful machine for its interactive capability. For example, the land-use planner is able to request maps, search procedures, and other spatial information by simple commands. In the third section of the book some of the future land-use planning scenarios are discussed with reference to remote sensing and computer technology.

CONCLUSIONS

Land-use planning has been modified primarily by many incremental technological changes since the dawn of industrialization. Currently, new technological developments have spurred major changes which are expected to alter radically land use and the procedure of land-use planning in this century. Among the most significant agents of change are: the shift from exhaustible to renewable energy; the opening up of the ocean as a new resource base; the combining of the electronic computer/video technology with the electric vehicle to speed up decentralization and provide many with new lifestyles. All these changes will challenge and significantly alter current land-use planning.

Increasingly more powerful computers, combined with such automated data acquisition devices as the multispectral scanner relaying ever more accurate and ample data to users, are changing the context of land-use planning. Even spatial data is being handled electronically and manipulated by numerical procedures. Just as the entire world is heading toward paperless transactions so are the maps and reports of planners being transformed by machines into numbers which can be retrieved in the form of brilliant colors, three-dimensional pictures, and even spatial sequences.

These new technologies are both promising and sobering. The potential for helping people to achieve a greater degree of individual fulfillment and productive work is enormous. Yet the absolute necessity for a massive job redesign to mitigate job displacement and for making enormous changes in land uses mostly by shifting population from highly centralized to decentralized areas is clear. The greatest challenge seems to be how to make technological choices to minimize the potentially negative effects of these enormous changes. The attitudes that we hold toward technology, science, and land-use issues, and the organizational capabilities of our society are yet another set of attributes which are affecting land-use planning. An analysis of them is in order and it is the focus of the next chapter.

CHAPTER 4

VALUES AND ORGANIZATIONS

Attitudes affecting land-use decisions have been increasingly polarized between the social, public, and community values on the one hand and the individual and business/corporate values on the other. This polarization has been aided by the tendency of both the public and the private sectors to centralize their respective organizations. For this reason, values and organizational capabilities are believed to be highly interactive. They are, therefore, discussed together in this chapter.

Of course, the land-use issues discussed in Chapter 1 are also interacting with values of people and the current organizational capabilities of our society. But if an organization such as a government body places little value on a land-use issue, such as flood hazard, it is simply ignored. Organizations such as governmental agencies can place much or little value on scientific knowledge. If a governmental agency places much value on a scientific finding, it may have a significant effect on landscape decisions and vice versa. In the case of water quality issues, the scientific community has greatly influenced the values of the Federal government. As stated earlier, the government spent over 140 billion dollars during the 1970s to clean up the nation's rivers and lakes. And finally, the adoption of any new technology, whether it is nuclear power to generate electricity or solar power, depends on the value or values that our society places on them and on our ability to set up an organization to implement our decisions.

One of the underlying themes of this book is that the emerging role of land-use planners is that of a catalyst for learning and action. If polarization exists between the public and private values or between the public (governmental) and private (individual and corporate) organizations, it will certainly obstruct the implementation of viable solutions, and will probably create bad feelings and much unwelcome struggle between the groups. Land-use and landscape planners therefore need to understand the origins of the often very diverse values of our society, how these values have changed through history, and how our organizational capabilities have evolved from a diffuse to a highly centralized organization. The major challenge for land-use planners appears to be how to arbitrate the conflicts among the various values of our society, and especially between the two polarized groups representing the public and individual interests. Finally, we need to speculate on how planners can adjust to the emerging organization which is changing in our current world from a highly centralized to a more balanced, centralized-decentralized mode.

SOURCE OF VALUES

Each of us has many values, biases, and opinions toward land uses or land-use issues. We may like or dislike shopping centers. We may be concerned or neutral about decentralization, or "sprawl," as it is labeled by many planners. We may fight against the construction of a nuclear power plant or be willing to accept the risk by not opposing it. In short, all of us have values which we may or may not express, but when we are not articulating our values we imply our *de facto* values by our very inaction. Some of our values seem to be more basic, cultural values and alter little over time, others can change more rapidly. In relation to basic cultural environmental factors, we may speculate that the values of a Midwest farmer in the United States toward the environment and land-use changes will be significantly different from those of a member of a collective farm in the Soviet Union. In the case of more changeable values, the nuclear power accident in 1979 at Three Mile Island in Pennsylvania presents a good example. It has influenced the attitudes of many against the use of nuclear power. Similarly, books and the lectures of articulate people are continuously changing or modifying our values. Finally, the results of public surveys can also exert such an influence.

In the past, land-use planners did not need to pay much attention to the values of ordinary people. For example, Le Notre, the planner of Versailles, the palace and the surrounding new town designed in the 17th century to house the French government, needed to concern himself only with the desires of the Sun King. It is well documented by Mumford (1961) and others, that for a long time planners were the agent of the rulers or the ruling class. They were mistrusted, and rightly so, by the common people. Some degree of mistrust still exists. However, contemporary land-use planners are well aware of the fact that they must cultivate a better understanding of public and individual values and their sources. For the purpose of this book, four basic sources are examined: environmental/cultural; objectivity based on science and technology; values generated by articulators; and public surveys when their results are disseminated.

Environmental/Cultural Sources

We have a good understanding of the ways in which the environment and cultural heritage shapes people's basic values toward the environment. These two factors always work in combination, their effect is certainly universal although either the cultural or the natural may predominate. For example, the Navajo Indians, who once occupied large areas of what are now the states of New Mexico and Arizona, had a significantly different attitude or value system toward their environment than the white men who emigrated from an industrializing Europe. The Navajo Indians had to live in harmony with nature; they did not have the means to do anything else. It seems that the natural environment factor had a greater influence on the American Indians. The Europeans, however, were able to exploit the land and build large cities, where before tribes were barely able to survive. The overwhelming attitude of the new Americans in the Southwest today is that technology will somehow assure them of the continuous growth which they perceive as essential for prosperity. For example, basically only a few scientists and planners are truly aware of the rapidly lowering water table, as available supplies are greatly abused by the invading masses. In this example, the cultural factors seem to be more dominant at present.

When we analyze Russian culture, it appears that the character and values of the Soviet people have been greatly influenced by the severe environmental conditions of the U.S.S.R. Burke (1956), a geographer who studied the relationship between man and nature in the Soviet Union, found that severe climatic conditions are the major reasons for repeated, large-scale crop failures. According to records, Burke found that there were 40 individual years during the 19th century when either severe winter cold or drought and dry winds destroyed the bulk of the Russian agricultural food supply (Burke, 1956, p. 104). We have been made well aware through the news media of similar conditions during recent decades. The harsh environment has produced a desire to control nature, going back many centuries. About 200 years before the Bolshevik seizure of power in 1917, Peter the Great, personally, and with great diligence, tried to import the newly developing industrial models from Western Europe and establish them in Russia to overcome the natural forces which produced periodic starvation. Similarly, in this century, the government announced in 1948 the "Great Plan for the Transformation of Nature," which called for large-scale afforestation, the planting of shelter belts, and huge irrigation projects designed to create an improved microclimate to overcome nature. This ambitious plan had only limited success, but it also demonstrated the need in the U.S.S.R. for a collective land-use system, which has been the basis for national survival for a very long time. Just imagine how few of the homesteaders who settled the hospitable midwest America during the last century could have survived on the inhospitable farms in Russia? In short, the severe climate of Russia is not only responsible for the desire of her people to dominate nature but also has greatly influenced the national land-use system, which was collective in nature during the feudal period. The Bolsheviks in 1928 acted to perpetuate this deeply rooted and perhaps essential land-use system of a harsh environment.

Science and Technology

In the previous two chapters, a case was made for better and more extensive use of scientific knowledge and for the important role of technology in dealing with land-use issues. Planners need to include these factors in land-use decisions, and the public needs to be aware of the pros and cons of both science and technology. We have plenty of evidence that both these factors have already influenced the values of many decision makers and a large sector of the public. Science and technology also provide many with a false sense of "confidence," "rationality," or "objectivity." The enormous success of transportation and water resource engineers in land-use planning during past decades can be attributed in part to their ability to use the "facts" and "figures" to impress on people that they indeed have the "right answer." They show charts, explain things through "numbers, quantities." The wizardry of the engineers, as they have used computers more extensively, has impressed many. There is a danger, however, that science and technology may be overvalued.

A case in point: on a professional tour of Portland, Oregon, some time ago, I was driving through the builtup flood plains of the city, where labels high on the walls marked the levels of floods over time. When I asked our tour guide, a land-use planner, about the chance of future flooding, his answer was simple. "The U.S. Corps of Engineers took care of that problem. They built plenty of dams on the Columbia River," he said. Others have total confidence that science and technology will solve our current energy crisis. For instance, a judge in Holyoke, Massachusetts, told me recently that "nobody needs to worry about the oil shortage. Exxon already has the answer!"

This optimistic attitude, this over-dependence on science and technology, has increasingly concerned many humanists. One of the most articulate philosophers and social critics, Michael Novak, wrote (1970):

> The American (and probably other western countries) way of life has brought to the surface of daily life a basic contradiction between science and humanism. The more science and technology advance,

the clearer their inner dynamic becomes. They are not directed toward the good of concrete, individual human beings but toward efficiency. The primary goal of scientific knowledge is power; the primary goal of technology is efficiency.

Concerns such as Novak's should have a sobering effect on those who have full confidence or faith in either science or technology. Land-use planners need to take note also, since in the learning process of planning, it is the land-use planner who should help to balance the overly optimistic and pessimistic views.

The Articulators

People who write books and articles, journalists of all kinds, lecturers, vocal advocates of all land-use issues, are all articulators who, in a lesser or greater degree, will influence the values of few or many. The articulators are the first to voice a problem or an issue. These people stimulate general interest in threshold events, an example being the continuing controversy over the Love Canal hazardous waste issue in Niagara Falls, New York. Others use their skills to create a crisis situation from a common problem. They have the ability of the cartoonist, but use words instead of drawings. Articulators are among the most effective opinion makers. They can be educated or uneducated, conservative or liberal, religious or atheistic, advocates or opponents of science and technology, they may come in all sizes, ages, and races, and are representatives of both sexes, but they all shape our values.

Articulators often create organizations ranging from small local groups opposing condominium conversion, a subdivision, or the filling of a wetland to those who, over the years, become mammoth organizations such as the Sierra Club, which has professional lobbyists in Washington to influence legislation affecting land uses or other matters. Some local bodies eventually become regional or even national organizations. The proliferation in America of conservation commissions as discussed in the chapter on land-use issues is a good example to demonstrate how opposition to the filling of a local wetland can generate much wider concern (Scheffey, 1969).

Articulators and the organizations that they help to establish often exaggerate and even distort information to achieve their objectives. Land-use planners find them on opposing sides at many land-use planning hearings and meetings. The planners' role once more is to bring the opposing parties to an acceptable solution. Through mediation planners often find that the disputes are much narrower in scope than they perceived at the outset.

Public Surveys

Opinion polls are being conducted for all issues at all levels and are not limited to political issues. In itself, a survey does not appear to influence our attitudes. Surveys, however, can become very important agents of change when they are disseminated, just for that purpose, to influence the opinion of others by proving a point of view from the survey results. Public survey results, just like scientific data and technological information, can be misused since they are analyzed by various statistical methods, each designed for varied purposes. A great many surveys must be analyzed by pseudo-statisticians who use an incorrect method or false application which distorts the results. Other statisticians may knowingly distort the findings in an attempt to change public opinion. Both groups fit Mark Twain's description: "he uses statistics like a drunk uses the light post — not for light but for support."

This discussion of the sources of our values is certainly not exhaustive, but even this brief summary demonstrates that our perceptions and values have many origins and that many of our values are highly changeable. It is essential that land-use planners acquire a basic understanding of this very complex human phenomenon. As reasoned earlier, values are the basis of every land-use decision. Value-free planning is nonexistent.

VALUE CHANGES IN HISTORY

Two contradictory attitudes toward land use and land ownership prevail in the United States and to a great degree in other western cultures. One represents our value for the public and the other for the individual right. Our public value is based on the notion that land, like air and water, is essentially a public good and the efficient use of which is beneficial to all citizens. The benefits won by resource conservation and by developing land which is best suited for development, and the costs avoided by restricting the development of poor or hazardous land, accrue to the population at large.

The individual value is prompted by an attitude that the individual's right in land-use decisions should not be restricted. It is marked by two beliefs: first, that individuals may own land in an absolute sense, and second, that they should be free of almost all restriction on its use. The underlying assumption is that this concept of property best advances the general welfare of the nation. In our society, vocal advocates for both beliefs generate enormous conflicts in the debate over land-use decisions. Each of these beliefs has an historical base. It is therefore essential that land-use planners acquire some knowledge of how these two prevailing values have polarized contemporary western societies.

Origins of Opposing Values

Public concern toward land goes back to the origins of most cultures. This tradition holds that God is the owner of land and that man acts as His trustee. In the Judeo-Christian tradition the Bible says that the land shall not be sold for ever: for the land is mine: for ye are strangers and sojourners with me. Ninety percent of the land of Israel today is managed in accord with this Biblical teaching. The government acts as trustee and leases land for terms not in excess of 49 years. The European feudal system was similar:

> The sovereign held land by divine right, and all others held it as tenants or sub-tenants. The tenants' interest was called fee title. The term fee was synonymous with feud or fief and meant that the fee title holder owed rents or duties to the holder of the superior title (Strong, 1977, p. 18).

American Indian theology concurs with the belief that land belongs to God but places the trust with all men in common rather than with government. The Calvinists held ideas similar to those of the Indians that mankind in common was God's trustee but held that, on creating government, men transferred trusteeship to that body. These beliefs are all variations on the single theme that land is owned by God, and a natural law governs its use. Man, acting either collectively or through the agency of governments, has the duty of a trustee to use and preserve the land resources. The rights of any individual are limited in time and extent by natural constraints and by rules established by the trustee.

During the 16th and 17th centuries, most colonial settlements were literally shaped by these views. For example, in all the English colonies, the King owned the land in his capacity of trustee, while the colonists were fee title holders who owed him stated obligations. Charters from the crown for establishment of towns tightly regulated the use of the land. For example, in 1666 the Connecticut colonial legislature granted all towns a right of preemption: no private owner could sell land without first offering it to the town. That is, the town's common interest took precedence over the fee holder's interest (Strong, 1977, p. 19).

The concept of land ownership under discussion met a major challenge from John Locke. It was Locke (1690) who proposed that all value in land results from the human labor expended to realize that value, and that by reason of that labor, man "annexes to something that was his property," that is, his own labor. Thus by the exercise of "improvement" a person elevates land from its natural, commonly held state to something which may rightfully be claimed as private. More importantly, perhaps, Locke also proposed that the appropriation of land by an individual by dint of his labor "does not lessen but increase the common stock of mankind." This notion that the public good is best furthered by private enterprise became a fundamental tenet of the American ethical order which has affected the general attitude toward land throughout that nation's history.

From the independence of the United States and throughout most of the 19th century the prevailing sentiment favored rapid transfer of land from public to private ownership. Settlement and resource extraction were perceived as serving the public interest, and there was little thought of how many settlements in what locations might most benefit the nation. The belief of the immigrants' forefathers that man was a caretaker, with an obligation to manage land resources wisely so as to maintain them for future generations, was almost totally discarded. There were a few exceptions, such as grants of land to the state to provide school and university revenues. Generous grants to railroads also helped to open up the country rapidly. The vast public domain was given or sold free of restrictions on alienation of use.

Challenges to the Lockean Thesis

Early challenges to the views of Locke had their origin in a concern for aesthetic and natural landscape values. The development of large industrial cities and regions of Europe and the rapid growth of American cities during the 19th century focused the attention of concerned people on the loss of natural and aesthetic values within these population centers. This romantic sentiment gave rise to the development of public parks in every major city by the end of the 19th century (Fabos, Milde and Weinmayr, 1968). The aim of the park planners was to "bring back a bit of nature" into the cities. The first truly public park was the Birkenhead Park in the industrial hinterland of Liverpool, England. Frederick Law Olmsted, Sr., the father of park and landscape planning in America, was greatly impressed by a visit to Birkenhead Park in 1850. Later, he wrote: "Five minutes of admiration and a few more spent in studying the manner in which art had been employed to obtain from nature so much beauty and I was ready to admit that in democratic America there was nothing to be thought of as comparable with this People's Garden" (Fabos, Milde and Weinmayr, 1968, p. 23).

For Joseph Paxton, the planner and designer of Birkenhead Park, for Olmsted, and for their contemporaries on both sides of the Atlantic, natural beauty was equated with Romantic settings, which was a response to perceived destruction of nature by the rapid growth of industrialization. The introduction of public parks also meant, to Olmsted, democracy. He liked to call Birkenhead Park the "People's Garden."

The rapid move to park planning and implementation was perhaps the first major challenge to the Lockean thesis of absolute ownership of land by individuals. This was soon followed by the preservation movement, and the development of public recreation areas, especially from the 1920s on. By the early 1960s, the attention of some articulators focused on ugliness and finally during that same decade efforts were made to plan the total environment. All branches of government have aided the reversion from individual ownership and rights. It is inevitable that this process will continue as we learn more and more about the cause/effect relationship of land uses and environment. To better understand this renewed public concern, each of these movements is further discussed.

Preservation Movement

Determined "to avoid the mistakes of the East," Olmsted was one of the many 19th century reformers who participated in the effort to create national parks throughout America, a many-sided battle which he himself saw as "a spontaneous movement...which we conveniently refer to as the genius of civilization" (Fabos, Milde and Weinmayr, 1968, p. 42). These articulators realized that the fierce beauty of Yosemite Valley (Figure 8) could not be created by human hands, but this and many other spectacular landscapes could be preserved from human destruction. To achieve this objective, Olmsted helped to prepare a national bill making the Yosemite Valley and Mariposa Big Tree Groves into state reservations. The legislation for Yosemite provided an early precedent for the national park movement, which began officially with the establishment of Yellowstone National Park in 1872. In 1916, the National Park Service was established to manage the growing numbers of national parks in the United States.

More importantly, the national park movement together with other emerging concerns toward public lands slowed down the rapid transfer of land from public to private ownership. As a result, today about one-third of the nation's land is still publicly owned and managed by the Federal government of the United States. Most of this public land is managed by the U.S. Departments of the Interior and Agriculture using strict management policies to protect the public interest. Transfer of this public land into private hands has not only stopped in the United States, but in this century the Federal government has purchased back large acreages from private owners especially on the Eastern seaboard, which was the first to be subdivided.

Also during this century, states and local governments have joined these preservation efforts. New York State, for instance, established the Adiron-

FIGURE 8   *Yosemite Valley (Ansel Adams photograph).*

dack region as a state park, some 6 million acres in extent, and at the local level, communities have preserved millions of acres of coastal and inland wetlands and beauty spots which have significant perceived value to state and local populations.

Public Recreation

State governments have made numerous attempts, starting with Yosemite Valley — initially preserved by the State of California — to establish public recreation areas. For example, the establishment of the Trustees of Public Reservations in Massachusetts in 1891 provided large parcels of land for recreation within the 250-square-mile area of the Boston Metropolitan region. The year 1895 marked the start of the first country park organization, in Essex County, New Jersey; and the first private acquisition of portions of the Palisades of the Hudson, across from New York City (Newton, 1971, p. 560). During the first two decades of this century, state parks for recreation were established in such states as Minnesota, Wisconsin, Pennsylvania, North Carolina, and Indiana. Yet historians mark 1920 as the beginning of large-scale establishment of public recreation landscapes.

One of the primary catalysts of the movement to create public recreation landscapes was Stephen Mather, the first director of the National Park Service. He had the sensible notion of promoting an ample, nationwide system of state parks to serve as a buffer to protect the great national parks from a dangerous avalanche of visitors in automobiles. To bring the attention of states to this problem he started to organize in 1920 a national conference, and a year later, 25 states attended the first Conference on State Parks. This event established a national movement for the development of public recreation areas. Ever since, the Federal, state and local governments have systematically acquired land, planned, and developed millions of acres, ranging from huge to small areas, for recreation. This large-scale recreation planning effort culminated in a voluminous study prepared by the Outdoor Recreation Resource Review Commission and completed in 1962.

The most important aspect of the development of public recreational landscapes was that it further limited the role of the private sector in land-use decisions. It has been the government's role to provide the population with most of its outdoor recreation opportunities.

Amelioration of Scenic Misfits

By the late 1950s, a new wave of aesthetic consciousness spread over the developed countries. It was a fight against ugliness. Articulators of this issue, such as Peter Blake, who wrote a provocative book, *God's Own Junkyard*,

became prominent. These spokespeople focused their attention on bill-
boards, unplanned developments, junkyards, strip developments and the like.
This movement gave the impetus to Federal, state and local legislation, all
designed to ameliorate what were perceived by these people as scenic misfits.
The zenith of this movement in the United States came in 1965, when
President Johnson, influenced by his wife, Lady Bird, called a White House
Conference on Natural Beauty. The dominant theme of the conference was,
however, how to eliminate "misfits." Between 1965 and 1968, 34 states
held similar conferences on "natural beauty."

The amelioration of scenic misfits did not require land acquisition.
Implementation came instead through police power. While police power did
not change the ownership of land, it clearly added a restriction on land uses
in many areas. The underlying assumption of these regulations is that this
concept of control best advances the general welfare of the nation.

Environmental Planning

From the late 1960s to the first part of the 1970s, was the decade of the
environmental movement. It also gave rise to the concept of total planning
of the environment. Of course, concern for the environment began well
before this decade. Reference has already been made to early environmental
advocates such as George Perkins Marsh, whose powerful statement, *Man and
Nature*, appeared in 1864. At the turn of the century, environmental
concern was also growing at the local level. For instance, zoning, another
policing device, has been used increasingly since its origins in early 19th
century New York (Toll, 1969). In fact, for many land-use planners who
have written on this subject in recent decades, and for practicing planners,
land-use planning has been synonymous with zoning, subdivision control,
and other regulations, all of which have been designed to limit the right of
the individual in developing private lands (Haar, 1971; Patterson, 1979).
This limited view of land-use planning will be challenged in subsequent
chapters.

Comprehensive environmental planning was not, however, institutional-
ized in the United States until the 1960s. During this decade at least two
major pieces of Federal legislation called for total planning of the environment and land uses. One was the Water Resource Planning Act of 1965,
which mandated that all water and related land resource planning must integrate environmental, economic, and regional development objectives (Water
Resources Council, 1968). The other was the National Environmental Policy
Act of 1969 (Zube, Brush and Fabos, 1975, p. viii) which requires that all
agencies of the Federal government include an environmental assessment in
each case of land-use planning and that all development is carried out in such

a way that negative consequences are minimized. Individual states soon after proposed and enacted similar legislation.

These developments, and many others which are not discussed here, have brought about a significant reversal of the Lockean thesis of 1690. This reversal has been an essential response to industrialization and its profound effects on the environment and land uses. A central element in Locke's reasoning, which while perhaps arguable in the late 17th century, contains a fundamental error when considered today. For Locke, the appropriation of land by an individual did not prejudice the well-being of anyone else because there was an abundance of land. He drew an analogy with drinking from a river: "Nobody could think himself injured by the drinking of another man ...who had a whole river of the same water left him to quench his thirst, and the case of land and water where there is enough for both, is perfectly the same." The point is, of course, that there is not "enough for all." Even water, which Locke obviously considered to be unlimited in supply, has proven to be a very limited commodity indeed in many parts of the world, especially in large urban regions (Fabos, Greene and Joyner, 1978).

EVOLUTION OF ORGANIZATIONS

Land-use planning, like any other human activity, has been greatly affected by the organizational capabilities of societies in historical time. The term "organization" is defined here as all governmental functions and individual and corporate management activities which are set up to plan and implement all plans. In analyzing the evolution of the organizational capabilities of western culture, we can see a significant correlation between organizations and land-use actions throughout history. An analysis of this evolution helps us to understand some of the current developments, for instance, how the "new federalism" and the "block grant program" in the United States represent changes and developments in organization by shifting much of the decision making to the lower levels of government.

The thesis presented here is that these current organizational developments represent a major or contextual change from our previous, highly centralized or pyramidal organization to a new centralized/decentralized mode of which the latter delegates power to the lower levels of government. This organizational change parallels changes in land use, in science, technology, and our value systems. In land use, we have experienced a major reversal from a previously ever-increasing centralization of rural population in cities to a decentralization and a move back to rural areas. Scientific developments such as operations research and other mathematical capabilities combined with high technology give an impetus to the current decentralization of decision making and the shift of population to rural communities. Our polarized value system has produced so great a range of values that we often refer to developed countries as highly pluralistic societies. A highly centralized society cannot respond well to the needs of a pluralistic society. For these reasons, our centralized organizations derived from past centuries can no longer sufficiently serve us.

Prior to discussion of the organizational change which is taking place in our society at present, a review of the evolution of previous organization is needed.

The Pyramid Organization

An increase in city population from a hundred thousand during the Italian Renaissance of the 15th century to over 10 million in today's largest cities took less than half a millenium. This period was without major change in organizational mode, which may best be represented by the simple pyramid model, characterized by a single central authority at the top and various levels of subordinates (Figure 9). For instance, the city state of the

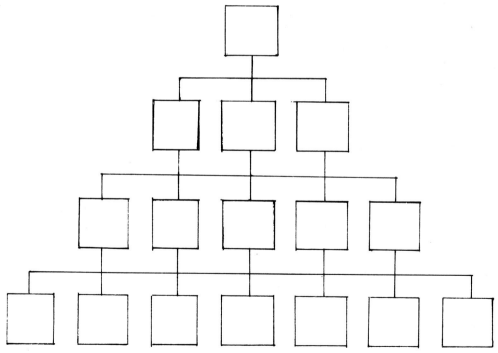

FIGURE 9   *The pyramid organization.*

Renaissance period consisted of a central city of about one hundred thousand housing the government, the merchant class, and the guilds of various crafts. This small city was supported by some 10 times as many farmers, peasants who provided the food for the city population. The sphere of influence of these city states was only a few hundred square miles. During this period, an attempt was made to systematize the cities. For example, Antonio Filarete's plan for an ideal city, Sforzinda, a star-shaped design with its radial road pattern, was an attempt to order the organic pattern of previous cities built during the Middle Ages (Giedion, 1967, pp. 46-47). While the ideal city was never built, the Renaissance era nevertheless adopted systematized elements, such as piazzas or city squares and streets.

During the Baroque period of the 16th and 17th centuries, incremental systematization and specialization created a more effective and efficient bureaucracy for tax collection, planning, and management: in short, the organizational pyramid was enlarged and improved. By the end of the 17th century, some cities attained a population of several hundred thousands. According to some estimates, London reached about 700,000. The Baroque order, with its wide boulevards, was overlaid on all cities which were controlled by the western powers. The same force also reshaped the countryside. In England, for instance, a series of enclosure acts produced a well-managed, orderly landscape, where hedge and tree-planting enclosed each 10- or 12-acre parcel (Hoskins, 1955, p. 152). The Baroque organization was developed sufficiently to enable western countries to colonialize the world. By the dawn of the Industrial Revolution, a handful of European countries were able to control the greater portion of the globe. It was a phenomenal development of highly centralized governments.

The industrial period of the 19th and early 20th centuries further developed this already impressive pyramidal organization mode, which was adopted by industry, and produced such well-known, giant international companies as Coca-Cola and General Motors. This central organization was also used by organizers of labor unions or by revolutionaries such as the Bolsheviks. This was the era of imperialism: the imperial capitalism, the imperial communism, the imperial corporate power, or, for that matter, the imperial power of some religious groups, such as the Catholic Church, which was controlling the religious beliefs of almost one-fifth of the world's population by the early 20th century. And finally this organizational knowhow permitted not only massive industrialization, development, power, and control, but it also brought on this century's two world wars, only 20 years apart from each other.

A Model for Change

The limits of the pyramidal organization mode were reached by the early part of this century. Its maturity and even decay took many forms, the most visible perhaps, being inefficiency or, in some cases, complete breakdown. As the chain of command was lengthened over the centuries through the continuous proliferation of the influence of a centralized government, or corporation, or religion, major changes have occurred, especially during the mid-20th century and those changes are continuing.

On the international scene the end of the colonial period came through the independence of colonies. The former colonies of the western countries broke away one by one. The world map was reshaped within a couple of decades. This independence movement which is, for all practical purposes, complete, also brought about the nationalization of corporate property belonging to the mother countries. In the communist world, the same disintegration has occurred. First, Yugoslavia broke away from the Soviet Union in the late 1940s. Then China, Albania, Rumania, and the communist parties of the western European countries created an ideological split, each of them attempting to interpret communist doctrine a little differently. During this period, the communist world often had to resort to force to preserve its cohesion.

While the dismantling of the centralized powers of the communist and western blocs at the international level went on during the 1950s and 1960s, centralization still increased at the national levels during the same period. In the United States, for instance, the Federal government continued to gain more power, especially during the 1960s when Federal legislation proliferated. Much of the massive Federal effort was an attempt to correct the enormous problems of centralized urban America. Crowded and inefficient cities had perforce led to bankruptcy of life. In spite of the immense Federal effort, the urban poor turned to violence, burning down their own neighborhoods and commercial areas in the 1960s. John Lindsay, then the mayor of New York, wrote an eloquent book (Lindsay, 1969), on the problems of the largest U.S. city of that period, which represents the plight of all large cities. While he proposed many innovative solutions, he claimed that New York is unmanageable.

Perhaps the essence of the centralized, Federal effort to solve urban and other problems was that all aid from that source was very rigidly allocated, most often did not respond to local need, and consumed large portions — estimates ranged from one-third to two-thirds — of its various programs in bureaucracy or red tape. It also meant that the beneficiary of any given program, under this highly centralized system, received only between one-third to two-thirds of the allotment.

It became obvious to some planners that drastic or contextual change in organization was needed to overcome these problems. The solution proposed during the early 1970s was "New Federalism," a device which has attempted to cut the "red tape" by allocating Federal funds to states and local communities with greatly reduced bureaucratic requirements or with much greater autonomy for the beneficiaries.

Is the "New Federalism" the new device of the Federal government or was this invented prior to the 1970s? Donald Schon in his book *Technology and Change* (1967) argues that corporations discovered the need for a new model during the 1950s. He calls this the "new corporate form or model." According to Schon, as industries expanded their research and development programs after the Second World War, many of their research efforts characteristically tended to yield unexpected results. For instance, companies in the food business found themselves in "possession of new devices for extruding plastics. Paper companies developed new textile fiber. Electrical firms gave birth to the new technology of powder metallurgy" (Schon, 1967, p. 120). Corporations saw a new opportunity and tended to be flexible and adaptive in their ability to commercialize unexpected technical blessings. To illustrate this development, Schon (1967, p. 121) uses the 3M company as the "most famous example":

> It began with sandpaper, moved into commercial coatings, marketed Scotch tape and then moved in rapid succession to magnetic tape, cleaning products and games among many other products.

All these businesses have built on the parent company's central research and development program. In each case, 3M formed a new management group and a new business was launched as a virtually autonomous division of the company. Most importantly, the pyramidal organization was replaced by a more horizontal structure (Figure 10). This diagram, when compared with the pyramidal organization mode (Figure 9), represents the most profound change, equaling in significance the potential effects of emerging high technology or current scientific developments. This new corporate model has provided an attractive alternative to the pyramidal model, which has become increasingly inefficient and rigid. The most salient aspect of the new corporate model or, for that matter, the "New Federalism," is its greater efficiency and flexibility, and thus greater responsiveness to new or local needs. This new organizational mode seems to be able to respond to the many values of our increasingly pluralistic societies.

John Naisbitt, in his recent book *Megatrends* (1982, p. 189) expands on this idea of moving toward decentralization and local decision making. He contrasts the pyramid or hierarchial models of the industrial era with a new

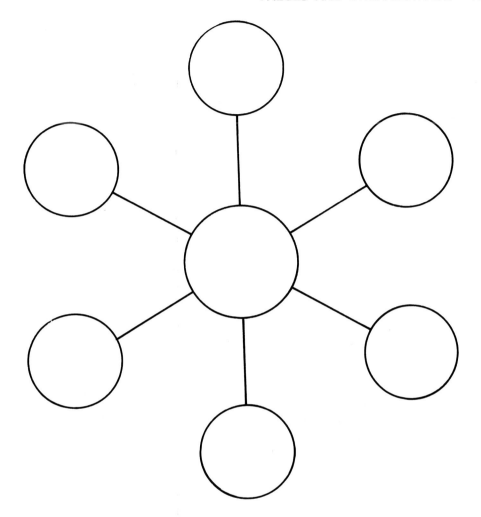

FIGURE 10 *The new corporate model.*

management style he calls "networking." Naisbitt claims that this emerging organizational model increases the communication "that creates the linkages between people and clusters of people. In his view, networks exist to "foster self-help, to exchange information, to change society, to improve productivity and work life, and to share resources" (Naisbitt, 1982, p. 192).

These two concepts, the first by Donald Schon and the second by John Naisbitt, both complement each other and support the thesis of this book. The new organizational model, with networking, will increasingly aid land-use planners in making intelligent local land-use decisions in the context of the larger environment. Among the networking examples Naisbitt cites, perhaps the exchanging of information is the most pertinent to land-use planning. Information on landscape/natural resources, on effects of hazards such as hazardous waste disposal problems and other development-related issues, can all be included at the local level. Yet most of this information has been generated by Federal, state and regional agencies. Networking aided by high technology can bring up-to-date information to the local users. Networking tailored to the needs of planners is becoming available (Figure 11).

CONCLUSIONS

The claim is made here that the interface between human values and organizational mode is very significant, and that major changes have occurred in both areas in recent decades.

Our values have originated from two sources. Our public or social value derived from theologies, while the values which express our individual interests have their origin in the Baroque era and were first expressed by Locke (1690) in the *Second Treatise on Government*. While a majority of

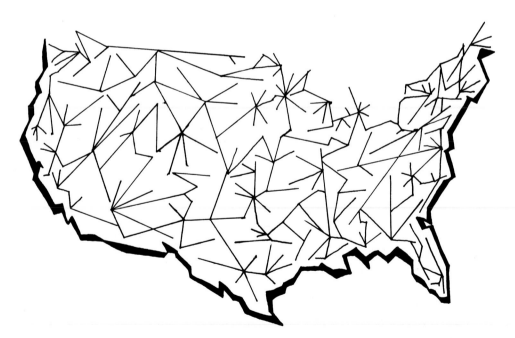

FIGURE 11 *LOGIN, the Local Government Information Network. This networking was developed recently by Control Data for information exchange connecting local governments with junctures to their common problems. The majority of these planning decisions do affect local land uses.*

people in western societies is affected by both these historically dominant value systems, one or the other may dominate various groups. As values originate in different sources, western countries, and especially the United States, have evolved into highly pluralistic societies, where each of the many subgroups or interest groups holds a different set of values.

The pyramidal organizational mode which dominated western societies for the past five centuries became increasingly rigid, inefficient, and inappropriate for pluralistic societies of the developed countries. A change came about, however, from a new organizational mode developed by corporations. This mode, while it maintains a central authority, provides the subunits with great autonomy. Thus this new mode is much more flexible, more responsive to current or local needs, and more efficient. This new corporate model combined with networking has started to change the previously highly centralized governments in recent years. The Federal government in the United States, for instance, has started to adapt this mode under the term "New Federalism." Predictions are that this new "corporate model" will replace the highly centralized pyramidal model in the coming decades. This new organizational mode is not only more appropriate for our pluralistic societies but it is also compatible with the decentralization of our large urban populations and with the high technology which is further aiding this trend.

CHAPTER 5

THE CULTURAL LANDSCAPE

The forces discussed in the previous chapter have produced what is called for present purposes, the cultural landscape, which is, in fact, several landscapes. The millions of individual land-use decisions which have been the influential forces already discussed in previous chapters, have resulted in huge monolithic urbanized and agricultural landscapes. The modern agricultural landscapes are often described as monocultures, meaning that the land is used for growing only one type of crop. The monoculture is the most common type of agricultural land use in developed countries. Highly specialized food production has resulted in there often being millions of acres of one type of crop. Similarly, the other land uses — the urban, the forests, and even the wilderness preserve — reflect this baroque order of specialization. The product of the previous five or six centuries can be labeled as "monocultural landscapes."

These monocultural landscapes have achieved many human objectives, through their very efficiency, but they have also created problems of enormous magnitude and have limited many options or flexibility in terms of unforeseen repercussions. Monocultural landscapes do in fact violate basic ecological, economic, and landscape/land-use principles by increasing vulnerability to manmade and natural hazards such as flooding and disasters like infestations of disease: they have cast a long shadow on the future. This chapter further illustrates the characteristics of the monocultural landscapes: the importance of diversity; the vulnerability of monocultural land uses; and some of the future land-use options which could minimize future uncertainties, while increasing land-use options.

MONOCULTURAL LANDSCAPES

The natural landscape is the resource base for the cultural landscape, and it has influenced the development of cultural landscapes throughout history. Regardless of which continent one analyzes, the major component of the natural landscape can be easily divided into several natural landscape types based on landform between the mountains and the coastal areas. Most often coastal areas are bordered with flat lands followed by undulating land, rolling hills, steep hills and mountains. This landscape continuum from coastal areas to mountain tops can range from a few miles to many miles. The greater the distance or the larger the land areas in the least constraining flat, undulated landscapes, the greater opportunity it provides for cultural activities.

The cultural landscapes have been superimposed on the natural landscapes and reflect a similar but reversed continuum. High-density often high-rise center cities are most frequently built in coastal areas or near major rivers, which give way to intermediate densities, then fringe or suburban areas which usually fade into farm landscapes up to the steep hills, where forest or unforested wild land takes over (Research Planning and Design Associates, Inc., 1970, p. N-19). Often these cultural landscape types (Figure 12) occupy large areas ranging from many thousands to several millions of acres of homogeneous land uses. Indeed, planners often refer to them as suburban, farm or wildland landscapes. Jean Gottman, the French geographer, found that urbanized areas often grow together to form what he called an urban megalopolis (Gottman, 1961). In the case of the Eastern United States, Gottman discovered that urbanization was almost continuous between Boston and Washington by the late 1950s (Figure 13). Not only the agricultural and forest landscapes have been characterized by monoculture, but these large regional developments of urban areas have similar homogeneous characteristics, and they too, can be labeled as monocultural landscapes or urban scapes. Land-use diversity, at least on these large regional scales, has been greatly reduced over the past five centuries as the forces of development converted the rural lands to urban and high-intensity agricultural uses.

IMPORTANCE OF DIVERSITY

These monocultural landscapes or large monolithic land uses seem to violate basic ecological principles and economic, aesthetic, and planning norms. But prior to discussing the vulnerability of monocultural land uses, one needs to understand the basis for these principles/norms.

To date, probably the ecologists have developed the most convincing argument for the importance of diversity. Margalef (1971) states that "the ecologist sees in any measure of diversity an expression of the possibilities of constructing feedback systems" which imply increased ecological stability based on longer food chains, more symbiosis and reduced oscillations or

FIGURE 12 *Natural and cultural landscape continua.*

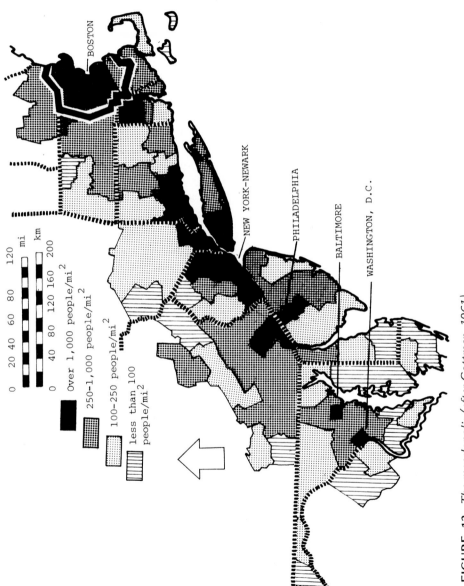

BOSTON

NEW YORK–NEWARK

PHILADELPHIA

BALTIMORE

WASHINGTON, D.C.

Over 1,000 people/mi^2

250–1,000 people/mi^2

100–250 people/mi^2

less than 100 people/mi^2

mi
0   20   40   60   80   120

km
0   40   80   120   160   200

FIGURE 13   *The megalopolis (after Gottman, 1961).*

fluctuations. Ecological diversity means the presence of more species or in other words the total opposite of monoculture. The more species present, the greater the possibilities for adaption to changing conditions, whether these be short-term or long-term changes in climate or other factors. Or to put it another way, the greater the gene pool, the greater the adaptation potential. Eugene Odum, the noted ecologist, urged the adoption of naturally diverse communities in the planning of agricultural ecosystems: "It would seem to be most risky for man to depend on only one or a few varieties of wheat or pine trees just because the yield happens to be highest at the moment. Should a sudden disease or climatic change occur, specialized species or varieties could be wiped out" (Odum, 1963, p. 34).

The trend in land-use decisions has clearly run counter to this ecological principle. We have not only reduced the number of species used in agriculture, but have converted naturally diverse landscapes into single uses, whether the new use is a large wheat field, pine forest or monolithic suburbia.

The economic norms in regard to diversity are very similar to ecological principles. The discussion of the evolution of organizations in the previous chapter suggested that the more successful corporations have discovered the need to diversify. Indeed, the organizational framework of the "new corporate model" is fully based on the concept of diversity. Over the past 30 years, successful corporations have systematically diversified their operations by two means. First, they have achieved their aim by creating new products as byproducts of their research and development — the commercialization of "unexpected technical blessing," as was illustrated by the 3M company. Secondly, corporations have merged to increase their diversity. A highly specialized small company, for instance, which is fully dependent on Federal contracts, may be wiped out by a change of policy as easily as a specialized plant species or variety of wheat by a sudden disease or climatic change. Large corporations, through this "merger" device, have been able to deal with uncertainty much more effectively, just as more diverse ecosystems are able to do when sudden unexpected changes occur. For many centuries, artists and designers have also recognized diversity or landscape complexity as the major contributor of aesthetic quality. More recently much work has been done by experimental psychologists dealing with the phenomenon of "diversity" or "complexity" of the landscapes around us. Using abstract symbols and simulating landscape scenes scaled for relative diversity/complexity, (Berlyne, 1963; Vitz, 1966; Day, 1967; Munsinger and Kessen, 1964; Terwillinger, 1963; and Wohlwill, 1968) positively correlated stimulus complexity with individual preferences. These scientists postulated that landscapes which are visually more diverse or complex provide a greater degree of "pleasingness" or "interestingness" than do undifferentiated (or monocultural) landscapes, provided they are not so complex to be incomprehensible.

Common sense planning norms constitute another set of reasons for the importance of diversity. From the landscape/land-use point of view, at least four working principles or norms, when implemented, would result in a more diversified landscape. These principles are discussed elsewhere, but they are pertinent here and are, I believe, worth repeating. These landscape planning principles are as follows (Fabos, 1979, pp. 56–57):

1. Development should be discouraged in areas of significant resource value. Many of the requirements and amenities of modern urban life — ranging from food to attractive scenery to gravel for concrete construction — are currently available only outside of our urbanized areas. Much of this local or regional scarcity can be avoided by preserving these biological, physical and aesthetic resources within the region and by acting to prevent their needless elimination, degradation or obliteration.

2. Development should be discouraged in areas of natural and manmade hazard. The losses and hardship that result from such natural hazards as floods and such human-caused hazards as noise and air pollution occur not only to the people and properties immediately affected, but also to the wider society that is called on to provide relief to the victims. By keeping developments away from such areas as flood plains which are most often vital, highly productive agricultural lands, we not only reduce hazard but provide additional options, an essential attribute of increased diversity.

3. Development should be encouraged in areas best suited for it. The costs associated with developing land for typical urban uses often increase owing to unfavorable site conditions such as slope. The cost of living on a site, once developed, can also increase owing to the nature of the site. It costs more and uses more energy, for instance, to heat a house in New England when it is located on a north-facing slope, exposed to winter winds and receiving less sun, rather than on a protected southern slope. Third, amenities, such as visual qualities or the proximity of recreation areas, constitute another important suitability factor.

4. The ecological "carrying capacity" of the regional environment should not be exceeded. Land-use/landscape planners have been influenced by ecological models such as Odum's "compartmental" model of ecosystem development (Figure 2), which implies that it is possible to determine the sort and amount of development that is conducive to maintaining an optimal degree of ecological diversity, which would result in greater stability and productivity. If a value is to be put on minimizing the unnecessary degradation of the environment, then its "carrying capacity" — its ability to accommodate human activities without being irreparably damaged — must be identified and respected.

Each of these four arguments provides powerful reasons for the importance of diversity, yet past and many current land-use decisions violate these principles and norms. We have reduced the natural diversity of our local areas, regions, and much developed land by creating monolithic, monocultural landscapes, by filling marshes, developing flood plains and other unsuitable areas, by ignoring inherent site suitabilities and the very important resource base. These resources are essential to maintaining populations on a continuing basis. Most importantly, past land-use decisions have increased our vulnerability in regard to environmental, aesthetic, economic, and social consequences.

MONOCULTURAL LANDSCAPES AND VULNERABILITY

The primary reasons for planning are to achieve human ends, to increase or maintain options, and to minimize uncertainty or maximize certainty. The lack of land-use diversity or our extensive monocultural land uses have made us especially vulnerable in the areas of limiting our options and increasing uncertainties. A long time before I became a landscape planner, these issues came forcefully to my attention.

As a young boy in Hungary during the Second World War, I grew up with the depressing news of war torn Russia. The tragic destruction and vulnerability of urban populations were the most shocking daily news events. The demise of Leningrad especially frightened my family. As the war turned its direction to the West, we had to live with the coming threat of war on our doorstep. We were prepared for the worst. We were well aware that one could survive injuries or escape death, only to succumb to lack of food or shelter. For years, my father was carefully planning to meet the worst eventuality.

My family was fortunate to live on a farm. Unlike the highly specialized farms to which we have become accustomed in the United States, my father's farm was most diversified. It had several acres of orchards producing dozens of kinds of fruits and nuts. It grew all the grains of the region. It raised hundreds of poultry, hogs and had a herd of milk cows and beef cattle. It had several sheep and six horses, in spite of the fact that our farm was among the most highly mechanized in pre-war Hungary.

In the early years of the war, we had to hide food from the German and Hungarian armies, which raided us regularly. Then it was the coming front, the Russian army, which forced us to use every kind of ingenuity we had. In preparation for this takeover, we spent many dark nights digging holes in remote areas in which to hide potatoes, carrots and beets. We made tunnels deep in the huge hay stacks to hide grains, meat and other food products which could be conserved in dry places. We sealed most of our clothes in waterproof barrels and buried them behind basement walls. My father put away much more of everything than was needed for our family. We needed seeds for the post-war era to plant the fields, but we were also concerned about our relatives and friends living in cities.

On December 4, 1944, the Soviet army invaded the area. My home town and our farm became a battleground for the following four months. During this time we stayed with relatives some 30 kilometers from the raging war, while my father returned frequently to the area to take out some very much needed food from the hiding places to replenish our supplies. We had plenty of food left after the war. We were able to plant all the fields and distribute much food to relatives and friends. We could do all this, not only because we were farmers, but because our farm was highly diversified. Just imagine how well an American wheat farmer would fare in a similar situation.

This example is probably too dramatic and many would think that there is no need to be concerned about this magnitude of uncertainty. Nevertheless, this story shows the incredible interaction between diversity and resilience, thus providing the most powerful argument against the huge, highly centralized, monocultural land uses if we are concerned with maintaining our options and decreasing the uncertainties which can result from them. We can also find countless and often dramatic examples resulting in large part from our highly specialized monocultural land uses.

The widespread urban riots in America during the 1960s, discussed earlier, were similar in nature to devastating destruction of huge wheat fields by a disease. Urban/social disease and plant disease can move rapidly in monolithic agricultural lands or urban areas.

The current depression in the state of Michigan is attributed to the problems of the auto industry. This highly centralized, monopolistic, inflexible industry is not only affecting the lives of its workers but has had an adverse impact on the population of the entire region.

The homogeneity of Howard Johnson's restaurant-hotel chain all along America's interstate highway system has proved vulnerable to a similar depression resulting from the two oil shortages of 1973 and 1979. Its stock value plunged and eventually the company was sold at about half of its value prior to the energy crisis.

Undiversified, single-purpose recreation industries, too, have experienced periodic slumps. A slump may result from a lack of snow for the ski industry or of gasoline to bring visitors to remote recreation areas. There are many other similar devastating circumstances which are beyond the control of the owners of these enterprises. Their primary problem always is that they are dependent only on a single activity, hence they are incredibly vulnerable to many unforeseeable circumstances.

These monocultural uses at the regional and often national scale, however, make us most vulnerable. For instance, the blackout of the electric power network in the Northeast in the fall of 1965 paralyzed the whole region instantly. Most of us have experienced major transportation strikes which have similar paralyzing effects on a region.

In short, any major concentration of land uses, activities, any monolithic institutions, any system or land use which does not provide alternative possibilities, are creating vulnerability. Land-use planners have to take note of the importance of diversity in spite of the fact that homogeneous, monolithic uses are often attractive because they seem to be more efficient. So-called urban sprawl, or the desire of the middle class to move into suburbia in the post–war era can be directly attributed to the widespread perception of the problems of living in huge conurbations. Suburbia, however, has been in many ways another monocultural land use. That is probably the reason why millions of Americans have moved further out into rural communities, which are much less centralized and much more diversified, offering people more options and a better chance to adjust to uncertainties.

FURTHER OPTIONS

The cultural landscapes and urban scapes have clearly resulted from the enormous forces discussed in previous chapters. We have responded to those forces, but the results are less than satisfactory. We have responded to issues as they appeared. We have directed much of science and technology to help us to solve land-use issues. We have modified our values and enlarged our bureaucracies through increasingly centralized governments and other organizations to respond to problems. Yet we have been unable to keep ahead of our land-use problems. The major challenge for the future is to find ways to act positively and creatively by foreseeing and avoiding problems, by finding opportunities instead of being the victims of circumstances.

Let us examine in greater detail each of the major forces which are covered in the previous chapters, and speculate on plausible options to better deal with those forces. In the chapter on land-use issues it was pointed out that there is significant interdependence among the seven land-use issues discussed. Yet land-use planning seldom deals with more than one or at the very best only a few of them. When we have growth pressures, we plan for them. When we need additional resources to maintain our population, we search for those resources. When our community or region is declining, only then do we worry about it. Similarly, we are concerned with impacts only when they become evident.

In comparison to this reactionary approach to issues, intelligent people, when planning their lives, deal with a multitude of issues simultaneously. A sensible couple, for instance, plans for the needs of their children during each phase of their development. They buy life insurance for them while young, set up a savings program for the college years. They have a retirement program and possibly some investment program to ensure an adequate standard of living during their less productive years. They plan for future uncertainties with health, life, and disability insurances. If they own land or property, they attempt to find an optimum time for use or sale.

This sensible approach has much applicability to land-use issues. A region or community which is impacted by great growth pressures, for instance, should deal with all the seven issues discussed in Chapter 1. By dealing with the population maintenance issue, planners may find that growth must be curtailed to ensure a steady supply of necessary water, sand and gravel and the like. Planners need to know something about the life expectancy of new industry, commerce or the like. If the community or the region has any resource base, even if its utilization may not be feasible now, it should maintain access to it by preserving it. Similarly, the potential impacts of further land–use changes should be evaluated prior to implementation. Such a comprehensive approach would result in a diverse landscape which would ensure a greater stability.

Similarly our response to science could improve greatly. Much of the current application of science to land-use decisions is also reactionary. As was pointed out in Chapter 2, most current scientific efforts deal with problems such as how to reduce the stresses we have created by urban concentration or through any of the monocultural land uses. Applied science would be more useful in helping us to determine the carrying or holding capacity of landscapes, or in providing land-use planners with opportunities for growth and options for a greater degree of landscape utilization, instead of focusing on corrective measures. Science, for instance, could help us greatly to find ways of disposing of our waste by researching how much waste the various ecosystems could assimilate without ever reaching a threshold condition, or, in other words, to determine the environmental holding capacity for waste and natural regeneration.

In regard to technology, it appears that the major, or contextual, technological developments will help to diversify and decentralize existing land uses. Our response to each new technology should take the course of a careful and detailed impact assessment, with adoption only possible when the impacts are acceptable.

Our response to human values should have one major objective: that is, to lessen the polarization between two extremes of views. The development of useful approaches to the problem will be discussed in parts two and three of this book.

Finally, our developing organizational capability promises to give land-use planning a more balanced approach in regard to land-use issues. New organizations must be capable of dealing with global issues on the one hand and local issues on the other. The former need increased centralization through creation of global federations if we wish to respond to worldwide environmental stresses. Secondly, land-use planning must respond better to local needs, but land-use planners must understand the consequences of local decisions on the larger environment.

PART TWO
PLANNERS' RESPONSES

CHAPTER 6

EVOLUTION OF LAND-USE PLANNING

Planners have responded to land-use issues for several millenia. The roots of contemporary land-use planning in Western culture, however, stretch back only into the 15th century, which marked the start of the Renaissance period in present-day Italy. Filarete's star-shaped city "Sforzinda" was an early attempt to organize the land use of an entire city based on the Renaissance theory of the centrally organized building (Giedion, 1967, p. 44). Another attribute of this *citta ideale* (ideal city), was that it provided its residents with better protection from attackers. Its central observation post was to give a clear view of the entire city and its surroundings. The encircling wall of this imaginary city would have been designed to include a series of regularly indented bastions from which flanking fire could be directed upon the attacker (Figure 14). The nature of these and other land-use issues was perceived by Renaissance planners as physical problems.

Land-use planners offered mostly physical solution to land-use issues until this century. The introduction of zoning during the early 20th century provided a new, nonphysical or legal device to deal with land-use issues (Toll, 1969). Since the introduction of zoning, land-use planning has been greatly expanded by many additional legal devices and numerous economic, social, and policy-planning actions. Land-use planning has become a highly complex activity pursued by numerous public agencies at all levels of government and by private planners ranging from the large interdisciplinary planning teams of corporations to individual land-use planning consultants. Land-use planning has been influenced and shaped by all those forces which are discussed in part one of this book and probably many others.

As land-use issues proliferated, so did land-use planning, expanding from local to large-scale regional, statewide and even national activity. The powerful forces of scientific findings, new technology and changing social values all have been contributing to the fascinating and often rapid evolution of land-use planning. To better understand this phenomenon, six areas of

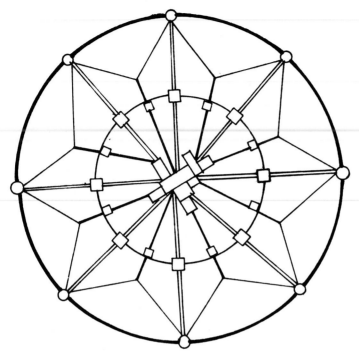

FIGURE 14 *Filarete's "Sforzinda," the star-shaped city with its radial road pattern. Sixteen main streets radiate from the central piazza to the eight city gates and the eight corner towers. Midway, each street crosses an open square, eight of which have a church in the center.*

concern are analyzed in this chapter. First, the changing role of land-use planners will be discussed. It will be followed by an analysis of the proliferation of disciplinary planners and the emergence of professional planners. Thirdly, public and private land-use planning activities will be summarized. Fourthly, the development of increasingly sophisticated planning processes or models is presented. It is followed by a brief discussion on the expansion of single-purpose planning to multipurpose or a more comprehensive approach. Finally, it will be shown how the planning hierarchy has developed over the past centuries.

THE CHANGING ROLE OF LAND-USE PLANNERS

The dream of an "ideal city" or a plan of a "perfect physical environment" was for centuries the principal interest of land-use planners. Although some land-use planners still maintain this interest, it is clear to most planners that their role has been changing significantly, especially during the past century. Contemporary land-use planners are being perceived increasingly as facilitators of an ongoing planning process, acting as synthesizers of the many factors of concern and as catalysts of the often lengthy debate on the tradeoffs, land-use options and environmental, economic, and social consequences of alternative plans.

The traditional role of the land-use planner as a form giver is, however, still an important one. The physical arrangement of land uses and their interrelationships greatly determine their functional use and their aesthetic quality. Innovative planners such as the English inventor Ebenezer Howard, the father of the concept of the "garden city," and Frank Lloyd Wright, the proponent of "Broadacre City," were essential visionaries, who are still very much needed to stimulate land-use decisions. The utopians of the 19th century also had profound effects — sometimes beneficial, sometimes regrettable — on land uses. A brief review of them is in order.

Recent Utopians

The Scottish mill-owner Robert Owen was one of the first utopians of the 19th century to implement his vision. In responding to the problems of the industrial society of his time, he proposed the establishment of small communities the initial economic basis of which would be agricultural, to be followed by manufacturing as the community coalesced. Buildings were to be "planned square, with communal arrangements for domestic chores" (Harrison, 1969, p. 29). Although a few Owenite communities, such as New Harmony, Indiana, were actually begun, each of them proved to be impractical and quickly failed.

The "garden cities" proposed by Ebenezer Howard in the 1890s were similarly motivated by a desire to overcome the problems of industrial cities. Howard envisioned the creation of small communities of 30,000 people each on 1,000 acres. They would be located in the countryside, separated from existing urban areas by a "greenbelt" of permanent rural land, 5,000 acres in extent. Homes would be laid out on a circular pattern of streets (Howard, 1965).

Both Owen's and Howard's schemes dealt only with certain problems of industrialized cities. Nonetheless, they anticipated some essential human desires. The current out-migration from large urban areas in the United States is indicative to some degree of the desire of many for a safer and more rural environment. The garden city idea has also greatly influenced the concept of planned unit development (PUD), which has been widely utilized by land-use planners over the past decades.

Some utopian consciousness is also found in the 20th century. Of the more modern proponents of ideal cities, three planners emerged who believed that they could tackle the problem or urbanization as a single entity. The first was Charles Edouard Jeannerett-Gris, who called himself Le Corbusier, whose proposals in *La Ville Radieuse* (first published in France in 1933 and translated by Knight under the title *The Radiant City*, 1967) and in *L'Urbanisme des Trois Establissements Humains* (Le Corbusier, 1959) called for the building of high-density cities characterized by huge high-rise structures (Doxiadis, 1966, p. 34). This monumental approach to land-use planning has been favored by autocratic governments. For example, all new towns in the communist countries closely resemble the concept of Le Corbusier's *ville radieuse*, and they are undesirable environments for people at best.

The second visionary often cited in planning books is the American architect Frank Lloyd Wright. In 1937 Wright first proposed his plan for a model city called "Broadacres" and recommended that each family in the community should live on at least one acre of their own land. The third, and probably the best-known living utopian is Paolo Soleri. From his compound in the American Southwest, Soleri has published plans for "objects of immense size that can support as many as a million people per cubic mile" (Soleri, 1971).

Of course, Soleri's utopia is far from unique in its apparent impracticality and its logical lacunae. All three of the 20th century proposals outlined above, for instance, failed to reckon with recent decentralization and the current out-migration movements from older, centralized cities, with the single exception of Wright's Broadacres. Yet even Wright took little cognizance of the inherent qualities of the land in his vision of a homogeneous land-use pattern. None of the utopians except Howard seems to have understood the complex economic, legal, social, environmental, and political aspects of current land-use planning. Utopian planners have seemed to be preoccupied with shapes and forms. They are more interested in finding a solution for the question of "how" than in considering the more basic initial questions of "what" needs to be done, "where," and "why." To answer all these questions sufficiently may be beyond anyone's ability, which may be the reason why the role of utopians has been increasingly disregarded by democratic societies. Land-use planners with a vision of powerful urban forms to shape and reshape central areas are still, however, often in demand. Large corporations all over the Western world and even some powerful politicians such as Gov. Nelson Rockefeller in Albany, N.Y. have used the services of visionary form-givers as land-use planners. The role of these planners is similar to that of the land-use planners of the Renaissance and Baroque periods, who acted as agents of the ruling class. As the democratization of planning continues, it is hoped that form-giving will be increasingly placed in the final or design phase of the planning process. This move is most appropriate since forms should not be devised prior to the making of acceptable decisions on the "what," "where," and "whys." Indeed, the final phase of the analysis of the changing role of land-use planners supports this argument.

Land-Use Planners as Catalysts for Learning and Action

The first major change in the role of land-use planners occurred sometime during the 19th century. One important proponent of this change was Frederick Law Olmsted. Albert Fein (1972) an historian of Olmsted's works and life, has contrasted him as a "democratic planner" with Richard Morris Hunt, whom he calls "an aristocratic designer." Indeed, it was Olmsted who became immersed in the politics of planning when in 1863 he joined the preservation movement, which succeeded in placing Yosemite Valley and the Mariposa Big Tree Groves in state reservations (Fabos, Milde and Weinmayr, 1968, p. 42). Perhaps the most important aspect of Olmsted's contribution was his expansion of the role of land-use planners beyond the traditional bounds of conceptualizers and form-givers. Olmsted had a clear idea of "what" must be done and "where," and he wrote eloquently on "why" preservation should be mandatory. The means to achieve preservation of unique landscapes was not through physical planning, but instead through legislation or other legal means. Indeed, he supported the use of legal devices to preserve large spectacular landscapes in the West almost half a century before the first enactment of zoning, which became a popular land-use planning device only during the early part of this century.

Zoning was in its own right a major catalyst for change and action. It brought the public increasingly into the planning process, as communities were presented with the pros and cons of the planners' rationale which outlined the limits of land uses. Since zoning has often had profound consequences on the rights of individuals, public debate has sharpened in the course of this century.

Public concern for land uses reached a threshold during the years immediately following the Second World War. This concern was precipitated in great part by large-scale redevelopment efforts in the central areas of old cities. In Boston came the demolition of the old West End to give rise to the Charles River Park luxury housing complex. In New York, it was Stuyvesant Town and Fresh Meadow; in Chicago, the bulldozers made way for the Hyde Park-Kenwood development; in San Francisco the Golden Gateway area was developed for the affluent; in Stockholm new office towers and commercial development replaced older buildings next to City Hall, and projects of these kinds were repeated in almost every major city.

These actions created reactions. Public outcry intensified as bulldozers displaced people and destroyed the entire social fabric of their neighborhoods. Jane Jacobs was among the first to launch a public attack on the planners of these massive redevelopments. In her powerful and articulate book *The Death and Life of Great American Cities* (1961), she dramatized the many harmful effects of this limited approach to land-use planning. As a result of these public concerns, planners quickly changed their procedures.

As a young professional, I entered the field of planning at the time of this change. I was fortunate to get a job with the Boston Redevelopment Authority, headed by Edward Logue, one of this century's most skillful planners. He was among the first to change planning strategy from redevelopment to rehabilitation. But most importantly, he started to change the planning process to a learning process by including the people of the community in a joint effort. His slogan "planning with people" dominated all our efforts.

For many, this organized effort by planners did not go far enough. Young planners, especially, frustrated by the failures of senior planners, joined the dissatisfied public by organizing advocacy planning groups. One of the most outspoken young planners of this era was Robert Goodman, who not only helped to organize advocacy groups in the Boston area, but also stimulated a new consciousness through his book *After the Planners* (1971). Since the 1960s, advocacy planning and more recently public involvement have become an important part of all land-use planning. All Federal and state legislation enacted since the early 1960s mandates the need for public involvement, thus more than anything else modifying the role of the planners.

The environmental movement of the 1960s added reasons for public involvement. As described in the first part of this book: land-use issues proliferated; scientific findings have added new concerns and provided modified land-use solutions; the technological choices have been placed under increasing public scrutiny; and social scientists have found better ways to include the values of the public at large. In short, the role of the land-use planner has changed to: a *synthesizer*, who organizes the many factors included in these increasingly complex procedures; a *catalyst* who helps to clarify needs and objectives and bring forth alternative plans addressing those needs within the environmental and social context; and finally the contemporary land-use planner is a *facilitator* for an ongoing learning process which debates the consequences of the various alternatives on people, on the environment, on the economy, and on the government. Indeed, the complexity of land-use planning is better understood today. Fewer planners dare to come forth with a simple solution to complex contemporary land-use problems. The question inevitably raised is: who are these land-use planners who can perform this new role described here?

DISCIPLINARY AND PROFESSIONAL PLANNERS

According to a frequently repeated story, a professor of planning at Massachusetts Institute of Technology some 20 years ago listed all the courses that he thought a planner should take: the total came to over 270. Today one could easily double the list of desired courses. This anecdote, together with the previous discussion on the changing role of land-use planners, suggests two things. First, no individual planner will be sufficiently knowledgeable to tackle all the problems encountered in land-use planning. This is the primary reason why so many land-use planners are having additional training in engineering, architecture, and landscape architecture, among many other disciplines. Land-use planning has become teamwork, depending on knowledge generated by many disciplines. The size of the team and the number of disciplines required usually grow with the complexity and the magnitude of the problem. Second, it is safe to say that neither land-use planning nor planning *per se* is a discipline. A professional planner is most often a generalist, manager, or facilitator. He or she may have more knowledge or expertise in certain areas, but never enough to enable him or her to bring forth conclusive plans single-handedly. Within these two broad categories are many kinds of land-use planners. Each may have a unique contribution to the ongoing planning process, which is very much a learning process for all concerned.

Disciplinary Planners

Formal training in planning dates back only to the 1920s in the United States and in many other countries it is of even more recent origin, although planning has been going on for centuries. Who planned our physical environment before the professional planners and what were their backgrounds? History books make ample references to engineers, architects, and landscape architects all of whom were responsible for a great number of plans. But the list is also filled with popes, kings, governors, and presidents. For instance, Pope Sixtus V is credited with the baroque plan of Rome during the 16th century. The architect Christopher Wren drew the famous plan for the reconstruction of London after the great fire of 1666. Le Notre, the French designer of gardens, planned the new town of Versailles, which housed the entire government of Louis XIV in the 17th century. Olmsted, the father of landscape architecture, not only worked as a land-use planner for urban parks but also pioneered the concepts of national parks, community planning, regional open-space planning and campus planning.

All these disciplines have maintained their involvement in land-use planning. Architecture, engineering, and landscape architecture firms are not only involved but often devote a major portion of their efforts to planning. Training in these disciplines includes planning courses in preparation for real-life needs. In addition, several other professions have added planning education to their disciplinary training during the last few decades and thus contribute to current land-use planning efforts. They include foresters, who often focus on resource or recreation issues, geographers and geologists in many areas of physical and land-use planning, and several others. Professionals such as historians, lawyers, political scientists, and sociologists, who usually lack planning training, often find their disciplinary knowledge in demand.

In spite of the development of professional planning education, it seems that disciplinary involvement in planning is also on the increase.

Professional Planners

Professional planning education has been initiated by various disciplinary programs. In New Zealand and Australia, for instance, professional planning was derived from surveying and architecture. In Hungary, it was an extension of architecture. In the United States, the Harvard School of Landscape Architecture offered the first city planning option toward its master's degree in landscape architecture, followed in 1929 by the establishment of a separate Harvard School of City Planning, under the chairmanship of Professor Henry Vincent Hubbard, a landscape architect and partner in the firm of Olmsted Brothers (Newton, 1971, p. 424). Half a century later, in 1978, the American Society of Planning Officials reported on the existence of 84 professional planning programs in the United States and Canada. Although these programs represent a broader range than land-use planning alone, the graduates of these planning schools are frequently involved in land-use planning.

Initially, professional planners were physical or primarily land-use planners. But as planning issues proliferated, and the planner's role changed to become more of a catalyst for learning, so planning developed several general areas of concentration or specialization. Burchell and Sternlieb (1978) distinguish four "Principal Currents" in planning, namely: physical, social, public policy, and economic planning. For instance, social planners may be involved in creating greater equity among citizens of communities by advocating greater educational opportunities for the disadvantaged nonwhites. This type of planning is remote from land-use planning. But social planners are also interested in ensuring an equity in the quality of the living environment, which is definitely a land-use planning issue (Davidoff, 1978, p. 69).

Contemporary professional planners often have a disciplinary training prior to entry into professional school, ranging from sociology to landscape architecture. This disciplinary-professional education has many advantages and is a common practice these days. This trend further supports the notion that both disciplinary and professional training continue to be essential to produce a diverse planning group which can address the complex problems of land-use issues more adequately.

PUBLIC VS. PRIVATE PLANNING

In a previous chapter on values and organizations, two opposing values, public and private interests, were discussed. This same distinction is also very much evident in land-use planning. The public sector plans and manages all public land and increasingly controls land-use decisions in the private sector. On the other hand, corporations and millions of private individuals do the majority of land-use planning in Western countries and especially in the United States, while forced to conform to a greater or lesser degree to public needs as they are specified by regulations or legislated by the public sector. The notion of what constitutes the role of land-use decisions by the public and private sector has been fiercely debated for many decades and is a direct outcome of our polarized historical development between the Lockean thesis on the one hand and the public social concern for the land on the other, which preceded the Lockean thesis and was reviewed during the 19th century.

This issue also concerned President Lincoln over a century ago. He articulated a sensible compromise for these opposing interests as he defined the role of government: "The legitimate object of government is to do for a community of people whatever they need to have done, but cannot do at all, or cannot so well do for themselves" (Clawson and Held, 1957, p. 5). This Lincolnian doctrine has guided public and private land-use planning ever since. One should understand, however, that such a general statement as this may be subject to as many interpretations as there are people to interpret it. Up to the great depression of 1929, this doctrine was interpreted, at least in the United States, in favor of private interests. The swing toward social planning of the post-depression era interpreted the "object of government to do" increasingly more for the "community of people."

As one could expect, public and private planning has polarized during the past 50 years. In the majority of land-use decisions, the private land-use planners have become the plan producers or proponents of action while the public planners have become reactionary, primarily by creating regulations and writing legislation to control the private sector in the interest of the public. The review of current land-use planning literature on the role of the public planner suggests that the majority of land-use planners perceive land-use planning as a means to control private developers. For instance, Patterson (1979) describes land-use planning primarily as the implementation of zoning, subdivision, and supplementary regulations including health and sanitary codes. Four other current books on land-use planning (Mandelker, 1963; Haar, 1971; Delafons, 1969; Bosselman and Callies, 1971) all devote themselves to descriptions of legal devices, controls and regulations, at all levels of government in the United States.

Both the literature and this review of current land-use practice suggest that the perception of the majority of land-use planners in the public sector is that the private sector cannot be trusted. Of course, this perception is not entirely irrational. Countless developers have disregarded basic social and environmental considerations in an attempt to increase the profit margins of their developments. Land-use planners in the private sector have often been the agents of these developers. On the other hand, many land-use planners in the private sector perceive their public counterparts as agencies with countless regulations and controls which slow down developments and escalate costs.

As a land-use planner, I have worked in both capacities, and it seems to me that there is much truth in these perceptions. This situation is, however, unhealthy. There is an urgent need to expand the learning process of planning not only toward the public at large but also between land-use planners of the public and private sectors. We need more planners in the public sector who can go beyond regulation, who have creative ideas to solve problems, and who can search out viable and acceptable opportunities to improve our environment. At the same time, land-use planners in the private sector must become much more cognizant of public needs.

Planners have made numerous attempts to bridge this apparent gap. Some of the case studies reviewed in the following chapters are selected to illustrate this development.

THE PLANNING PROCESS

Land-use planning is similar to many other planning processes. In its simplest form it can be a common sense process consisting of a few basic steps, that is: identification of problems or opportunities or needs; assessment of the environmental, social, and economic resources which are needed to solve the problem or satisfy needs; the setting of plausible goals and objectives; development of alternative plans; and selection of an alternative for implementation. Perhaps every sensible human being uses this procedure implicitly or explicitly for the majority of human activities. A simple process such as this is sufficient for many land-use decisions.

For instance, a homeowner wishes to find a suitable site for a vegetable garden on his home site. He may define his need as having enough vegetables for the household during the growing season. He then may need to consider a few factors only, such as variation and wetness of soil, slope, existing vegetation, access to sun, location in relation to other uses, some aesthetic considerations, and possibly a few other factors. Then he would analyze these factors individually and in combination to ascertain the relative appropriateness of the various homogeneous areas of his home site for this purpose. He may conclude that among the three possibilities he has an area in the southeasterly corner of his land which would be most suitable and is large enough to provide him with enough vegetables not only for seasonal use but also to be conserved for the off-season. He may modify his need by setting an objective to exploit this opportunity and select the site at the southeasterly corner.

This overly simplified land-use planning problem takes into account only a few factors, and as shown, the gardener can make a decision without any formal planning. In fact, it is so simple that one can consider three or four steps simultaneously, such as the assessment, setting goals and objectives, developing alternatives and selecting one of the alternatives. This can be done because we know that most human beings are capable of considering from 7 to 10 factors at once.

The bulk of land-use planning, however, includes many more factors than shown in this example. For this reason, planners also need to make their procedures explicit so that the decision makers and the public can see the rationale used in the process. This apparent need has given rise to the development of clearer and more comprehensive planning procedures. Some of these procedures will be discusssed in the following chapters by using actual case studies.

As land-use planners are faced with increasingly complex problems, land-use planning is becoming more and more quantitative, often using highly sophisticated mathematical models. Quantitative techniques such as linear programming, network analysis, gaming, and various simulation models have been widely used in industrial, military, and other planning activities for several decades (Hiller and Lieberman, 1968). Quantitative planning affecting land uses was first introduced by transportation planners in the late 1950s (Boyce, Day and McDonald, 1970, p. 1). By the 1960s, water resource planners developed what they called multiobjective planning procedures, which were designed to evaluate environmental, social, and economic factors in water resource planning (Bishop, 1972). By the early 1970s the use of mathematical models for various kinds of urban and regional problems was commonplace (Perraton and Baxter, 1974). Responding to this trend, current planning education is also becoming more quantitative. Land-use planners are among the last groups who are being affected by this change. The reason for this trend has already been discussed in Chapter 3.

TYPES OF PLANNING

The bulk of land-use planning has been carried out to solve a need for a land-use problem. This type of planning is called single-purpose or mission planning. For example, a land-use plan may be needed to provide new recreation facilities for a growing population, or find a new water supply, or deal with any number of those issues discussed in Chapter 1.

At the other end of the continuum is planning which attempts to solve the majority of land-use needs or problems simultaneously. Planners label this type comprehensive or place planning. Of course, in between these two extreme approaches are all possible combinations or degrees of comprehensiveness. For example, a search for a new water supply may necessitate the inclusion of the planning of all land-related activities within a given watershed, because the various land uses affect the water quality and supply differently.

Single-purpose or mission planning is done at all scales ranging from local to global levels. At the local level, for instance, planners may need to find an appropriate site for a new school. An example at the global level is the current search for an appropriate dumping site for nuclear waste. Recently, an Australian desert site was suggested as the candidate area for waste disposal. On the other hand, planners can take a very comprehensive approach to planning for a small area. For example, the location of a school site may be part of a comprehensive land-use plan for a community, which includes planning all land uses for the foreseeable future.

Land-use planning as a whole is becoming more comprehensive for those reasons discussed in part one of this book. First, planners and the general public comprehend that in most instances the solving of one problem may lead to the creation of another problem. Hence, we have a greater desire to anticipate such potential problems and attempt to deal with them. Secondly, the scientific community has challenged land-use planning decisions and has aided the inclusion of factors which planners could easily disregard previously. Thirdly, the new technology and the development of quantitative tools enable planners to take a more comprehensive approach. And finally, as the public has increased its role in planning, it has raised additional issues sometimes overlooked by planners.

HIERARCHY OF PLANNING

Ever since the Baroque era of the 16th and 17th centuries a planning hierarchy has evolved, and is now widely used all over the world. In land-use planning at least four distinct levels of planning activities are evident, ranging from the most general to site-specific or design solutions.

The first level of planning has several names. In England, Australia, and New Zealand it is called "strategy planning." In the United States, it has at least three names — "policy planning" or "framework planning" or "planning for planning." All these terms imply a first cut, or very general planning effort which guides the rate, the type of land-use conversion and its general location. This first level is appropriate for global, national or state level planning, but it is also often the first planning done at regional and even at local levels. In the private sector, corporations have a similar starting point and hierarchy for planning.

The level two planning effort is called structure planning in England and the countries of the Commonwealth. In the United States, it is called meso-scale planning, often so designated by government bureaucracy. This level of planning includes more specific physical delineation though it does not yet provide site-specific descriptions of proposed land uses. It is carried out most often for various regions or metropolitan areas. Regional planning in the United States can include several states, but at this level most often means a sub-state or smaller regional planning effort. Both level one and two planning tend to be long-range or at least longer-range efforts, which attempt to guide land-use changes or land management for between 10 or 50 years.

The third level of planning is most often done at the local and community levels. At this level, land-use boundaries are site-specific. A typical example of a level three planning effort is community zoning, which specifies the type of land uses, their densities, and other regulations such as specifications of setbacks, height of structures, street width, and the like. But it is still not a design.

Level four is the final phase of land-use effort. This is the phase which gives the form of new land uses, structures, and all the specifications which can be implemented by contractors, or in the case of preservation planning it is a set of specifications for the ongoing management of a site. This description serves also as a definition of both planning and design. Indeed, the simplest distinction between planning and design is that land-use planning is only a guide for action, but it lacks a set of detailed specifications. It is the design phase which provides sufficient instruction for the implementation of both planning and design decisions.

While design most often is a local or small-scale effort, it is possible to design at a regional or even at the national scale. For instance, the rectangular land survey of the United States, which was implemented during the 19th century (Clawson and Held, 1957, p. 23) and laid out 6 mile by 6 mile townships and homesteads for each farmer, was indeed a design specification, although it was set forth by legislative effort. It has had a lasting effect on the national landscape (Figure 5).

While the hierarchy from the level one or policy planning to the site-specific decision is the most logical and sensible approach to land use, this hierarchy is not followed in many of the planning-design decisions. There are many decision makers and designers who start with the design by specifying objects on the land and bypassing or ignoring the many planning questions which should be dealt with prior to design. In other words, this limited approach pays only lip service to the basic questions of "what," "where," and "why" land-use change is necessary and jumps into "how" it should be done. With increased public concern and development of this planning-design hierarchy, this limited approach has fallen into disfavor during the recent past.

The following three chapters are organized in a hierarchy from the global-national to local level planning and design efforts. At the end, each chapter is analyzed in relation to the six areas of land-use planning concern discussed in this chapter to make the necessary link between this rapidly changing field of land-use planning and actual planning cases, which bring theory alive.

CHAPTER 7

LAND-USE PLANNING AT THE
HIGHEST LEVELS OF GOVERNMENT

The general perception of the public and even of some professionals is that land-use planning is a local and most often a site-specific activity. The construction of a large housing development or a highway, the opening of a regional recreation center, the building of a sewage treatment plant, the damming up of a river for water supply are all visible changes which create concrete images in people's minds. Yet the most important land-use decisions are often made at the highest levels of government. They are often not labeled as such, but governmental policies, whether they are controls on developments or blank approval of individual rights, are determining the cultural land use of the world, nations, and states, or provinces within them.

The purpose of this chapter is to show the importance of policy-level decisions which have significant and often enormous and long-lasting effects on land uses. The intent is not to provide an exhaustive survey of policy planning, but rather to sample some pertinent activity and to analyze the trend in land-use policymaking at the global, national, and subnational levels. The land-use or related policies at these levels of government are direct responses to the forces described in part one of this book. These forces will inevitably stimulate land-use policy formation at all levels of the government in future years for the reason that land-use issues will increase instead of decrease. The scientific community will continue to surprise us with findings of undesirable environmental consequences of many land-use decisions which do not yet concern us. The technological choices and many of their potential impacts will continue to proliferate. The divergent interests of the populations of the globe, of nations and their subareas will multiply. If past responses of planners to these forces continue, the policymakers' ability to deal with uncertain futures may improve.

Perhaps the most exciting aspect of policy planning is the apparent move from single-purpose land-use policy formulation through a more coordinated approach to a more comprehensive or integrated approach. This evolution of land-use policymaking is illustrated in a case study following a brief analysis of policymaking at the global, national and subnational levels.

LAND-USE PLANNING AT THE GLOBAL LEVEL

As one would expect, land-use planning or land-use policymaking at the global level is very limited at present. Global land-use policies to guide growth-related, population maintenance, decline, and reclamation issues are practically nonexistent. The formulation of policies to guide the resource exploitation of the world, preservation of significant landscapes, and the minimization of global land-use impacts are only in their initial or formative stage. Yet one should make note of current responses with some degree of encouragement. The evolution of our responses to planning issues at the global level is taking the same predictable course as were our responses to issues at other levels. The primary difference is that the comprehension of global issues is coming later than those at lower levels of land-use planning.

The evolution of our responses to global issues follows a textbook pattern. These responses consist of two stages of development. As elsewhere, responses to global issues have started with eloquent articulators of relevant problems. Their work has been further pursued by various organizations and governmental bodies such as the United Nations, which represents the governments of all member nations and multinational task forces interested in subglobal issues.

The individuals, organizations, and those governmental bodies interested in planning the land use of the globe all share similar concerns: all are speculating on or estimating the resource availability to sustain present and future populations and the likelihood of new technologies which may affect resource utilization and pollution.

The Articulators of Global Issues

A healthy debate is going on among individuals who have focused their attention on global land-use problems. On one end of the continuum are people sounding an alarm, and at the other are the optimists or those who propose a technical solution to global problems. A review of current literature suggests that the alarmists constitute the majority of this group.

Benton MacKaye, one of the fathers of contemporary regional land-use planning, warned in the 1920s that "the problem [of planning] is nothing less than the control of the world's birth rate" (1962, p. 154). He claimed that if population growth is not controlled soon, the decline of our civilization will be inevitable. Other articulators have focused their attention on world resources and the limitations of science and technology in supplying the apparent need for increased resources. Commoner (1966), for instance, believes that the age of "innocent faith" in science and technology may be over. In *The Closing Circle*, Commoner (1971) sees that as older production technologies are displaced by new ones, global pollution will increase. Mesarouil and Pestel (1974) in *Mankind at the Turning Point* consider all worldwide land-use issues and perceive a steady global deterioration. All these and many other writers have, to various degrees, forecast doomsday. They have also been a very important catalyst in generating public concern for the world as a whole.

In contrast are the optimists, such as John Maddox, a leading British scientist (1972), who, against current trends, has great faith in human nature and in the evolution of contemporary society. On the subject of resource availability, Maddox believes that the "exercise of human ingenuity" will be sufficient to overcome the apparent resource shortages which will be an intermittent worldwide phenomenon. He also sees that technology will continue to be used not only for resource substitution but also for pollution control and further reduction.

Buckminster Fuller, the great inventor, went one step further. In his book, *Earth, Inc.* (1973) he proposed to replace current technology with new forms which would ensure an "intelligent and responsible production of a total-humanity sustaining system," a universe with no pollution or waste. He believed that humanity could acquire the technology for the purpose of total success and enduring peace.

The Role of International Organizations and Institutions

While individuals have continued to stimulate land-use and related issues, activity in recent years has been dominated by the proliferation of international organizations and institutions, all committed to influencing global land-use policies. A quick survey of any major library catalogue file can produce information on hundreds of international organizations which meet at annual congresses, conferences, or symposia devoted to such topics as food and fiber production or agricultural and related matters or even biological control. Others focus on energy, population growth, water pollution, waste, and ecology. These international activities are sponsored by at least three different groups or institutions — the professional organizations, several nations, and finally the United Nations, which is perhaps responsible for more debates on land uses and related concerns than the other two combined. Numerous research studies on the subjects of population growth, maintenance, and decline, have been sponsored by several of these inter-

national organizations. Recently, much attention has also been given to resource exploitation. Among all land-use issues at the global level, preservation probably has the longest history. Finally, waste and environmental
impact issues have dominated many international gatherings and generated
many studies.

Population Growth, Maintenance, and Decline

Population growth is the major change agent for land-use conversion and
has been the focus of global planners. Yet there is no global policy, neither
on population control nor on food supply. However, there is a growing worldwide realization that there is a possible limit to growth and food supply.
Among the many studies on the interrelation of growth and food supply,
perhaps the reports of the "Club of Rome" have received the most attention.
Their first study was an attempt to understand the unprecedented tangle
which they called the "World problematique." They sponsored a "world
simulation model" realized with the system dynamics technique of Professor
Jay Forester of the Massachusetts Institute of Technology, which culminated
in the well-known study published in 1972 under the title *The Limits of
Growth* (Meadows, Meadows, Randers and Behrens, 1972). In it, Professor
Meadows and his team projected into the future a number of interacting
critical phenomena with a view to indicating what might happen to the
world system if present trends were allowed to continue. While this study
illuminated and dramatized several major global land-use issues, its limitation
was its adaption of worldwide aggregation.

The Second Report to the Club of Rome adopted a new "world model,"
based on developments of the "multilevel hierarchical system theory"
(Mesarovic and Pestel, 1974, p. 203), which divides the world into ten inter-
dependent and mutually interacting regions of political, economic or
environmental coherence, and is capable of breaking down its data into still
smaller units, such as that of a single nation, if necessary. That means that its
findings can be relevant to national policymakers. The study claims that "for
the first time it is now possible, by...confronting the policies of different
groups competing among themselves within the finite capacity of the planet,
to delineate areas of conflict or incompatibility inherent in national or
regional policies."

An application of their model resulted in five future scenarios, (Mesarovic and Pestel 1974, p. 127) from which the group formulated "the only
feasible solution." It requires: "a global approach to the problem; investment aid, rather than commodity aid...; an effective population policy; and
worldwide diversification of industry." The land-use implications of these

policies would be enormous. This so-called "only feasible solution" or rather policies which resemble it, have already been implemented in several parts of the world, especially in Asia, which has experienced the "green revolution."

One of the most celebrated successes of this approach can be seen in Punjab state and its neighboring areas in northern India, where three rivers, the Ravi, the Beos and Satluy, have been completely diverted to irrigate over 15 million acres to date and are capable of supplying a large portion of India's food supply. Here current science and technology was applied to create dams of enormous size, and canals as large as the Connecticut River in the United States, but dug by human hands. In line with Maddox's criticism of the alarmists, one wonders if human ingenuity could do better than this. Several agricultural and food scientists are now forecasting developments in science and technology which will not only surpass the effects of the "green revolution" but may change agricultural production more than any previous innovations. That would add perhaps the most significant parameter to the Mesarovic and Pestel model, by markedly altering the limits to growth.

In addition to growth and population maintenance issues, the United Nations is especially interested in reversing insidious desertification in many parts of the world. Desertification has contributed to the most severe decline of several countries and regions, as overgrazing and cultivation have decimated vegetation. Increased scientific knowledge and new technology may be the basis of future global policies to change this devastating phenomenon.

Global Resource Utilization

The earth under the ocean waters is the new frontier for resource exploitation to satisfy much of the food, mineral, and energy needs of future generations. Recent international debates on fishing and oil rights have been followed by intensive negotiations over future mineral exploitation of the ocean floor, which occupies over two-thirds of the surface of our planet. Large-scale resource utilization is inevitable and will surely change many coastal land uses. Land-use planners therefore have a great interest in this development. Another, perhaps more important, aspect of this international debate is that the utilization of the ocean floor demands international cooperation. While this debate has been going on for more than a decade, and any resolution seems to be far in the future, nevertheless, a useful model for global land-use policymaking may evolve from this exercise.

The International Preservation Movement

Attempts to preserve international resources are almost as old as the preservation movement itself. In a pioneer example of international cooperation, both Canadian and New York State officials labored for a score of years to rescue spectacular Niagara Falls, which had been threatened with encroaching industries. They succeeded in 1883 (Fabos, Milde and Weinmayr, 1968, p. 46). Ever since, international organizations interested in natural landscape qualities, vegetation, wildlife, unique geological formations, and cultural landscapes, have placed pressure on governments to preserve our global natural and cultural heritage. The success of these groups is impressive. The hunters of precious wildlife in Africa and Asia are being replaced by nature-loving visitors to large wildlife preserves. The preservation of unique natural landscapes and the restoration of treasures of earlier cultures are being supported by international fundraising efforts often combined with national cooperation. It is not suggested here that the international preservation groups have completed their task. They are far from doing so, but their success should provide inspiration to others interested in influencing global land-use policies.

International and Global Environmental
Impact Issues

International environmental problems are often well defined. When a Liberian oil tanker dumps thousands of tons of oil into the English Channel, the oil spill can damage several countries. The environmental impact is very obvious and measurable in a number of ways. Similarly, the slow, incremental deterioration of the Mediterranean Sea can be traced to the practice of surrounding countries disposing their waste in it over the centuries. International efforts to deal with this type of environmental land-use issue have begun. Amelioration of such a neglect of chronic problems, however, will not happen overnight.

At the global level, we still are lacking clear, specific problem definitions. We have ample hypotheses and even some theories on human impact on global air quality, climate, water pollution, radiation, and the like. But until these theories are more conclusive, planners will have difficulty in influencing policies to alleviate them.

LAND-USE PLANNING AT THE NATIONAL LEVEL

Land-use planning or land-use policy at the national level dates back at least to the 16th century. For example, in Sweden, "plans for new development in towns [during the 1500s] had to be ratified by the king before building could start" (Strong, 1977, p. 21). Yet the greater part of national planning to guide land uses has developed only during the 19th and 20th centuries in response to problems and opportunities created by the industrial revolution and to needs which were generated during those times. National land-use planning can accomplish three things. It can aid the exploitation of the riches of virgin land. It can minimize environmental land-use problems resulting from human activity. It can even search out new opportunities by reclaiming land which has been degraded by previous cultures.

National land-use planning efforts have often incorporated all the above three aspects. However, in most countries, specific problems and opportunities seem to result in one primary focus, which dominates national land-use policies. For instance, in the United States, Canada, and Australia the existence of enormous unused land resources has meant that resource exploitation or utilization has been the cornerstone of national land-use policies. On the other hand, the dominant focus of national land-use planning in Europe has been more a response to the problems arising from the superimposition of industrialization on the "old world." In some countries, such as Israel, the national aim has been the creation of a productive land from a landscape which had degenerated into desert over past millenia.

The availability of scientific and technological know-how was the same in each of these countries. However, the issues which generated the national planning problems and opportunities, combined with the history of each of these countries or continents, have been very different. It is no surprise that national attitudes toward the landscape and land use, and thus the national focus on planning, are also very different. The following illustrations of land-use planning at the national level are selected to demonstrate these very important differences.

Focus on Landscape Utilization

The prevailing trend among land-use planners in the United States, Canada, Australia and some other "new world" countries rich in land resources, is that they do not pursue national land-use policies or planning. One of their most prominent critics is Ann Louise Strong, who recently declared that in the United States "there are no agreed upon land use goals or standards" (Strong, 1977, p. 1). Others claim that in these countries land-use decisions are based on speculation, and that this pioneer or cowboy mentality results in the squandering of natural resources. Failure to provide a suitable living environment for people is blamed on the lack of a national land-use policy.

If we compare the land-use controls of these countries with those of several European countries, such as Switzerland, these criticisms are valid.

These contemporary critiques seem to imply that land-use policy means control, and that policy which sets out to utilize land resources is not valid. But if we define a conscientious national effort at land utilization as planning, then indeed the new world countries also have national land-use policies. We may not like many of the consequences of land uses. Nevertheless, the new world countries have often had very clear land-use goals and well-defined procedures for their implementation.

As it was pointed out earlier, the United States has had a series of national land-use policies starting with an ordinance passed by the Congress in 1785 to provide for a "system of rectangular surveys" based on the meridian lines in the Western territories (Kemmerer and Jones, 1959, p. 112). Townships of 6 miles square were surveyed; each township contained 36 sections of 1 square mile or 640 acres (Figures 6 and 15). This was a very powerful and pioneering national land-use policy, which made possible rapid and orderly land utilization of vast areas of highly productive virgin land.

The 1785 ordinance of rectangular survey has been complemented by many acts and policies which have reinforced the initial national policy of

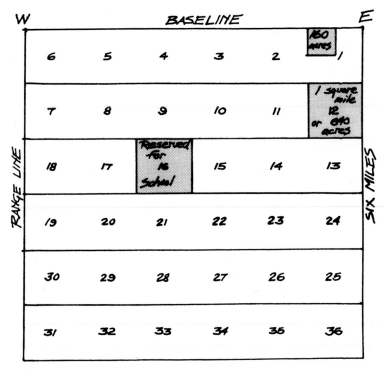

FIGURE 15 *Survey of a township under the Ordinance of 1785. (Drawn by D. L. Kemmerer.)*

public land disposal into agricultural utilization and other private uses. For example, the Railway Land Grant of the U.S. Federal Government gave 174 million acres to railroad companies between 1850 and 1871 to encourage them to build across the Western Plains. The grant achieved that goal. The Homestead Act of 1862 provided 160 acres of land to individuals for a small registration fee. After 5 years of cultivation they received full title to them. Other acts of land disposal included the Morrill Act of 1862 to encourage the funding of state colleges and universities; the Timber Culture Act of 1873 to increase wood production; the Desert Land Act in 1877 to promote use by irrigation of the arid regions. The era of land disposal continued into this century.

The next major stage in the history of Federal land-use policies was the reservation era, which arose from a growing concern with the land disposal process and its consequences. Starting with the preservation of Yellowstone National Park in 1872, approximately one-third or 756 million acres of the nation's land of 2,300 million acres has been retained in public ownership. While the primary intent of the Federal land reservation was to limit the land disposal and initiate land preservation, modifications have been effected by several land management policies which have promoted intensive management of Federal lands from the 1930s to the present day (Clawson and Held, 1957, p. 35). A relatively recent report to the President and the Congress on the use and management of all Federal land (Public Land Law Review Commission, 1970) underscores this intent. This report calls for the "highest and best use" of land and support for the multiple use concept which has been expressed by the Multiple Use Act of 1964 (Public Land Law Review Commissions, 1970, p. 43). It seems that the significant aspect of Federal land policy is that its primary aim is "land utilization" to benefit the nation's population.

Similarly, a series of land development policies of this century has reinforced this trend in national land-use policy. Perhaps the two most important interrelated policies have been suburban land conversion and the planning and implementation of the huge, 45 thousand mile long interstate highway system. The Federal government has stimulated suburbanization by various assistance programs to finance home buying and construction and a Federal income tax provision which has provided significant tax exemptions (Clawson 1971, p. 41). The interstate highway program, which cost almost a hundred billion dollars by 1970, provided the accessibility and an unprecedented mobility.

In summary, this brief case history of the United States proves that indeed this nation has had not only land-use goals but also very powerful policies which it has implemented. Decentralized suburban developments have provided the "suitable living environment" (as perceived by the majority of the public) for millions of Americans in natural settings. Of course, these policies have created many undesirable environmental, economic, and social problems. Policies were also advanced to mitigate these problems. Some of them will be further discussed in this and in following chapters.

Focus on Land-Use Controls

At the dawn of the Industrial Revolution, European countries were almost uniformly settled. With the exception of the rugged mountains and steep hills, most land was in human use. The railroads had to be built through cultivated land unlike their counterparts in the New World, where they were used to open up virgin land. Industrial regions were superimposed on agricultural settlements. The population of many of the European cities reached half a million prior to the era of industrialization, when the rapid influx of city dwellers aggravated the already severe urban problems.

It is not surprising that in these circumstances, national land-use planning efforts took the form of a more reactionary response. The effects of industrialization in Europe were perceived more as problems, in contrast with the New World, where optimism and a sense of opportunity prevailed. National land-use policies have evolved in the Old World with a much greater emphasis on control when compared with those of the New World.

In addition to the pressures of industrialization, environmental constraints have been factors to a greater or lesser degree in the Old World countries. This difference can be well illustrated by comparing the land-use controls of France with those of Switzerland. The natural environment of France is much more adaptable to human exploitation than the mountainous landscape of Switzerland. The greatest portion of the French landscape is productive flat or undulating agricultural land. Mountainous areas are limited to the Pyrenees at her southern border with Spain and the western end of the Alps, which spills over into her territory at its southeastern borders. Land-use controls in France until the mid-19th century consisted primarily of curbs on urbanization in the Baroque tradition. Environmentally based controls were nonexistent. According to a recent brochure of Ambassade de France, the concept of what the French call organization of the territory is relatively new in France, where the formulation of national land-use policy controls were added to their fifth 5-year economic plan (1966–70). The underlying emphasis of their land-use policy, even with the addition of environmental considerations, is how to aid the decentralization of the Paris region, to lessen the disparities of the country. In short, their national land-use planning policy is designed to direct or control urban growth and industrial development.

The control of urbanization or urban growth is evident in every European country. Land resources are limited, which mandates the creation of increasingly stringent controls. In addition to this ubiquitous problem of limited land for a growing and increasingly more affluent population, Switzerland has special problems in that her mountainous landscape is much more vulnerable to human use and abuse. Because of this environmental constraint, Switzerland pioneered very powerful land-use controls at the turn of the century. In 1902, legislation was passed to control development on about three-quarters of the nation's land.

Let us analyze this severe environmental constraint which appears to be the basis of this unprecedented land-use control. The Swiss landscape can be easily divided into four major types, each of which covers approximately one-quarter of the country. Starting at the top are the rocky, mostly snow-covered steep mountain peaks. This is the country's major aesthetic resource. Immediately below are the alpine meadows, which have been in community ownership and control. Only grazing and limited recreational use is permitted in these areas. Then there is the third layer, the forests, which cover all the steep foothills of the Alps. Finally, a quarter of the country's total land area is in the form of valleys spotted with lovely chalets and neat villages.

The Industrial Revolution in Switzerland did not mean the building of industrial regions like those in England, France or Germany. But it did entail the building of roads and railroads to provide access to the valuable forest resources. The impact of large-scale forest harvesting was swift and dramatic. As these fragile steep hills were denuded, flooding, mudslides, and avalanches destroyed hundreds of alpine settlements or parts of them. The need for national control was mandatory. The forest protection law was enacted in 1902 (see Eidgenössische Oberaufsicht Über die Forstpolizei, 1971), which was designed to maintain forest land as a protective zone. This law is so strict that it requires an immediate reforestation of all forest land on which cutting is permitted. The law spelled out full protection, and policing of forest use by trained foresters, coupled with public education. Since the traditional use of alpine meadows has been maintained under public control, and since the snow-covered rocky peaks and the alpine meadows have always been in public ownership, with the addition of this forest protection law, some three-quarters of Switzerland's land area has been highly controlled since the turn of the century.

Switzerland's second major land-use policy was established after the Second World War in response to food shortages experienced in wartime. A policy was devised to protect most of her agricultural land from development, a step made possible only by massive subsidy, which the Swiss decided to pay in order to minimize future uncertainty in case of another war. An additional benefit of this policy is that the open farm valleys provide a great cultural setting to the foothills and often to the mountain peaks of their spectacular landscape. Just imagine Switzerland without its open farmlands! If farmland were replaced by forest or urbanization, much of this scenic resource would be impaired. The Swiss pay for this, in at least two ways. Food prices are significantly higher, since these marginal farms could not survive without massive subsidies. Secondly, because they limit severely the conversion of agricultural land to urban uses, the majority of Swiss have no other choice but to live in high-density apartment complexes. A detached house on a tenth of an acre is considered to be a luxury.

In conclusion, the two extreme national policies discussed above have very different results. While the national land-use policy of the United States has emphasized land utilization, the "highest and best use," the result is greater individual choice in housing, and perhaps at the cost of the public landscape. In contrast, Switzerland has one of the most highly managed public landscapes, but her population is forced to live in high-density environments, against the will or preference of many. This contrast is also useful for land-use planners because it demonstrates that indeed there is no clear consensus on what constitutes a so-called "suitable living environment." The greatest challenge for planners is to help societies to find "the proper balance" between public and private values. Of course, the difficulty in reaching this general objective is that the interpretation of what constitutes "proper balance" is highly personal.

STATE AND MULTISTATE LEVEL LAND-USE PLANNING

In large and complex countries, such as the United States, policy-level planning continues at the state and multistate levels. Up to about 1970, the major focus of state and multistate planning was on policies designed to accommodate growth. The emphasis of these plans was on land or landscape utilization. During the late 1960s, which marked the period of the environmental movement, an interest developed in land-use control. This focus on control dominated state-level policy planning during the entire decade of the 1970s.

Land-Use Policies to Accommodate Growth

In America, as early as the 1920s, some states initiated statewide recreation planning. For instance, the governor of Massachusetts appointed an Open Space Commission in 1928 to deal with the state's recreation needs

(Figure 16). Although this plan was never implemented, it provided the basis for an open space requisition and recreation development policy. State-level policy planning for recreation and guidance of all growth and land-use conversion proliferated during the 1950s and 1960s. Wisconsin's statewide recreation plan was among the most ambitious efforts of this period.

In devising the Wisconsin plan, planners directed by a distinguished landscape architect, Phil Lewis, identified 220 natural and cultural "landscape resources for recreation." Through a simple overlay, generalized mapping, and map analysis, they attempted to identify those co-occurrences where several of those valuable landscape resources were located. They found that these resources occurred together in corridors throughout the state, hence they named these linear resource concentrations "environmental corridors," (Lewis, 1964, pp. 100–107). These environmental corridors became the basis of the "Wisconsin Heritage Trail Proposal" (Figure 17). This statewide policy plan also included detailed recommendations on how recreation development should be carried out in harmony with the existing natural and cultural resources. During the same decade, Wisconsin's Department of Resource Development expanded the statewide recreation planning to include policies for economic, population, land-use, transportation, and facilities planning (Zeidler, 1968).

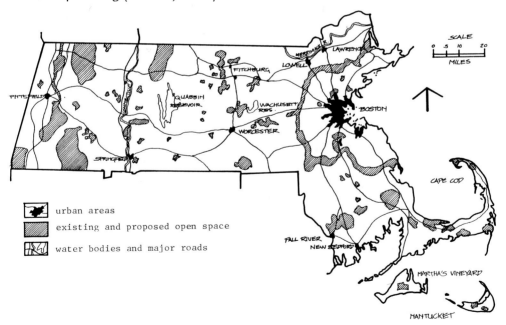

FIGURE 16 *Open space plan for the Commonwealth of Massachusetts, 1928.*

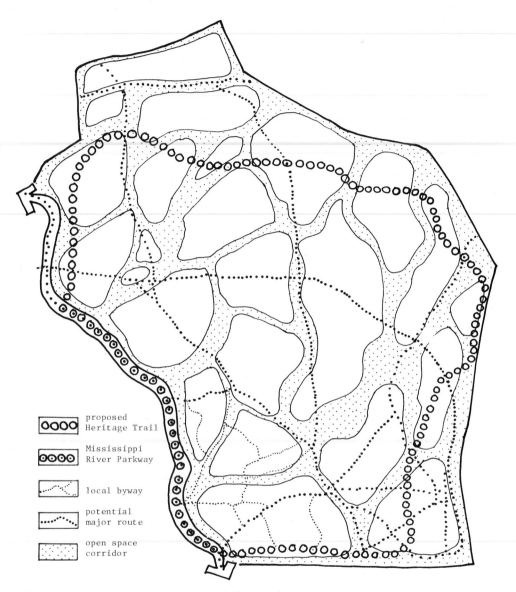

proposed
Heritage Trail

Mississippi
River Parkway

local byway

potential
major route

open space
corridor

FIGURE 17 *Wisconsin Heritage Trails Proposal.*

Although several states have developed land-use policies for growth similar to Wisconsin's the most ambitious land-use planning has been done by the state of Hawaii. This small state of eight islands has perceived its landscape resource limitations more clearly and much earlier than the states of the mainland. One can see the limits of land and growth much more readily on an island, hence the pioneering work of Hawaii's more comprehensive land-use plan. The result was that Hawaii was the first of the 50 states to have a "General Plan" (Eckbo, Dean, Austin and Williams, June 1970). With the aid of a large land-use planning firm in California, boundaries of four land-use districts were delineated, including urban, rural, agricultural, and conservation areas (for illustration see the land-use map of Kauai, Figure 18). This pioneering statewide general plan of 1961 was approved by resolution of the legislature, followed by a land-use law designed to enforce it.

Impatient with state planning efforts of the 1960s, private organizations in several states proposed policies for land-use planning. One of the most visible of these organizations was "California Tomorrow." This group has published the quarterly magazine *Cry California* with the aim of identifying land-use issues. The same organization developed a plan to guide land-use policies in the state and published it under *The California Tomorrow Plan* (Heller, 1971). To dramatize future uncertainties, they projected a plan based on existing policies, which they named "California One, in which the quality of life becomes seriously impaired before the year 2000" (Heller, 1971, p. 109). They contrasted it with alternative two, labeled "California Two, [which] attempts to deal with disruptions in a systematic way through a process of comprehensive state and regional planning."

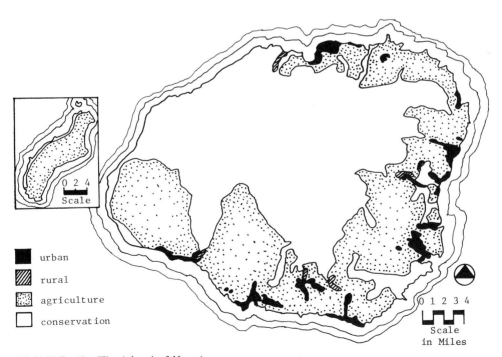

urban
rural
agriculture
conservation

0 2 4
Scale

0 1 2 3 4
Scale
in Miles

FIGURE 18 *The Island of Kauai.*

Land-Use Policies Through Control

The states active in developing statewide land-use plans had already accepted in the 1960s that their most effective and least expensive device for implementation of land-use policies was land-use control or some sort of police power. In the United States, local government had long ago received these powers from the states. In the late 1960s and early 1970s, several states decided to take back some of these powers. This era has been described as the "quiet revolution in land-use control" (Bosselman and Callies, 1971). These emerging state land-use controls were similar to the national land-use controls in Europe, and also a logical response to our national policies, which were primarily designed to utilize land resources.

The roots of these statewide land-use controls are found in the environmental movement of the late 1960s, which generated a new public interest in land-use planning. The public as well as the state decision makers realized that the plans prepared during the 1950s and 1960s had very little effect on development. The controls that they initiated usually arose out of a specific issue, such as the development of wetlands. Hence they initiated single-purpose controls of wetlands, flood plains, or other fragile areas — from developments. Later, states began to develop more comprehensive sets of controls to guide the majority of land-use conversions.

Today, virtually all the states in the United States, including several which planners do not usually associate with state planning, have some sort of regulation of procedures for local planning. The most ambitious of these controls were enacted by Hawaii, Vermont, California, and Florida (Healy and Rosenberg, 1979). A brief review of the Vermont Environmental Control Act (Act 250) of 1970 and over a decade of experience with this comprehensive state land-use law, amply illustrates the development of state-level controls (see Healy and Rosenberg, 1979, pp. 40–79).

The Vermont act includes four land-use controls, namely a permit procedure, a set of performance standards for development, a property tax relief for those who keep their land from development, and a capital gains tax on land sales. The backbone of the system is the "nine district commissions, each made up of three unpaid citizens appointed by the governor" (Healy and Rosenberg, 1979, p. 72). The performance standards that these commissions enforce are part of the law itself. Appeals may be made to the state environmental board and to the courts.

Experience with this form of land-use control in Vermont during the 1970s suggests that it has been more effective in improving the quality of development than in stopping it outright. However, several land-use planners believe that Vermont's strict controls may have led to far less growth than would have otherwise occurred. In particular, Act 250 may have saved

Vermont from the proliferation of shoddy developments that have sprung up in neighboring northeastern states. In spite of this success, land-use controls even in the strictest states of the United States fall far behind such European countries as Switzerland.

Toward Integrated Planning

Throughout this chapter and in the previous chapters, implications have been made about the evolution of the planning process from a single-purpose to a more comprehensive approach. Early land-use plans, and many current plans, have dealt with a problem without much concern for any other related issues. The limitations of single-purpose planning have long been recognized. The first corrective step was introduced decades ago, when several agencies within the Federal and state governments were asked to coordinate their efforts from time to time. Coordination involved agencies informing other relevant agencies of their intent, with a view to making changes if an inter-agency conflict was discovered. Coordination improved planning to some degree. It did not, however, produce comprehensive planning.

Signs for the development of an integrated approach can be traced in the land-use plans of Hawaii and the plan for Wisconsin. Those state plans were comprehensive in that they attempted to deal with population growth, economic and transportation issues, and land conversion for housing and recreation. However, they were the responsibility of a single agency. The next step in the evolution of planning came when the Federal government started to mandate an integrated approach. The Nation's Water Resource Act of 1965 (Water Resources Council, 1968, p. v) was one of the early acts which made integrated *water* and *related land resource planning* a legal requirement. This act created a "cooperative framework between the Federal government, state, local governments and private enterprise."

The water and related land resource planning which was overseen by the Water Resources Council was actually carried out by 18 regional groups, each including several states. The North Atlantic Regional Water Resource Planning area is used here as a case study to illustrate how the mandatory integrated approach was effected (North Atlantic Regional Water Resources Study Coordinating Committee, 1970).

The land and water area of the North Atlantic Region extends over 13 states and includes the watersheds of 21 river basins. The region extends from the North Carolina border to the Canadian border. It is approximately 900 miles long, averages about 200 miles wide and comprises 167,000 square miles. The area houses about one-quarter of the nation's population. The overall focus of this study was the optimum development of water and related land resources over a long-range planning period extending to the year 2020, with intermediate benchmark years set at 1980 and 2000. The three major planning objectives which were set by the Federal mandate were to achieve maximum environmental quality, regional development, and national efficiency.

The North Atlantic Regional Water Resources Planning Study Coordinating Committee was established within the U.S. Army Corps of Engineers to manage the study, which included significant input from seven other Federal agencies, thirteen state agencies, and several groups of consultants with various specializations in water- and land-use planning.

The integrated approach was achieved by the establishment of a significant framework by the coordinating committee prior to the involvement of the other groups. The committee also took responsibility for the preparation of the final integrated plans. The 6-year planning effort had three major phases: the identification of needs; the planning for each need; and the integration of all needs into three alternative integrated plans and the preparation of the final plan for the U.S. Congress.

In the first phase, the coordinating committee *identified* 18 specific *needs*, to satisfy the region's growth in terms of municipal and industrial water, water for the industrial processes, rural water supply, irrigation water, water for industrial cooling, water for power cooling, water for hydroelectric generation, development of navigation, development of recreation, development of fish and wildlife resources, plans for waste disposal, waste discharge, flood protection, drainage, erosion prevention, health maintenance, and utilization of visual and cultural values, all to be considered within the available legal framework. This extensive set of needs demonstrates two important things. First, one cannot plan for water without planning the land uses. Much of the water is collected on land surfaces, where its quantity, quality, and use is affected by land use. In turn, flood water affects land uses. In fact, all these needs are interrelated. Second, this list demonstrates the importance of a comprehensive and integrated approach. The major impetus for this approach came after the prolonged drought on the East Coast of the United States in the late 1950s, where previously planning had been carried out in response to short-range problems, with major water shortages, and several other unwanted consequences as results.

The coordinating committee set up separate teams for the planning phase for each of the 18 needs listed above, and established a critical path, which specified clear tasks, deadlines, report format, meeting schedules with the coordinating committee, and some general criteria for evaluation. The second, or planning, phase was done by each of the 18 study teams, separating in three stages to include resource inventory/assessment, development of planning strategy, and development of three alternatives for each of the needs.

The resource inventory and assessment stage was done to identify all available resources and their quantity, quality, location and distribution within this huge region. In certain instances, such as the assessment of visual cultural resources, a methodology had to be developed first, since there was none available at this general policy-level planning. This assessment was further complicated by the fact that separate procedures were needed to assess the natural and the cultural resources and yet the team had to produce one composite assessment as the requirement for their particular "need." Figure 19 shows the combined visual/cultural landscape qualities. What does the assessment of visual and cultural values have to do with water resource planning? I was part of the study team which debated this question for years. The longer we worked on it, the more relationships we found between visual/cultural values and water resources. The essence of our findings was that water resources in the form of impoundments add to the visual quality of landscapes. Similarly, major installations like power plants are more appropriate in areas where they would not impair existing visual and cultural qualities. If these assumptions are true, then this level of visual and cultural assessment is indeed a useful input for regional water and related land resource planning.

The second stage of the planning phase was the development of the planning strategy. This process required from each team the further identification of its "needs" in more specific terms. In areas of limited existing resources, the teams were asked to supply concepts and devices to develop needed resources. The teams also had to develop priorities to satisfy each of the three study objectives within each of the three planning time frames (the years 1980, 2000, and 2020).

The third stage of this second planning phase required each of the 18 teams to come up with three alternative plans. Each of the alternatives had to be biased toward one of the three study objectives, namely environmental quality, economic efficiency, and regional development.

The third and final phase of this water and related land resource planning study was the plan integration phase. This phase was also divided into several stages. First, each team had to review the alternatives of all the other teams and to comment on their effects on their own plans. In the second stage, representatives from each of the 18 study teams met within several sub-regions to work out the conflicts between the various needs and alternatives. Following this, the coordinating committee integrated or combined all the 18 sets of plans into one integrated environmental plan, one integrated economic efficiency plan and one integrated plan which was biased toward regional development.

The final stage of plan integration was the development from the three biased plans of a compromise plan which was then debated in public hearings

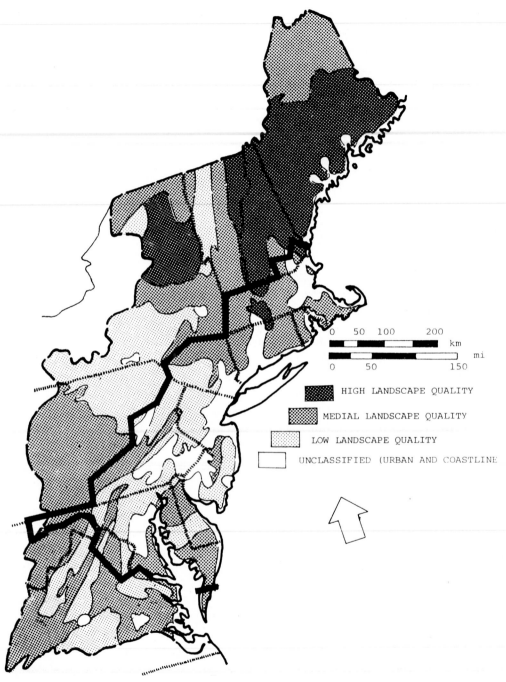

FIGURE 19 *Megalopolitan development has occurred largely within the Atlantic Coastal Plain. Almost all the highest quality landscapes spread outside the megalopolis (heavy black line).*

in several parts of the North Atlantic Region. It was revised through this public participatory process and a final set of recommendations was drawn up for the use of the Congress of the United States. As planning went from more general to more specific, from a higher level to a lower level, this large regional, multistate policy or level one planning formed the basis for determining the level two planning in several parts of this region. That next level of planning is presented as another case study in the following chapter.

AN ANALYSIS

This chapter has discussed land-use policy planning at various levels of government. The previous chapter presented the evolution of land-use planning in six areas of planning concerns including: the changing role of land-use planners; the difference between the disciplinary and professional planner; the role of private and public planners; the various planning processes; the types of planning; and finally the hierarchy of planning. In this chapter, implications were made throughout in regard to these six concerns. This brief analysis is designed to make a clearer link between the evolution of land-use planning and its effect on policy planning.

The traditional role of land-use planners in policy planning has been as a catalyst for learning and action, Olmsted's preservation efforts being an excellent early example. Such planners have been aiding the decision makers in their understanding of the total planning process from problem identification to plan evaluation. More recently, as shown through the North Atlantic Regional (NAR) Water Resources Planning Study, planners have also been required to communicate their plans to the public.

The analysis of the NAR case study also implies that this large multi-departmental planning was also multidisciplinary in nature with specialists for each of the 18 separate planning activities. Similarly, other types of policy planning, such as the plan for Wisconsin, call on expertise in economics, transportation, recreation, and so on. Among all the examples cited above, none was carried out by the private sector. Although it is common knowledge that corporations such as giant paper companies, which may own millions of acres, do undertake policy planning, the bulk of policy planning seems to be done by various governmental planners.

In the analysis of the evolution of the planning process, it is clear that some earlier policy planning, such as the determination of the settlement pattern of the United States through the "system of rectangular survey," demanded a very simple intuitive approach, while later studies — for instance the work of the Club of Rome — have used a highly advanced mathematical model to assess global uncertainties. The NAR case study also required a highly advanced "critical path" just to manage the huge study. Similarly, many of the 18 separate teams needed sophisticated models for assessing and planning for water supply, navigation, and most other factors. Indeed, systematic, quantitative planning approaches are used increasingly in policy planning as decision makers want to know "more facts" in order to appear "more rational" and more responsive to perceived needs.

It is also clear that policy planning has moved toward integrated planning, especially since the 1960s. More and more it is replacing single-purpose planning since planners and decision makers have discovered that the solution of one problem often creates another. We are now capable of dealing with several needs or issues simultaneously, and we should. Land-use issues are highly complex. One can hardly solve them with limited single-purpose planning. Finally, in terms of the hierarchy of planning, it should be clear that much more land-use planning is needed after land-use policies are formulated. The following two chapters discuss land-use planning at those lower levels.

CHAPTER 8

LAND-USE PLANNING IN METROPOLITAN
AND RURAL REGIONS

Policy planning such as that discussed at the national and state levels can be directly followed up by local planning units. For example, the United States' national policy on the system of rectangular land survey was implemented directly at the local level. These surveys outlined the initial land uses of each township in midwestern and western states during the last century. Similarly, the "performance standards" of Vermont's Act 250 have been enforced by state-appointed commissions at the local level since 1970. If this can be done, why is there a need for another planning unit between the broad policy and local planning levels?

This middle-level physical or meso-scale land-use planning has perhaps two distinct origins, namely metropolitan expansion and the development or use pressures on rural areas. The majority of metropolitan areas around the world have engulfed several of their local communities. Several planning issues have emerged in these metropolitan regions which go beyond local issues. Transportation, water resource, waste management, open space, and recreation are just a few which have required coordination and even integration at the metropolitan levels.

Similarly, some rural issues such as the planning of a large national park or national forest, which are often several million acres in size, have necessitated some sort of activity which is more specific than policy planning but more general than local or site-specific planning. In countries of the British Commonwealth these are referred to as "structure plans." The United States' Federal government often defines them as level two planning. The states themselves may call the activity regional, county, or substate planning. All these terms refer essentially to some sort of large-scale physical land-use planning which determines land-use allocation in an area including few or many local municipalities.

To illustrate the nature and importance of this level of planning, the two types, the metropolitan and rural, are here separately considered. The primary foci of land-use planning at the metropolitan level are the accommodation of growth and the protection of sufficient resources, such as water supply, for metropolitan populations. In addition, reclamation and impact — related issues are often part of metropolitan regional land-use planning. In contrast to this, rural planning is often done to develop and manage timber, recreational resources and the like, and to preserve or to set aside invaluable natural or cultural resources from human consumption or overuse. More recently, restoration, conservation, and environmental impact-related issues have been added to rural planning.

PLANNING IN METROPOLITAN AREAS

From the mid-18th century onward, the Baroque order established during the previous two centuries was extended into the metropolitan regions of large European cities. Haussmann was perhaps the most successful planner of that time. Between 1853 and 1869, he expended, directed, and supervised the expenditure of some two and one-half billion francs on the expansion of Paris (Giedion, 1967, p. 745). The fundamental aims of Haussmann's schemes were to create a modern metropolis to "control street fighting and riots; to ameliorate the state of health of the city through the systematic destruction of infected alleyways and centers of epidemics"; and thirdly "to assure the public peace by creation of large boulevards which will permit the circulation not only of air and light but also of troops" (Giedion, 1967, p. 746). The wide boulevards and the series of ring roads built in Paris became the major physical elements planners used to provide order and growth pattern for the new metropolises.

By the end of the 19th century, the introduction of a revolutionary technological innovation, the street car, greatly accelerated metropolitan growth. Built in a radial pattern, streetcar lines reached out 10 to 15 miles from central downtown areas, stimulating high-density developments within walking distance of the tracks. For example, most growth in the Boston metropolitan region, from the turn of the century until 1945, was controlled by the street car (Warner, 1962). Later the areas between the street car lines filled in as automobiles gave access to the more affluent people who could afford to purchase one (Figure 20). In short, earlier visions of planners combined with technological forces to set the pattern of metropolitan areas.

In response to this seeming uncontrolled and rapid metropolitan expansion, landscape planners began the task of balancing these developments with metropolitan regional planning of public open space. One of the most successful case studies is the landscape planning efforts of the Boston metropolitan region. The initial park system designed by Frederic Law Olmsted in 1878 was the first major linear open space for the growing city and

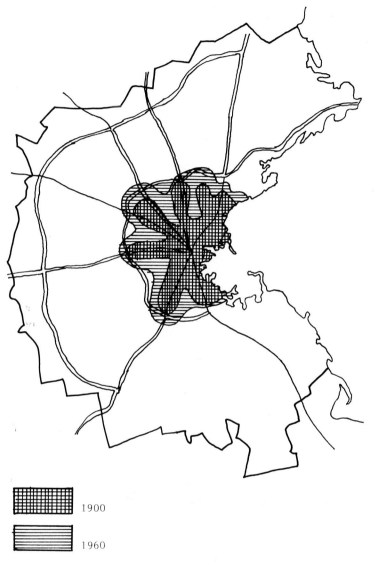

1900

1960

FIGURE 20   *The automobile was primarily responsible for rapid urban incursions into the rural landscape. The darker tone represents a densely populated urban Boston circa 1900. The lighter tone represents a decentralized urban Boston circa 1960.*

was often referred to as the "Emerald Necklace." Landfill operations had created the South End and Back Bay districts on both sides of the original neck that joined the city to the mainland. As the population of Boston grew, the city had also expanded its political limits to include the mainland, suburban townships of Roxbury (1867) and Dorchester (1868). The Olmsted plan used the Muddy River drainage area to create a link around the city between the large proposed Franklin Park and the Charles River, with another tie to the Common, the original public space of the city of Boston (Figure 21).

The second and perhaps the most significant planning effort for the Boston region was the work of Charles Eliot, who planned a public open space framework for the burgeoning Boston metropolis (Eliot, 1902). He proposed (and helped to implement) a regional development plan that allotted land along the trolleys to high-density uses but created an extensive park system in the interstices (Figure 22). This park system was designed, in Eliot's words, to place in public use the "spaces on the ocean front, much of the shores and islands of Boston Bay, the courses of the large areas of wild forest on the outer rim [of the metropolitan region] and numerous small squares, play grounds, and parks in the midst of the dense population" (Eliot, 1902, p. 381).

In summary, three types of metropolitan land-use planning can be identified during the 19th century. There were the planners such as Haussmann who attempted to satisfy several physical or land-use planning objectives. The single-purpose mission planners implemented such significant transportation devices as the streetcar, which had a profound effect on the growth patterns of metropolitan regions. The third type of land-use planning, for public open space, was to a great extent a reaction to seemingly uncontrolled urban growth. These three types of planning have continued into this century. A multipurpose land-use planning approach has been employed in many European metropolises. In the United States, in much the same way as the streetcar early in the century, metropolitan highway planning has had the most dominant influence on land-use allocation. Finally, reaction from landscape planners has continued. In some instances, this group has been able to contribute to more comprehensive integrated planning efforts. Each of these three types of planning is summarized below, concluding with a case study of a level two integrated planning approach to problems of metropolitan regional developments.

Multipurpose Planning

As discussed in the previous chapter, land-use control has been a more acceptable approach in Europe than in the United States. For this reason, European planners have been able to deal with multiobjective land-use planning within metropolitan regions. Recent planning for the outlying regional area of Stockholm, Sweden, and the plan for the Basel region of Switzerland illustrate this difference.

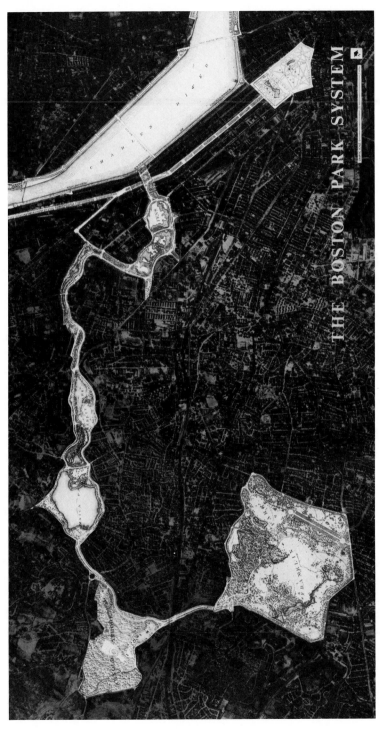

FIGURE 21 *Boston park system.*

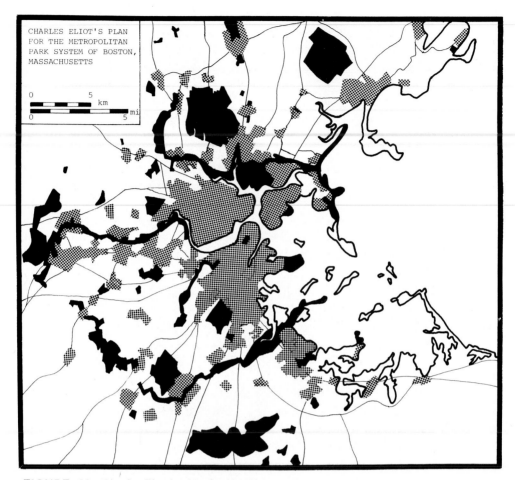

CHARLES ELIOT'S PLAN
FOR THE METROPOLITAN
PARK SYSTEM OF BOSTON,
MASSACHUSETTS

0   5
         km
0   5
         mi

FIGURE 22 *Charles Eliot's plan for the Metropolitan park system of Boston, Massachusetts.*

Planning for the Swedish capital has been carried out by a team of planners of the Regional Planning Federation of Stockholm. This group prepares a set of plans every five years. The first plan was published in 1952. The early dormitory new towns, Vallingby, Farsta, Skarholmen, and Jarva, are the successive physical manifestations of this early plan for the region. These new towns are connected to Stockholm by a clean, speedy, comfortable, and heavily-used subway, the T-Bana (Strong, 1971, p. 42). The town centers and the individual neighborhoods of these towns are skillfully placed in beautiful natural settings. In short, this early plan successfully achieved several planning objectives. It provided new housing, shopping and recreation for Stockholm's growing population; it used efficient transportation; and the developments were built in an environmentally sensitive manner. Later five-year plans have perpetuated this early, multipurpose approach. "The 1966 Outline Regional Plan," for instance, revised housing plans and residential standards, leisure and recreational areas, transportation and other "communications networks." Each five-year plan offers thirty-year projections. The revised plan of 1966 looks ahead to the year 2000 and to a population of 2.2 million (the Stockholm Regional Planning Office, 1968).

Switzerland's Basel regional plan was equally comprehensive. Although it did not advocate a satellite or new town concept, it revised the land areas previously zoned for development by the 76 separate municipalities of the region. This regional plan was able to increase the open space and agricultural uses within these towns. It also included a transportation plan with an emphasis on the improvement of public transportation facilities to help especially children and the elderly of the region. The third major component of the plan was a "landscape plan" designed to protect all significant natural and cultural landscapes of the region from development or misuse (Plattner, 1975, p. 192). The plan was unique in that it analyzed extensively the conflicts among the three areas of concern. The planning process included a significant public input, and was revised to better incorporate the desires of the population in the region.

Planners in the United States have attempted to make proposals similar to those of European planners of metropolitan regions. The Regional Plan Association, for instance, prepared two regional plans for the New York City metropolitan region which consists of 12,000 square miles around the city in New Jersey, New York, and Connecticut. The first regional plan was proposed in 1929 and revised in 1965. Both were financed by various foundations and by the membership of the association, and while they have had an impact on county and municipal planning, zoning, and acquisition and development of recreational areas their influence falls far short of European efforts in spite of the fact that several members of the association have been leading planners of the United States.

Comprehensive planning of metropolises has also been undertaken by numerous planning agencies in the United States. Two regional planning agencies in the nation's capital, for instance, prepared in 1961 the so-called "Plan For The Year of 2000." The comprehensive plan proposed six alternatives, including: a restricted growth plan; a plan placing the new growth in three new independent cities; a planned sprawl; a region with dispersed cities; a denser region with peripheral communities; and finally the radical corridor plan (Figure 23), (The National Capital Planning Commission and the National Capital Regional Planning Council). Neither of these plans, however, had much effect on the growth of the capital region.

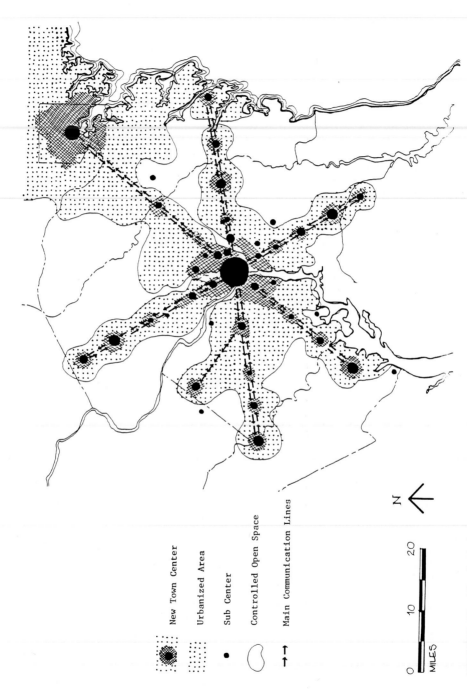

New Town Center

Urbanized Area

Sub Center

Controlled Open Space

Main Communication Lines

N

0   10   20

MILES

FIGURE 23 *The Radial Corridor Plan: National Capital Region.*

Single-Purpose Planning

A glance at any map of metropolitan regions or a visit to such an area in the United States reveals the immense impact of the highway engineer. One sees an impressive highway network crisscrossing the metropolitan regions. These highspeed, limited access highways form a radial pattern interconnected by one and often two belt highways from 10 to 20 miles away from the old downtown area. These highways have opened up huge areas for development. In the Boston metropolitan region, for instance, these superhighways enlarged the pre-war metropolitan region from 250 square miles to 2,500 square miles, a ten-fold increase within two decades of the end of the Second World War (Figure 24).

As illustrated in Chapter 3, the United States government accepted this auto-oriented technological development and through a massive highway program and complementary policies, discussed in the previous chapter, transportation planning became synonymous with metropolitan regional planning. The authors of a recent book on transportation planning (Boyce, Day and McDonald, 1970) entitle their book without any hesitation, *Metropolitan Plan Making*. For them, transportation planning also means land-use planning. They are indeed correct. People can build only on land which is accessible. This single-purpose, auto-oriented transportation planning has created what many planners call the "multinucleated metropolitan areas." The many small industrial and commercial centers in the belt areas diminished the prosperity of downtown areas since the belt had become the most attractive and economically the most feasible site for development. Transportation planners proved once more that accessibility is the most important component of land-use planning.

Perhaps the most important part of this autotransportation oriented planning approach is that the highway plans are based on very sophisticated travel forecasts. Planners start with extensive public surveys to ascertain the people's desire. Then highways and roads are planned and built to satisfy that perceived desire. The models generated by this approach are often called land-use allocation models (Putnam, 1975). In essence, the highway engineers who have emerged as metropolitan regional planners have attempted to simulate the future based on public preference surveys and through the planning of roads to provide a regional framework within which people can build their houses, industries, commercial areas, and recreation facilities. These plans are based on an assumption that the greater part of the land within this metropolitan landscape is developable. In the case of the Boston region, the highly complex mathematical model was based on the premise that 80 percent of the total area is developable (Boyce, Day and McDonald, 1970, p. 199). As a result, these highways have placed enormous develop-

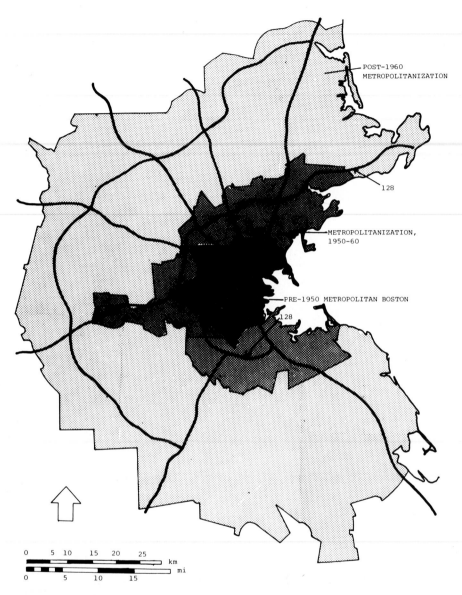

FIGURE 24 *The decentralized Boston metropolis after 1970 spread over one-third of Massachusetts. This lower-density development has an impact on about 2,500 square miles of landscape. This area is 50 times larger than the Boston metropolis at the turn of the century. Dark tone: Pre Route 128 development; Medium tone: Route 128 band; and Light tone: Route 495 band.*

ment pressures on the greater portion of the large metropolitan landscapes. The development of wetlands, productive agricultural lands, flood plains, and other highly productive lands aroused the same type of landscape planning concern which emerged during the streetcar era.

The Landscape Approach

In response to the large-scale developments in metropolitan regions of the United States, a new and vocal group of environmentalist landscape planners proposed an alternative approach to the allocation models of the engineers. The problem with the allocation model, they have claimed, is that it ignores the landscape and environmental side of planning, and concentrates on the supply side. They argue that the landscape should be developed in harmony with long-range objectives and that the failure to incorporate the landscape attributes in land-use planning will result in impairment and elimination of valuable landscape resources such as water supply, in the increase in natural and human-caused hazards, in unnecessary increases in development costs, and finally, in the case of a blanket, ubiquitous development, in harm to the environment when evaluated against pertinent ecological principles (Fabos, 1979, pp. 45–60).

Perhaps the most articulate landscape planner who has advocated this landscape-ecological approach is Ian McHarg. In *Design with Nature* (McHarg, 1969), he presented this landscape approach developed, over a decade, by him and his associates. McHarg asserted that the "intrinsic landscape attributes" should be the basis of land-use planning. One of his early works was *The Plan For the Valleys*, (McHarg, 1969, pp. 79–93), the study of a 70-square mile area within the developing Baltimore metropolitan region. After assessing the regions, he found four distinct landscape types (Figure 25). He concluded that the valley floors were unsuitable for development and proposed complete protection for them. For the remainder of the area, he recommended various types and densities of development which in his judgment were compatible with the landscape. He also analyzed the development demand and concluded that the area would be able to absorb the expected 110,000 new inhabitants if his proposed land-use plan were to be implemented (McHarg 1969, p. 83).

In later years, McHarg and his team developed much more sophisticated models to incorporate more landscape attributes or the supply side of planning into the metropolitan land-use decision making process. Their work for Staten Island, for instance, assessed 34 critical factors including several parameters of climate, geology, physiography, hydrology, pedology, vegetation, wildlife, and land uses. Through an overlay compositing procedure they were able to map land-use suitabilities which would provide a highly diverse

VALLEY FLOORS

VALLEY WALLS

BASIC AMENITY

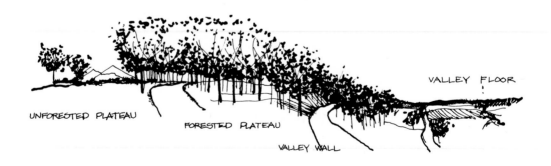

UNFORESTED PLATEAU

FORESTED PLATEAU

VALLEY WALL

VALLEY FLOOR

PHYSIOGRAPHIC SECTION

FIGURE 25 *The plan for the valleys.*

environment while achieving compatibility between uses and resources. The most intriguing feature of their proposed land-use map is that while the greater part of the land area is proposed for a given use, they found a significant percentage which would be compatible for several uses (McHarg 1969, p. 114). This approach makes their land-use plan suitable for public discussion, since it offers viable choices and gives some idea of possible consequences of alternative land uses.

The Landscape Approach as Part of
Integrated Planning

While single-purpose transportation planning has provided the land-use framework for metropolitan growth in the United States, land-use planning continued through the late 1960s and early 1970s, with the emphasis on water and related land resource issues.

In the case of the Boston region, this study was a follow-up to the North Atlantic Regional water resources planning study which is discussed in the previous chapter. The primary objective was to take the policy level information and develop a more specific land-use plan for the joint Boston and Providence metropolitan region. The planning framework was similar to the North Atlantic Regional Water Resources Planning Study in that this level two planning had to address both economic and environmental objectives.

The plan to satisfy economic objectives was in a sense a follow-up to earlier transportation or allocation models, which attempted to forecast development trends and locations. The plan to satisfy the environmental objective was based on a landscape approach similar to those developed by McHarg and other landscape planners during the 1960s. The important aspect of this planning effort was that the economic and environmental models had to be integrated into one plan which would satisfy both objectives as much as possible.

The most specific objective of the study was to direct metropolitan growth to suitable areas while protecting critical water and other related resources. The study also included planning for outdoor recreation, resource management, hazard prevention, and the general location of unwelcome facilities such as power plants, electric transmission lines and pipe lines.

The composition of the planning team was also similar to the level one North Atlantic Regional Water Resources Planning Study. An interdisciplinary group of planners and scientists from several Federal and state agencies and from consultancies were coordinated by the planners of the New England River Basin Commission. Once more, I was fortunate to work as a member of this multidisciplinary team, especially because this case study represented one of the earlier examples of the land-use allocation model being combined with a landscape supply or a landscape planning approach.

The economic model was based on detailed surveys to ascertain development trends. The landscape planning model was developed to assess all critical resources for preservation, the highly valued resources and hazard zones for protection from development, and for the rest of the area, it assessed the degree of development suitability, which specified the densities based on several land-use characteristics (Fabos, 1979, p. 162). Figure 26 illustrates the three-phase process used to generate these recommendations. Each of the critical, highly valued resource and hazard areas was identified and assessed by a team of specialists that included hydrologists, soil scientists, geologists, wildlife biologists, foresters, recreation specialists, and others. All these areas were mapped and then overlaid to produce composite maps for each of these three major categories: (1) preservation of critical resources, (2) protection of highly valued resources from industrial, commercial, and housing developments, and (3) developments (at various densities) for all areas found suitable for development. The three composite assessment maps were further combined to produce a "Development Capability Map." An abstracted version of this map for the Boston region is shown in Figure 27.

This map is significant since it represents the third generation of land-use planning effort in the Boston area. The first metropolitan land-use plan was the recreation open space plan prepared by Charles Eliot (Figure 22), who aimed to balance the metropolitan area development generated by the introduction of the streetcar with protection and use of public lands. The second generation of landscape plan was at the state level, which also included a detailed metropolitan area plan for the Boston Region. This effort was coordinated by Charles Eliot II, the nephew of the Charles Eliot who prepared the first plan (Fabos, 1973, pp. 27–30). This case study done during the early 1970s is the third generation of a metropolitan areawide land-use plan. All three plans are similar in concept. However, as data availability and accuracy increased, so planners were able to be more specific and the plans have shown increasingly more detail.

Another significant aspect of this work is that it amply illustrates the differences between level-one and level-two studies. At the North Atlantic regional scale, the smallest mappable unit was some 250 square miles or an area as large as the original metropolitan area of Boston. In this level two study, planners identified units as small as 50 or 100 acres. One should note that such attention to detail is only possible at the local level, where the final phase of site-specific planning can be done. Indeed, the planners of waste water management and local planning units have been using this level two planning ever since. Its major value is that it provides them with the regional land-use planning context which is essential for making local land-use decisions. This level-three or local land-use planning is the topic of the next chapter.

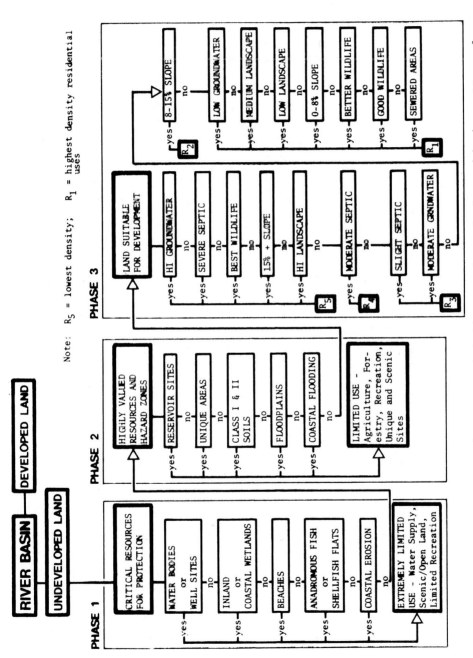

FIGURE 26 *This landscape approach attempts to deal with preservation, protection, and development types of environmental decisions. This planning process is abstracted from the work of T. J. Clapp and J. P. Wargo. The study was codirected by Dr. Ervin Zube and the author.*

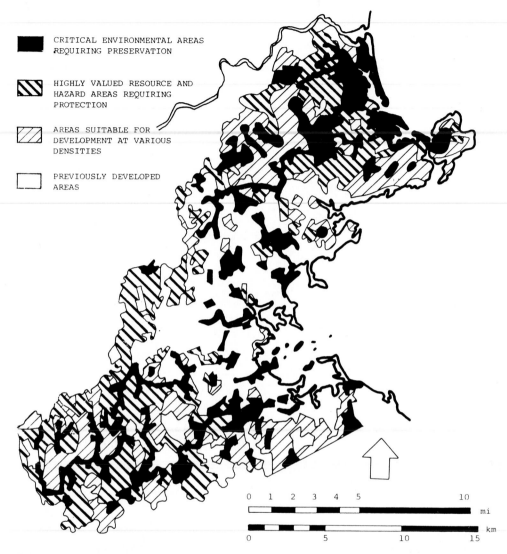

CRITICAL ENVIRONMENTAL AREAS
REQUIRING PRESERVATION

HIGHLY VALUED RESOURCE AND
HAZARD AREAS REQUIRING
PROTECTION

AREAS SUITABLE FOR
DEVELOPMENT AT VARIOUS
DENSITIES

PREVIOUSLY DEVELOPED
AREAS

0 1 2 3 4 5   10
                                        mi

0   5   10   15
                                        km

FIGURE 27 *This simplified development capability map shows that approximately half of the undeveloped landscape of this region consists of critical hazard and/or highly valued areas and should not be developed. Earlier development apparently neglected these considerations, as can be seen by analyzing the large continuously developed areas. This development capabilities map is being used by various planning groups of this region to guide future growth more sensitively and sensibly from the point of view of environmental constraints and opportunities.*

RURAL PLANNING

While planners in metropolitan regions deal primarily with development and land conversion issues, planners of rural regions focus mainly on resource utilization. These planners are managing the many vital public land resources for export into metropolises. In the case of timber, for instance, the wood is exported for construction and for conversion into other wood products. The large public range lands of the United States produce much of the meat supply for the urban population. In the case of rural recreation, wilderness, and wildlife resources, the urban population is attracted into these areas to use the resources. Rural planners, indeed, deal with significantly different issues and their procedures are often very different from those who are planning in metropolises, though aspects of planning are interchangeable. Because of these significant differences, rural planning at the regional scale deserves a separate discussion.

It should be noted that in certain countries such as the Netherlands or Belgium and even some densely developed American states such as Rhode Island and Delaware, rural planning at this level is often an intricate part of metropolitan planning. In these places, the predominant planning issues are related to growth and population maintenance. These areas are dependent on large quantities of imports from the rural areas of other countries or states. Countries rich in natural resources like the United States or Canada export large amounts of rural resources into their urban regions and to other, resource-poor, countries. For this reason, examples of rural planning are drawn heavily from the United States and Canada.

In the previous chapter, it was shown how national and statewide land-use policies have determined ownership and the general land-use patterns of the nations and the states. But just as in metropolitan regions, the Federal and state policies for rural areas need to be developed further at the regional level to provide the very much needed regional overview, context, and alternative choices before one can proceed with local planning.

Rural planning, much like metropolitan area planning can be classified into single- or multipurpose planning. Both these approaches are practiced today, and therefore these subcategories are used in this discussion. However, rural planning, whether it is single-purpose or multipurpose, differs from its metropolitan counterpart in that it is usually based on inherent landscape attributes or the supply aspects of the landscape. For instance, a rural landscape is developed for recreation or preserved as a national park because of its landscape characteristics. Similarly, the intrinsic landscape characteristics may suggest multipurpose use potential. For example, a large national forest may have attributes for simultaneous use for timber production, water supply, recreation, and wildlife resources.

Single-Purpose Rural Planning

When President Grant of the United States signed the bill on March 1, 1872 to establish Yellowstone National Park "in the Territories of Montana and Wyoming," (Newton, 1971, p. 520), the legislators established the need for regional-level rural planning, although at the time they did not realize what kind of planning was needed for the Yellowstone Park area, which is larger than the state of Rhode Island. The Yellowstone legislation itself was far from adequate for effective planning and management of this unique landscape. Today, the Federal and state governments have many regional agencies which are planning the use, preservation, and management at this intermediate scale of millions of acres each year.

In the case of Yellowstone, it took two decades before it was realized that a better understanding of the assets of the region was needed prior to the park's being used. Today, when a national or state-level land-use act or policy is established for preservation, recreation, or any other purpose in a large rural landscape, planning for the region becomes a logical first step. Federal and state agencies have established many regional planning groups which are continuously assessing, planning, and managing their rural regions.

In analyzing the evolution of regional rural planning one can identify at least three stages of development. The first was a response to Federal and state acts and policies which established a use or preservation of large areas, such as the Yellowstone Park area. Within these large areas, planners allocate the region to various uses. For instance, the large Gros Morne National Park in Canada has five established use areas: a special area with arctic alpine flora and fauna of scientific significance, which is open only to scientific studies; a larger wilderness area, mostly rugged tundra landscapes open to small groups for interpretation and education; natural environmental areas where higher intensity nature interpretation and educational programs can take place; a small portion of more resilient area set aside for general outdoor recreation uses; and finally an area for intensive use to house the administrative, operational, and residential areas (Figure 28).

The second stage of regional rural planning was a response to legislation which authorized feasibility and desirability studies to determine use potentials of a region. During the 1960s, for instance, the U.S. Federal government initiated many studies to establish national recreation areas. The acts which authorize these regional rural planning efforts did not define the area boundaries as did the legislation which established national parks and national forest areas. Instead, these level-two studies had to determine areas with boundaries in a coastal or a river basin region for public acquisition and use.

The Connecticut River National Recreation Area Study is a good example of this development (Department of the Interior, 1968). Instead of

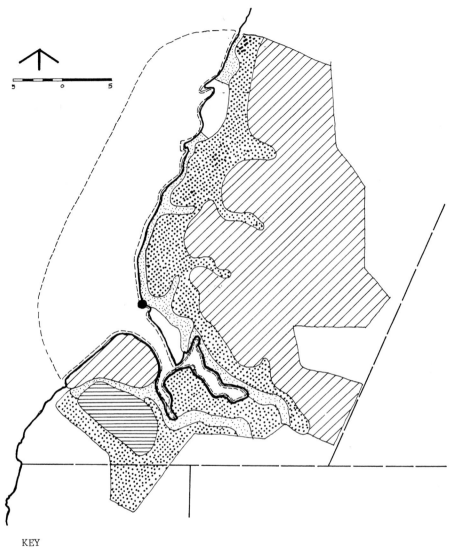

KEY

▤ special area

▨ wilderness area

▨ natural environment areas (land)

▨ general outdoor recreation

☐ natural environment areas

● intensive use area

FIGURE 28 *Zoning Plan Gros Morne National Park: Richard Strong Associates Limited.*

legislating an area for recreational use, the policy makers mandated a feasibility study to recommend appropriate areas for Federal acquisition and to create a total recreation plan which would link Federal lands to existing and proposed state parks in four river basin states and to cultural and historical areas of the valley (Figure 29). Although coordination of planning at this level was minimal between the planners of the Federal and state governments, and public involvement was absent, when part of this and other national recreation studies were carried to local-level planning, the involvement of states, municipalities, and the public increased significantly. The planning approach used in this and other studies was similar to the simple landscape approach illustrated in the previous section; that is, the acquisition of recreation areas as based on a few pertinent factors such as scenic quality and proximity to the river.

The third stage of regional rural planning was the development of more sophisticated procedures, especially those to assess the landscape resources and to evaluate the impacts of plan alternatives. In response to increased public concern toward the environment during the late 1960s, planners attempted to incorporate public values and viewpoints in their assessment and planning procedures. For instance, a wetland assessment procedure based its public values on preference studies and used these values to rank order the wetlands from most to least valuable. This procedure was applied to several regions of Massachusetts to aid in wetland preservation decisions (Smardon, 1975). In another procedure, which was designed to plan and evaluate alternatives for the location of electric transmission lines, a computer was used to include the values of the various interest groups, including the naturalists' (Murray and Nieman, 1975, p. 238).

During the 1970s this third stage of regional rural planning also changed the way planning documents were prepared. Before this time, plans were presented without any mention of the process used in preparing the planning documents. As public involvement, and therefore accountability increased, planners responded by making their work more explicit and even reproducible.

Multipurpose Rural Planning

Among the countries rich in land resources, the United States has led the way toward multipurpose rural planning. This level-two, or regional-scale planning has been initiated by land-use policies discussed in the previous chapter. The national focus on land utilization has manifested itself by two interrelated Federal policies, each of them designed to "maximize net public benefit" (Public Land Law Review Commission, 1970, p. 9). One is the change from custodial management to intensive management. According to

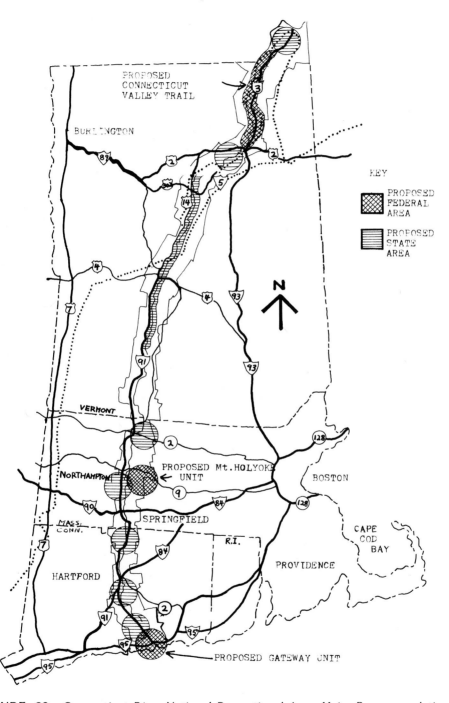

FIGURE 29 *Connecticut River National Recreational Area. Major Recommendations.*

Clawson and Held (1957, p. 36) the transition seemed to come in the post-war years of 1947 to 1950. This policy shift entailed considerable Federal investment in such areas as timber management and the building of access roads, and greatly increased the need for regional-level planning.

The second policy change was initiated by the Multiple Use Acts of 1960 and 1964 which "specify the number of uses that can be made of the national forests and the unreserved public domain lands administered by the Bureau of Land Management respectively" (Public Land Law Review Commission, 1970, p. 50). As a result of these acts and the recommendations by the Public Land Law Review Commission, rural land-use planning at the regional level has become more comprehensive. Agencies responsible for managing public land in the same region have also been required to integrate their efforts, both internally and among themselves. Just as single-purpose planning became more sophisticated during the 1970s, so did multipurpose planning. It even went one step further. Agencies such as the U.S. Forest Service and the Bureau of Land Management have developed comprehensive planning and management procedures involving timber production, range land use, water shed, wildlife, and visual resource management, including environmental impact statements for all eventualities. These procedures are well documented and form the basis for planning by the regional district offices of those Federal agencies responsible for the management of public lands (U.S.D.A. Forest Service 1973; Iverson, 1975; U.S.D.I. Bureau of Land Management, 1980). Similar to single-purpose planning, these procedures have also increasingly included the public in the decision-making process. Multipurpose rural planning at this regional scale is done by interdisciplinary or multidisciplinary teams including natural and social scientists, landscape architects, planners, engineers, and geographers among others.

AN ANALYSIS

This final section is aimed at analyzing the metropolitan and regional rural planning responses against the six concerns presented in Chapter 6, which are: the changing role of land-use planners at level-two planning; the input of disciplinary and professional planners; the role of private and public planners; the types of planning; the planning process used; and finally an analysis of this hierarchy of planning in relation to the other levels of planning.

The role of land-use planners on this intermediate scale has changed significantly. It seems that the earlier planners, such as the European comprehensive planners or the American highway planners, perceived their role as similar to that of the utopians, as form givers to large-scale, regional growth. However, increased public concern towards the environment, the landscape, and the social fabric in the rapidly growing metropolitan areas gave rise to the greater involvement of various interest groups. This review of several metropolitan and regional rural land-use planning studies clearly indicates that especially since the early 1970s planners indeed responded to this public concern, by including their values and participation in planning.

An analysis of the role of disciplinary and professional planners also shows significant differences between the two and various changes over time. In Europe, the professional planners have been much more influential at this level than their American counterparts. Highway engineers were the dominant plan makers of metropolitan growth in the United States for over two decades. Disciplinary planners coming from the natural sciences and landscape architecture have also been very influential in regional rural planning since these planning activities have been so much dependent on the natural resource base and the intrinsic qualities of the landscape. It is also evident that by the 1970s interdisciplinary planning teams in many agencies consisted of professional planners and colleagues from many other disciplines.

On the role of public versus private planners at this level, it appears that the public planners have had a dominant role. Planning consultants or private planners seem to have had an insignificant impact on aspects of metropolitan and regional rural planning. At this level, planning is more a long-range activity when compared to local levels, where it is more task-oriented. Metropolitan and regional rural planning is also more a continuous process. A bureaucracy is essential for such planning, hence regional and metropolitan planning agencies have proliferated over the past decades.

On the analysis of the types of planning, single-purpose planning dominated much of metropolitan and regional rural planning activities until very recently. While the integrated approach is becoming more common, single-purpose planning will continue, especially for rural areas. Issues such as large-scale recreation, location of transmission lines, exploitation of oil-shale resources and related impacts are among the many powerful single-purpose issues which will continue to dominate planning in many regional rural and metropolitan areas.

The planning process has shown great variety in its applications to metropolitan and rural regional planning, from overly simplistic, almost intuitive approaches such as in the case of the Year 2000 plans for the Washington metropolitan region, through highly sophisticated computerized allocation models of the highway engineers, to a more comprehensive and integrated approach used in both metropolitan and rural planning during the 1970s. An important aspect of this evolution was that these later procedures included both the demand and the supply of landscape resource sides of planning.

Finally, in the hierarchy of planning, the importance of this middle level or metropolitan and regional rural planning is increasing. As land-use issues have become more complex, as our understanding of the interrelationships between human activities and the environment have increased, as local areas have grown into metropolitan regions, this regional level planning has become inevitable. A significant growth in this area of land-use planning is vital and most likely to occur in the near future.

CHAPTER 9

LAND-USE PLANNING AT THE LOCAL LEVEL

For many people, land-use planning at the local level is the most significant because the result of it can be seen by all. Our housing, shopping, working, and recreation environments are all results of some degree of local planning. The majority of land-use planning books also focus their attention on this lowest level of local or community planning. Indeed, at this level, all of us experience daily the consequences of planning, and often the lack of it.

Land-use planners have responded to the problems created by unplanned developments or the misuses of landscape resources, and in a few instances, have conducted local planning as a follow-up to regional planning. The three major streams of land-use planning responses are: innovative approaches in physical planning; the proliferation of land-use controls and devices used primarily by the public sector; and some recent moves toward an integrated approach, attempting to combine the innovative physical planning with a variety of public land-use devices as part of the ongoing planning process. Analysis of these three streams of planning shows that planners have responded to all the emerging problems and issues which were discussed in the first chapter. This presentation also demonstrates the changing role of the planners; and clarifies the need for more disciplinary and professional planners; the roles of the private or more active and the public or more reactionary planners; the increased complexity of the planning process; some attempts which are designed to deal comprehensively with land-use planning; and finally the types of decisions made at local/community levels. The reader will also discover numerous shortcomings of local land-use planning when it is evaluated against an ideal hierarchical and comprehensive approach advocated by this author.

INNOVATIONS IN PHYSICAL PLANNING

Land-use planning during the past century has been, in the main, physical planning. Architects, landscape architects, engineers, surveyors, and various kinds of inventors were all surrogates for land-use planners. They were the inventors of most of the physical planning devices used today in planned unit developments, new town planning, recreation planning, and perhaps in all aspects of land-use planning. This group has operated under the notion that land-use planning is a creative process, similar to the design of a building or an urban center. Most physical planning has been done by the private sector. But even the planning which is undertaken by public agencies, such as redevelopment authorities, has involved planners and the developers of the private sector in a major way in the western countries. The accent of physical planning has been on action, when compared to the control-oriented or reactionary approach which has emerged in this century, starting with zoning and followed by other regulations.

These physical land-use planners have advanced at least two unique and important approaches during the past century. Those whose initial training has been in architecture and engineering tend to approach land-use planning as a creative, problem-solving activity to satisfy human needs and desires for housing, transportation, recreation, and so on. The second group of land-use planners can trace their origin to landscape architecture, and is inclined to believe that the intrinsic quality or attributes of the landscape or a local land area should be the basis for land use. This group has also advanced the landscape approach in regional planning discussed in the previous chapter. There are several commonalities between these two groups, but because of their different philosophical backgrounds, these two land-use planning approaches are discussed separately.

Physical Planning with a Focus on Needs

Physical planners have advanced many innovative ideas during the past four or five centuries. During the Renaissance, they planned public squares and places. During the Baroque period of the 16th and 17th centuries, land-use planners laid out boulevards and separated residential from commercial uses to satisfy the emerging needs of the bourgeoisie. In responding to the problems created by the 19th century Industrial Revolution and the 20th century dependence on the automobile, physical planners met social, functional, and aesthetic needs with physical planning solutions. In addition to dealing with growth-related issues, they have advanced proposals to halt the decline of the downtown areas of our cities, have advocated preservation, and also tackled some impact-related issues. However, physical land-use planners in this category have contributed mostly to growth- and decline-related problems.

Innovations in Community Planning

In dealing with growth, these land-use planners have focused on the interrelationships of the various land uses, area requirements, ideal densities for each use, and on circulation with a special focus on separating the auto traffic from pedestrian walkways. The plan for Radburn, New Jersey during the late 1920s is perhaps the most commonly quoted example to offer a combination of viable solutions to these requirements. Stein (1966, p. 48), one of the planners of Radburn, claims that the "modern neighborhood conception [for a new community] was applied for the first time and, in part, realized in the form that is now generally accepted" (Figure 30).

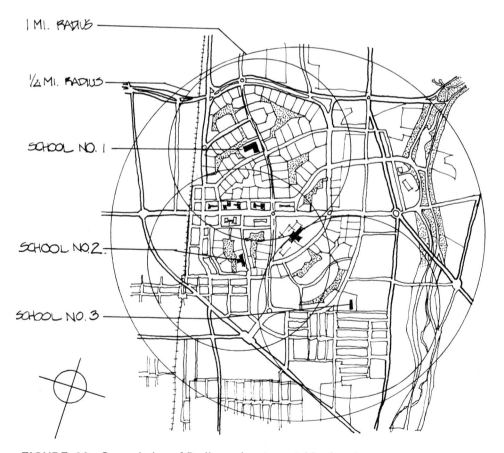

FIGURE 30 *General plan of Radburn showing neighborhood.*

An elementary school, playgrounds, local shops, and a church were planned for each center of the three proposed neighborhoods. The half-mile radius placed facilities within easy walking distance for all residents. Radburn was the first planned community for the "motor age." The safety issue was one of the most important concerns to its planners. To achieve their goal they took several design steps. First, they devised a hierarchical system of specialized roads and used cul-de-sacs in residential areas; second, they made use of superblocks; third, they separated pedestrian and motor traffic; and last, they employed a continuous system of interior park areas related to pedestrian movement (Figure 31).

Radburn, this planned, partially built settlement, represented the influence of English garden city theories and as such added several innovations to community planning. A contemporary critic, Eugene Ladner Birch, (1980, p. 424) claims that "Radburn's plan was so well designed and rationally organized that it has become a permanent resource for planners who in every generation examine and sometimes adapt it to solve contemporary problems." Indeed, its influence can be seen in most contemporary new towns of Western Europe and in all well planned developments in the United States.

Among recent works, the planning of Columbia, a new town in Maryland, half way between Washington, D.C. and Baltimore, is one of the best American examples, manifesting all the Radburn ideas, while adding some new ones. The plan resembled those of the English new towns, with its attempt to bring in industry and other employment opportunities to achieve self-sufficiency. It also expanded on the neighborhood idea by grouping five neighborhoods into a village with retail stores, high schools, and major recreational facilities. Furthermore, Columbia's 10 villages are served by a town center consisting of all necessary retail business, office, educational, and community facilities (Figure 32). Building started in 1964. At present, several of its villages are completed and its town center (Figure 33), designed to serve up to 150,000 people, is nearing completion. Another essential characteristic of Columbia and many other such new communities is that they are planned by an interdisciplinary team of developers, physical planners, engineers, sociologists, economists, legal experts, recreation planners, landscape architects, artists, and others. The majority of their social, safety, functional, and aesthetic objectives have been achieved, especially when these developments are compared with communities which are the result of less rigorous planning.

Unfortunately, the majority of community developments during the post-Radburn era have failed to benefit from the many innovative ideas of these physical planners. The proliferation of planned unit developments, which were very much an outgrowth of the Radburn idea, took over three

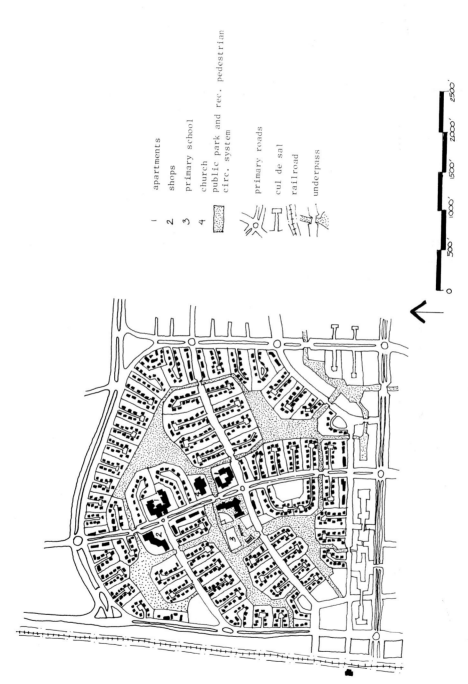

1   apartments
2   shops
3   primary school
4   church
     public park and rec. pedestrian
     circ. system

     primary roads
     cul de sal
     railroad
     underpass

0   500'   1000'   1500'   2000'   2500'

FIGURE 31   *Site plan as planned and partially developed.*

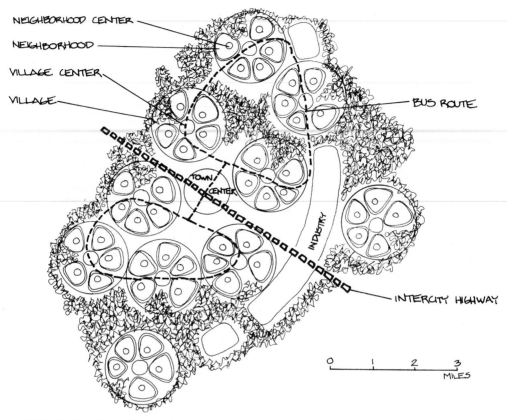

FIGURE 32 *Town Plan divided into villages with open space between them avoids the amorphous sprawl that plagues most suburban areas.*

decades but even this phenomenon influenced only a portion of the total built environment.

Responses to Urban Decline

Physical planners who were active in community planning were also most influential in the redevelopment of cities during the 1950s. Almost every major city established redevelopment authorities which often worked with private consultants on plans and implementation of massive urban revitalization schemes (see the discussion in Chapter 6 of land-use planners as catalysts for learning and action). Widespread public outcry quickly changed the planners' strategy from redevelopment to rehabilitation. It also changed their role from form givers to synthesizers whose ideas were shaped increasingly by the public interest groups which were affected by their plans.

FIGURE 33   *Town Center of Columbia.*

The rehabilitation effort carried out in the downtown area of Fresno City in California represents one of the early rehabilitation projects, which provided a useful model to communities throughout the United States for dealing with the decline of city centers. Fresno, a trading center in Central Valley, experienced a decline in its downtown area as new shopping centers around its periphery opened up different options for its growing population. Its problem was further aggravated by traffic congestion and lack of sufficient parking in the older business district. The need for revitalizing the downtown area became apparent to city officials, city planners, and the business community. These groups engaged Victor Gruen Associates, a firm active in massive redevelopment projects and the planning of shopping centers all over the United States.

The Gruen plan (*Observer in Progressive Architecture*, 1965, pp. 184–186) adopted several concepts of community planning discussed above. It created a superblock by building a freeway loop around the entire central area, replaced the previously congested commercial streets with well-designed pedestrian malls, and provided new parking facilities. The mall also served as a pedestrian link to the city's civic and cultural area and provided an expansion to a park and an existing medical complex. One of the unique aspects of this plan was that instead of rebuilding the commercial buildings, many of which had been long neglected, they made intensive improvement on those buildings. The success of this rehabilitation was overwhelming. It not only brought back many of the old shoppers but it attracted new ones. The planners proved that physical solutions can have beneficial effects on the economy and on the use of these areas while at the same time they greatly improve the aesthetic quality of these manmade environments.

Fortunately, this more sensitive rehabilitative approach has replaced redevelopment and it has also increased public involvement in the planning process. Physical planners have achieved a much greater overall success in these rehabilitation works than in their efforts in community planning. Perhaps their success can be attributed to the fact that the majority of the rehabilitation projects have been originated by public agencies which have recognized the need for and value of good planning. Indeed the majority of European and American cities from Vienna to San Francisco can boast of one or more success stories. Places such as the highly functional and beautiful Quincy Market area of Boston is a recent testimony to the kind of development which provides a delightful urban environment for thousands of people each day (Figures 34 and 35).

Physical planners who have focused their efforts on satisfying needs have also been involved in preservation work and have developed planning norms for uses within and surrounding preservation areas. They have been involved in many reconstruction efforts in historic towns and neighborhoods all over the world. They have also responded to manmade and natural hazards by developing physical devices such as floodwalls, buildings which are floodproof, and various barriers to reduce noise in urban environments. More recently, these planners have been developing fresh approaches to greater efficiency in land use. For instance, in places such as Portland, Oregon and Davis, California, physical planning devices are being devised to save energy through efficient land uses.

It is safe to say that during the 1960s and 1970s, local land-use planning was dominated by controls, with the result that the contribution of this group of physical planners was suppressed. Now, at the beginning of the 1980s, there is a renewed interest in physical land-use planning. This development is most encouraging. One could hardly expect a quality environment without a major contribution from physical planners, who have the visual literacy and sensitivity to improve the aesthetic quality of our environment.

FIGURE 34 *Quincy Market in Boston. Photograph by Barrie B. Greenbie from Spaces: Dimensions of the Human Landscape used by permission of Yale University Press.*

FIGURE 35   *An indoor/outdoor survey scene. Quincy Market in Boston. (Photographed by Barrie Greenbie.)*

Physical Planning with a Focus on Suitability

During the past century, a new type of local land-use planner, whose origin can be traced back to the foundation of landscape architecture, has been at work. Planners in this discipline, such as Olmsted and Eliot, developed regional plans dealing with growth, preservation, and other issues. Over the years, they have also made significant contributions to local planning. This branch of landscape architecture is known as landscape planning, its practitioners being augmented by physical geographers, soil scientists, foresters, and many others. They share a common belief that all land use should be based on what McHarg, its most articulate advocate, calls the "intrinsic suitability" of the land. They see their role as "matchmakers" who find the appropriate use for the land unit which has the suitability for that desired use. Consequently, by applying their philosophy, the proper use of a natural flood plain should exclude all developments with the exception of some recreation or agricultural uses; conversion of agricultural land to development also violates the concept of intrinsic suitability. They also have established criteria for suitability based on physical, topoclimatic and aesthetic factors. Because very strong philosophical differences exist between the community planners and this group, the contributions of landscape planners are often very different from the work of the other physical planners at the local level and deserve a discussion here.

While these community planners have concentrated on innovative ideas to solve a perceived need, landscape planners have approached planning from the landscape resource base. They have advanced quantitative methods to assess critical resource values, hazard issues, ecological compatibility, and development suitability, all based on scientific findings. They have also incorporated in their plans public preferences and values regarding these issues. By the late 1970s, landscape planners had adopted powerful geographic information systems using computerized graphic techniques for landscape assessment, plan formulation, and plan evaluation procedures. A recent study by Duane Marble (1980) found over 800 computer software programs used in spatial data handling. This adaptation of high technology is expected to alter significantly local land-use planning during the remainder of this century.

Suitability as the Basis of Community Planning

Olmsted's plan for Riverside, outside Chicago, drawn up in 1869, represents the first major effort to make landscape suitability the basis of community development. Before Riverside, American community planners followed the practice of imposing a grid pattern on whatever topography existed. Natural features such as hills and streams were treated as an inconvenience to be corrected or ignored (Fabos, Milde and Weinmayr, 1968, p. 48). In Riverside, Olmsted established the foundation for a landscape planning approach which made the existing landscape features the determinant for the physical form of the community. Here the natural water corridor of the Des Plaines River became the backbone for public open space and allowed the street plan to flow around the landscape in harmony with the meandering river (Figure 36).

Ever since Olmsted's plan for Riverside, landscape architects as land-use planners have developed increasingly sophisticated approaches to making landscape suitability the basis of community planning. As a matter of stan-

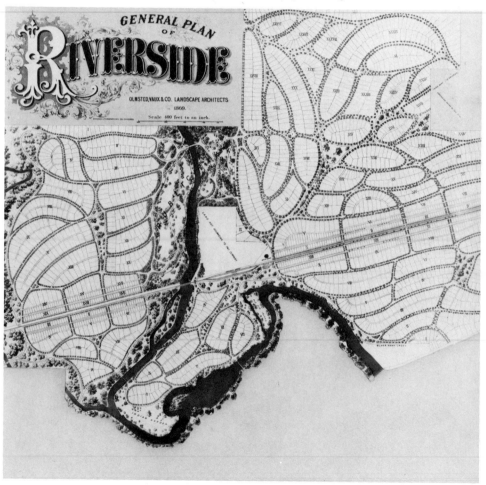

FIGURE 36 *Riverside General Plan by Frederick Law Olmsted, Sr.*

dard procedure, contemporary landscape architects are analyzing and assessing the major physical, topoclimatic, and visual characteristics of all areas prior to planning the land uses. For example, a composite assessment of a 100-hectare or 250-acre area (Figure 37) was the basis of a comprehensive urban development plan to house 1,400 families, offices, and retail stores, while providing recreation on areas less suitable for development. After it had been assessed against the major landscape planning criteria, the highest density area was located on the most suitable portion of the site (see area marked as "Important Vista" on Figure 37).

During the 1960s, the landscape planners joined scientists to develop advanced suitability assessment procedures with a focus on several landscape issues including development, preservation, and maintenance. The master planning of a recreation community on Amelia Island in Florida provides a good example of this development. To determine an ecologically acceptable development suitability, the landscape planners synthesized the work of different scientists — for example, ecologists, geologists, and ornithologists — to determine land-use suitability for development, and the preservation of critical resources (Figure 38).

Since the late 1970s, landscape planners have further advanced suitability assessment procedures to aid in local land-use planning decisions. Helped by computers and improved remote-sensing technology, land-use planners have been able to include more parameters and assess them more accurately by using quantitative methods (Mabbutt, 1968; Fabos and Joyner, 1980). Through these advancements, landscape planners have been able to place values on landscape resources expressed in terms of economics, energy, ecology or even the perceptions of representative segments of local populations. For example, several critical or special value resources can be composited and evaluated using economic valuation procedures (Figure 39). Another procedure forms composites of all pertinent special resource values, hazards, and development suitabilities (Figure 40). Landscape planners claim that such information is essential for making intelligent land-use decisions at the local level. As these procedures become operational in this decade, they are expected to improve significantly the land-use decision making process.

Suitability Assessment with a Focus on Resource Maintenance,
Preservation, Resource Utilization, and Environmental Impact Issues

Landscape planners use assessment as a basis not only for decisions on development but also for all other land-use planning problems. The approaches used for these problems are similar to the ones discussed above. The difference between the two sets of approaches is only one of emphasis.

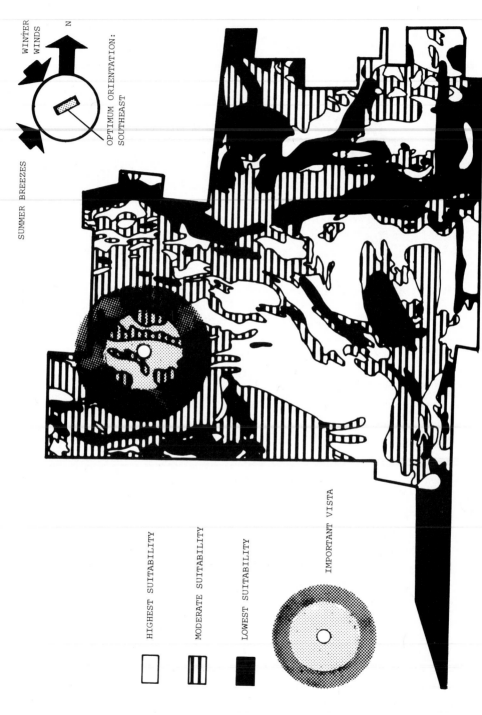

FIGURE 37 A composite site assessment map for Manchester site.

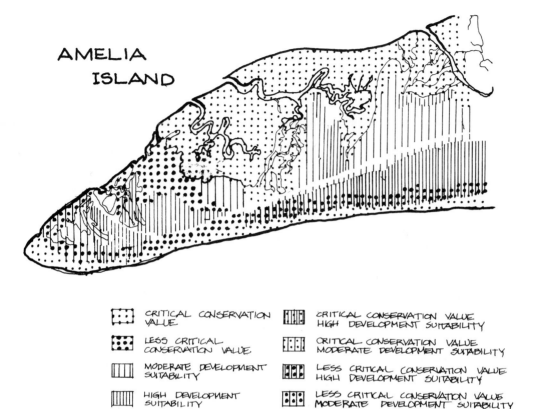

AMELIA ISLAND

CRITICAL CONSERVATION VALUE

LESS CRITICAL CONSERVATION VALUE

MODERATE DEVELOPMENT SUITABILITY

HIGH DEVELOPMENT SUITABILITY

CRITICAL CONSERVATION VALUE HIGH DEVELOPMENT SUITABILITY

CRITICAL CONSERVATION VALUE MODERATE DEVELOPMENT SUITABILITY

LESS CRITICAL CONSERVATION VALUE HIGH DEVELOPMENT SUITABILITY

LESS CRITICAL CONSERVATION VALUE MODERATE DEVELOPMENT SUITABILITY

FIGURE 38 *Syntheses of all land use suitabilities.*

While the community planning procedures focused on finding places for landscape-sensitive developments, these procedures place the accent on issues which, when taken into consideration, would preserve or protect land from development.

For instance, the soil scientists of the U.S. Soil Conservation Service during the 1950s advanced assessment procedures which determine the agricultural productivity of all homogeneous land parcels based on such physical properties as drainage, slope, and soil texture. Landscape planners expanded this procedure by estimating the degree of detraction of the various land uses. For instance, highly productive agricultural land, when used as tilled land, has no land use detraction. However, if the same highly productive land is abandoned for years, some clearing may be needed before it reverts to productive land for agriculture. If the current land use is industrial, that use has eliminated all its potential productivity for agriculture forever (Fabos and Caswell, 1977, p. 33). The effects of further develop-

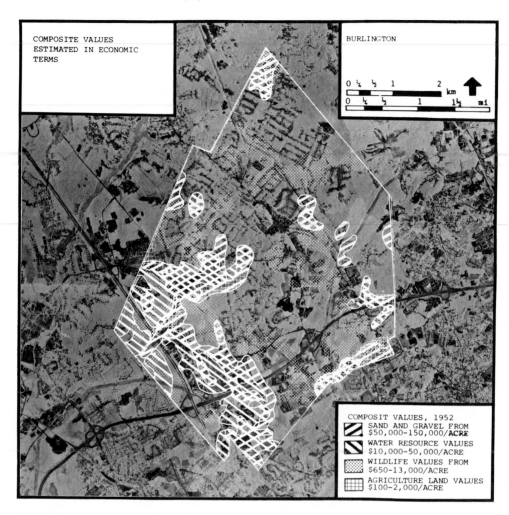

FIGURE 39 *This simplified composite special resource value assessment illustrates the parametric approach to environmental landscape planning. The values are estimated in economic terms as they existed in 1952. The estimated values range from $100 per acre to a possible $203,300 per acre in areas where water, wildlife, agricultural, and sand and gravel resources overlap. Note that on the 1972 airphoto beneath the resource areas a great portion of these areas was used up by housing, industrial, and commercial uses. The impairment and elimination of these resources is estimated at over $30 million. This composite map was abstracted from the work of K. H. Ferris and S. Coswell.*

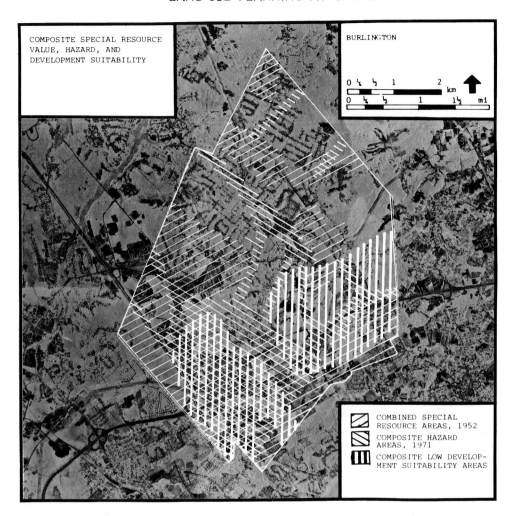

COMPOSITE SPECIAL RESOURCE
VALUE, HAZARD, AND
DEVELOPMENT SUITABILITY

BURLINGTON

COMBINED SPECIAL
RESOURCE AREAS, 1952
COMPOSITE HAZARD
AREAS, 1971
COMPOSITE LOW DEVELOP-
MENT SUITABILITY AREAS

FIGURE 40 *A simplified, combined value estimate of the environmental components included in this study. It reveals some severe environmental problems. Note that the most intensive development occurred on areas with high special resource values and low development suitability. New developments were concerned with neither natural nor manmade hazards. The type of assessment and planning synthesis presented here could minimize many problems of this kind. This map is based on the work of K. H. Ferris, a landscape planner of the University of Massachusetts landscape research group.*

ment on a vital landscape resource, as applied to a highly developed town in Massachusetts, is shown in an assessment of agricultural productivity (Figure 41).

One of the more successful landscape planning efforts of recent years, where suitability assessment was the basis for resource maintenance, preservation, and resource utilization decisions, was the Nantucket Island Study in Massachusetts. An interdisciplinary team of scientists coordinated by landscape planners, working closely with community representatives, prepared a series of landscape analysis and assessment maps for the island (Figures 42 and 43). A long-range implementation program, undertaken by two local conservation organizations, the Conservation Foundation and the Conservation Commission, during the 1970s has been able to place over one-third of the island's resources in permanent preservation and recreation use, while protecting much of the island's groundwater supply areas and the vulnerable southern coastline from developments (Zube and Carlozzi, 1966). This case study is a good example of how landscape planning, by providing pertinent information in the form of landscape analysis and assessment, can be used to limit local development on a fragile landscape.

Finally, in responding to environmental legislation, landscape planners have developed and applied in recent years numerous impact assessment procedures which have been designed to minimize the adverse effects of major developments, and to evaluate alternative plans and select an alternative with the fewest negative impacts. In the United States, impact assessment was initiated by the National Environmental Policy Act of 1969. The other developed countries established similar environmental legislation at about the same time.

The majority of assessment techniques involve the completion of a matrix in which existing environmental characteristics and conditions are listed along one axis and proposed actions that may have an environmental impact along the other axis. In the simpler techniques, the matrix is completed by entering "yes" or "no" for each combination of proposed action and existing conditions, depending on whether an impact of some sort is anticipated. The later and more sophisticated methods attempt to quantify both the significance and magnitude of the existing environmental characteristics, as well as the severity of the anticipated impact from each proposed action or alternative plan (Leopold, 1971; Burchell and Listokin, 1975). The majority of these impact assessment studies have dealt with local land-use issues, such as a by-pass road in a town or the building of major unwelcomed facilities such as power stations, refineries, and the like.

In summary, physical planning with a focus on suitability, or landscape planning, has become an essential part of many local land-use decisions. It is anticipated that its role will increase significantly in the future because of

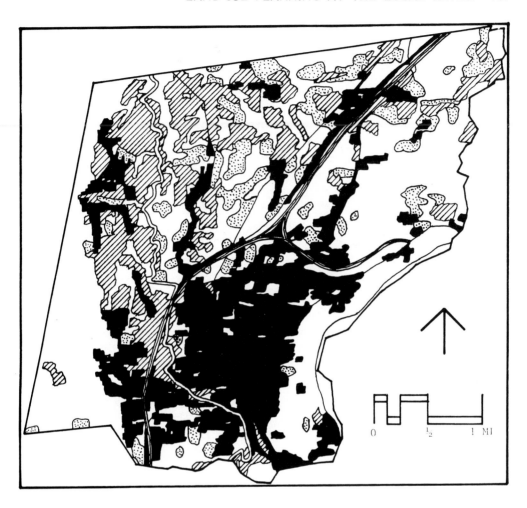

existing development

Class "A" 2444 acres

Class "B" 1621 acres

Class "C" 9034 acres

FIGURE 41 *Agricultural productivity assessment for Greenfield, Massachusetts. The "A" acres are the highest; "B" acres are medium, and "C" acres are the worst productivity agricultural lands. Source: METLAND Landscape Planning Research, University of Massachusetts, see Fabos and Caswell, 1977.*

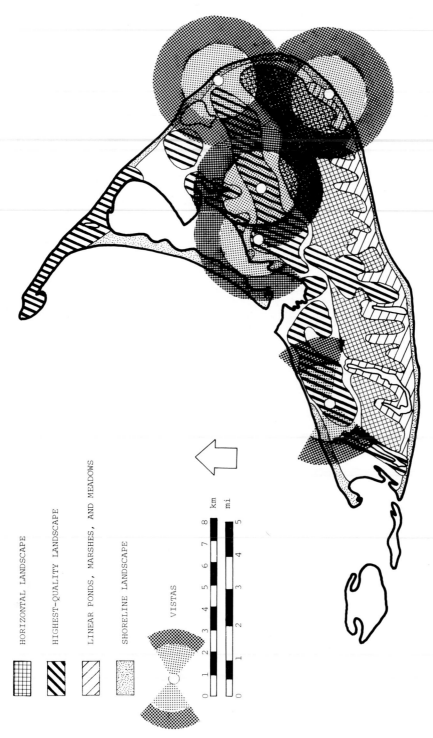

FIGURE 42 *This figure illustrates the significant visual quality and scenic view areas of the island of Nantucket. This visual assessment was prepared in 1966 by the author in collaboration with Dr. Ervin Zube, study coordinator. The process identified significant island landscape types of high scenic quality. These landscapes were ranked according to their perceived value for public use and to ensure their preservation and protection for future use.*

HORIZONTAL LANDSCAPE

HIGHEST-QUALITY LANDSCAPE

LINEAR PONDS, MARSHES, AND MEADOWS

SHORELINE LANDSCAPE

VISTAS

0 1 2 3 4 5 6 7 8 km
0 1 2 3 4 5 mi

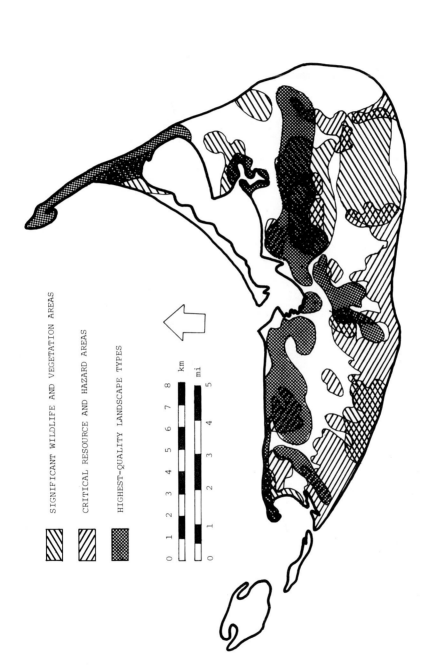

FIGURE 43 *Landscape synthesis Nantucket, Massachusetts. The three separate resource and hazard assessment maps were combined to show the amount, distribution, and overlap of critical areas when using the landscape approach. This composite map was drawn by overlaying the three separate assessment maps prepared by the author in collaboration with Dr. Ervin Zube, study coordinator.*

SIGNIFICANT WILDLIFE AND VEGETATION AREAS

CRITICAL RESOURCE AND HAZARD AREAS

HIGHEST-QUALITY LANDSCAPE TYPES

two interrelated factors. First, scientific findings will precipitate many more environmental crises or threshold events such as the recent revelation of the ubiquitous problem of hazardous waste. Secondly, the development of high technology aids landscape planners in several ways. As spatial data is becoming available in the form of electronic signals, landscape planners will have ready access to ever larger and more accurate data bases which can be retrieved easily. High technology also augments data analysis and assessment capabilities. But perhaps most important is the fact that, aided by powerful machines, landscape planners will be able to investigate far more alternatives and will be able to evaluate their consequences against an infinite number of criteria. This means that public involvement in the planning process can increase significantly. The development of interactive computer capabilities enables planners to simulate the cause/effect relationships of numerous plans, perhaps a plan suggested by each official decision maker or interested member of the public. In short, this emerging form of landscape planning may lead the way for planners to become more than ever a catalyst for learning and action in local land-use planning. Perhaps these developments will also make planning more democratic.

PROLIFERATION OF LOCAL LAND-USE CONTROLS

Ever since the development of the first comprehensive zoning ordinance in the United States in New York City in 1913, an important movement of local land-use controls was started. Zoning as a land-use control device proliferated rapidly. In addition, local land-use planners developed many more new techniques to control land uses. A recent study identified and described in great detail 57 different techniques (Einsweiler, and others, 1975, p. 293). Although many of the initial land-use control devices have originated primarily from social concerns, they have been augmented during the 1960s and 1970s by numerous techniques with a focus on environmental concerns. Several of these techniques, such as "public acquisition" and "impact zoning," incorporate both social and environmental concerns. Even more important, the intent of many techniques is changing from "control" to "growth management" or "growth guidance." This development is an important change. It shows that planners can be creative not only in the invention of physical devices, but also in the development of such nonphysical devices as zoning.

Although the development of a comprehensive zoning ordinance dates back in the United States only to 1913, land-use control techniques were applied well before this date. For instance, zoning was employed as a tool in California by the late-19th century primarily as an exclusionary discriminating device against Chinese settlers. Modesto, California passed an ordinance in 1885 making it:

> ...unlawful for any person to establish, maintain or carry on the business of a public laundry...within the City of Modesto, except that part of the city which lies west of the railroad track and south of G Street (Delafons, 1962, p. 19).

This ordinance placed a great number of Chinese immigrants in violation of the law, since virtually all of them lived and worked on the "wrong side" of the tracks.

Well before the practice of exclusionary zoning ordinances, the common law of nuisance gave legal effect to the ancient maxim "sic utere tua ut alienum non laedus," that enjoined a property owner to use his land in such a manner as not to damage the property of another (Reiner, 1975, p. 212). This brief historical account shows that land-use controls or nonphysical devices have been a part of land-use planning perhaps for as long as physical planning.

The majority of land-use controls or nonphysical techniques were advanced as a response to undesirable developments. The creators of these controls, therefore, have been most often planners who have worked for the public sector, although public agencies have often engaged the services of private consultants to draw up local controls, such as zoning ordinances and subdivision regulations. Perhaps this interaction between the public and private planning practitioners gave the impetus to a growth-management approach in place of reactionary controls.

To illustrate the proliferation of local land-use controls and growth-management devices, several of the important techniques or types of techniques are summarized under the three general headings of controls with a focus on social, environmental, and combined concerns.

Land-Use Controls with a Focus on Social Concerns

In the United States zoning is probably the most commonly used development control device at the local level. Conventional zoning is used to regulate the type of land use, the extent of land area or a lot which may be developed, the land-use density, and the height or bulk of buildings. The primary aim of zoning is to avoid unwanted or unacceptable side effects of individual development decisions. At least eight variations of zoning are practiced in the United States (Einsweiler, and others, 1975, p. 293), including: conditional zoning — this variation obtains a promise from the property owner to limit development beyond that required by the codes, to dedicate land, or to make other concessions of public benefit in return for a rezoning; contract zoning — this represents a commitment on the part of local government to rezone in exchange for incorporation of deed restriction by the property owner; planned unit development — this substitutes required specific plans, for conventional zoning, often providing incentives, such as permitting a higher density, for achieving a better development and more common open space; flexible zoning — this variation allows an adjustment in the location and density, such as development in clusters, so long as the total number of units does not exceed a specific overall density ratio; performance standard — this approach employs a set of standards relating to acceptable levels of nuisance or side effects of the development rather than specifying acceptable uses, and is often used for industrial developments; bonus and incentive — this category includes a variety of practices in which the community obtains such features or amenities in a development as, for example, an additional open space, by generating additional income to the developer; and others, such as special permits, variances, and the so-called floating zone used in some areas.

Subdivision regulations are the most common development control device after the zoning. These are used to control the process of converting raw land into building sites by ensuring adequate public improvements, enforcing certain lot sizes and set back, assuring buyers of developable, drained lots, and often enabling the local land-use planners to coordinate the work of adjacent developers (Patterson, 1979, p. 92; and Delefons, 1969, p. 69).

Tax and fee systems are normally employed to generate revenues. However, they can have a significant controlling effect on developments. Specific devices used in this category include: designation of separate urban and rural service areas — this distinguishes areas by the level of service they can be expected to receive and also therefore the level of taxation payable for those services; special assessment — this is a tax method in which the cost of the specific facility such as a road improvement, sewer, or water system is assigned fully or partially against the adjacent benefitting property.

Annexation is a particularly useful technique in regulating development when the community to which annexation is occurring is fully developed or nearly so. There is significant impact upon the annexed area, which represents a major land use change affecting lifestyle, taxes, and government of that area. Annexation also influences traffic patterns, police and fire protection, available services, and water supply. Developers seek annexation as a means of increasing profit by getting the maximum number of units per acre while using existing services. It is wise to review an environmental impact statement to determine the suitability of the boundary change before annexation occurs (Logan, 1982, pp. 104–6).

Official mapping helps to direct growth by providing information to the public. The mapping of proposed future facility locations such as roads, streets, parks, and drainage systems puts developers on notice as to improvements to be built within particular areas and also constitutes a commitment to others as to facilities the community intends to provide. Thus this device can assist in an orderly development of the community.

Capital programming is a schedule on the allocation of public investment and as such it is even more powerful than official mapping. Because it is a long-term plan for public projects, it improves the community awareness of problems and gives members a vehicle for controlling growth. Programming provides a plan for development over a number of years, along with cost estimates and methods of financing proposed projects. Developers are required to respond to the framework of existing and proposed services outlined in the capital program, and pressures for improvement on an ad hoc basis are reduced (Moss, 1977, pp. 340–41).

Public improvements include the provision of facilities such as roads, sewers, water, and other support facilities essential for development as a measure to influence its growth and location. The basic assumption is that these improvements provide sufficient incentive for the developers by providing access to existing facilities such as sewer or water lines or permitting a curb cut to a road.

Geographic restraints are control systems which identify the geographic area limits to developments. They may establish a long-term limit line or service area with a 15 to 20-year planning horizon, which identifies areas where urban development should occur within this time frame. Shorter-term service areas use the same geographic constraint concept, but this short-range plan identifies areas to be serviced in the near term or within the next 5 to 10 years.

Cost/Benefit or similar economic analyses are used by communities in evaluating the effects of major proposals on the community. These analyses question systems of control that allow unequal distribution of benefits from public and private land-use decisions. Through public interest, communities can determine who actually profits by these decisions and what the profits will be. Although many planners believe this to be a useful device, many social factors cannot be treated adequately by economic criteria alone.

"Retention of development value in the public sector, and compensation and betterment, are alternative systems of providing an equitable outcome from land use decisions," (Strong, 1981, pp. 230–31).

Land-Use Controls with a Focus on Environmental Concerns

Environmental concerns for local land-use planning are of very recent origin when compared with social concerns, and hence, the number of techniques used are significantly fewer when compared with the controls developed for social objectives. In the United States, planners use primarily two sets of environmental control techniques.

Controls for critical and hazardous areas represent one class of environmental controls. The control for critical areas, adapted or carried to local-level from level-two planning (of metropolitan or substate/regional) areas, was adopted by the American Law Institute under the "Model Land Development Code," which has been used by several state and local groups (Einsweiler, and others, 1975, p. 294). It generally refers to an environmentally sensitive area, such as wetlands, which has regional or statewide significance.

Local-level controls have been advanced for at least three types of hazards — flood plains, stream valleys, and shorelands:

> Many ordinances are of the specification type identifying express uses which are allowed or prevented or specifying exactly where that development may occur. Emerging controls are of the performance type in which a showing must be made that the natural process or critical resource is not damaged or infringed upon by the proposed development (Einsweiler, and others, 1975, p. 293).

Pollution controls may be in effect in areas of substantial developments or environmental sensitivity, where air and water pollution standards and limits may influence the location of further developments. Finally, an example of a special protection area is furnished by Sacramento, California, which has a seismic protection zone.

Land-Use Controls with a Focus on Social and Environmental Concerns

Several local land-use planning controls or growth-management devices which represent dual (social and environmental) foci have been developed in recent years. Some of these are mainly controls, while others are more creative approaches which provide incentives in place of controls. Land-use planning literature in the United States has identified at least six different techniques or sets of techniques which can be grouped under this title.

Public acquisition is perhaps the most powerful tool for managing land in the public interest, whether we fulfill a social or environmental objective. In the United States, four forms of ownership are used. These are discussed in order of degree of control and cost of acquisition from highest to lowest: fee simple acquisition — this is a process of acquiring full title to land for public purposes, such as parkland, recreation areas, open space, or school cites; land banking — in some instances, communities purchase land in areas where urban expansion is expected or desired and hold it for timely and appropriate use by the public or private sector; compensable regulation — this is a technique for combining compensation with constitutionally acceptable police power such as zoning, (for instance, a community may zone an area for a restrictive use, and then distribute the cost of this property on adjacent beneficial properties through a special assessment); and the fourth technique is less than fee simple acquisition and includes such items as rights of trespass or scenic easements on land which remains in private ownership. All these techniques can be used to achieve both social and environmental objectives.

Transfer of development rights has several variations. In general, it is a land-use plan which designates areas where development is restrained and areas where development is permitted. An owner in a restricted area can sell his or her rights through a market mechanism to an owner in a permitted area who may have fewer rights than he needs in order to develop. TDR is a land-use control device for preserving land and protecting its value, most often used for agricultural land. The right to develop property becomes a salable asset. TDRs give the restricted landowner the rights to develop on other land within the municipality. The landowner also has the option of receiving compensation for development restrictions imposed on his land by selling these rights rather than developing elsewhere. He retains ownership of his property, with compensation to ensure the preservation of the agricultural land. TDRs could also be used for scenic landscape and wetlands protection (Richman and Kendig, 1981, pp. 224–25).

Administrative processing and delay is a local public power to delay action, and by holding up a project long enough, it may render development costs prohibitive.

One stop permit is the exact opposite of administrative delay. It enables the builder to make one application and receive all permits necessary from all local agencies of concern.

Impact zoning is a more recent technique which is based on the analysis of the various social, economic, and environmental impacts of development proposals. Impact zoning aims at minimizing the negative impacts. Impact zoning "provides municipalities with an affirmative program for managing local growth while still accepting a fair share of regional growth." (Cerchione, Rahenkamp, and Yannacone, 1981, p. 153). Impact zoning is flexible and suggests alternatives for development, while allowing the orderly growth of the community. By determining ecological, societal, and economic capacities for growth, recognizing constraints, and realizing opportunities for innovative design, positive growth can occur with minimal adverse consequences.

Numerical restraints, and various quota systems employ a quantitative measure rather than an area as the limit for development. These techniques are designed to control the total population by annual permit limits or to set population and employment targets. The aim of no-growth control is reformation of inefficient land-use practices of fragmented suburban governments, that result in urban sprawl (Boyer, 1981, pp. 123–24). These restrictions attempt to achieve well-balanced, attractive communities that remain energy efficient and reduce urban sprawl. The problems with this type of control are that it restricts social and geographic mobility, reduces housing supply, and possibly discriminates both economically and racially (Zumbrun and Hookano, 1981, p. 161).

Land banking involves the governmental acquisition of large tracts of land to be set aside for controlled development of growth. This practice enables the government to plan the timing of release of land for development, as well as the type of development, by imposing restrictions that would promote energy efficient and ecologically sound land use (Harwood, 1977, p. 166). Land banking also provides the local government with the means for preserving agricultural land. Alternatives include the leasing of land to the farmer for agricultural production, or the selling of land to the farmer with restrictions prohibiting resale to developers.

The review of these nonphysical land-use planning techniques demonstrates not only their proliferation, but in many instances also their transformation into more positive incentives for creativity. Indeed, an interested community, with creative planners, can assemble from these techniques a sensible growth management program which would satisfy social and environmental objectives. An increasing number of communities have started to do this.

MOVES TOWARD INTEGRATED LOCAL LAND-USE PLANNING

The town of Ramapo in New York State is one of those communities which has initiated a "managed growth program" (Emanuel, 1975). The Ramapo experience started in 1964, with the preparation of a (physical) master plan. After several public hearings and modifications the master plan was approved in 1966, and with that, the town established a policy for managed growth. In 1967, the Ramapo town board adopted an official map for the town, which was derived from the master plan, particularly with respect to existing and proposed streets and highways, parks, sewer developments, and drainageways. These detailed proposals were later incorporated into the town's capital improvement program, which provided for the location and sequence of capital improvements for the following 12 years. This set of devices ensured the implementation of the necessary infrastructure and open-space system. To guide the implementation of the private development or to ensure a managed growth, the town adopted several zoning amendments, and the issuance of special permits which revolve around a "development point system."

The elements of the point system, namely sewer drainage, and recreation facilities, roads and firehouses, were principally derived from the scope of the master plan, official maps and the proposed capital budget. In attempting to arrive at a reasonable point system:

> a series of different overall scoring systems were [developed] and tested to determine the number of lots or building units which would become eligible for approval each year, based upon the projected capital budget and capital plan. These calculations also gave the town a measure of the probable annual rate of land consumption measured against its ultimate capacity (Emanuel, 1975, p. 308).

To ensure the preservation of critical and valuable areas for the town as a whole, this growth management was complemented by an easement acquisition program for the purpose of maintaining lands as open space, to control the rate of development, and "to enhance the conservation of natural and scenic resources" (Emanuel, 1975, p. 310).

Before the managed growth program, an annual average of 620 units was added to the town, which overloaded many of the public facilities and eliminated many of its valuable critical resources. This new, managed program created an orderly growth, by reducing the annual average growth rate to 350 dwelling units while providing good services and maintaining a quality environment. The Ramapo case proves that one can adapt useful techniques from this impressive list of nonphysical devices. In addition, the planners of Ramapo realized the value of physical planners, whose services they freely employed in preparing the master plan, the official map, and the proposals for easement acquisition.

Another impressive case study is the community development program of Germantown, Maryland. As in the case of Ramapo, this effort consists of coordinated and positive public land-use planning, capital improvements programming, public land acquisition, and innovative zoning and subdivision controls to encourage the development of a new community (Black, 1978).

A third case study represents another innovative and integrated approach developed for Lake County, Illinois. Under the name of "performance zoning," its principal author, Lane Kendig (Kendig and others, 1980), describes an entire "model ordinance" for orderly, managed growth. This new ordinance has attempted to incorporate the innovative nonphysical techniques with comprehensive physical planning including both social and landscape or environmental suitability concerns. The unique aspect of this work is that it integrates the nonphysical and physical land-use planning techniques to establish what are called "zoning districts," carefully designed "on the basis of use distinction [or consideration of human needs], geographic consideration [or physical suitability] and community fiscal and planning policy" to be achieved by nonphysical devices (Kendig and others, 1980, p. 75). The integration of these three factors results in the establishment of wilderness districts at one end of the continuum and urban core districts at the other.

While none of these case studies presented here has been copied extensively, they do however represent significant innovations in adopting nonphysical techniques which use both controls and incentives. They also show evidence of integration of these nonphysical techniques with physical land-use planning. If this trend was to continue, we would witness a more balanced approach to local land-use planning.

AN ANALYSIS

When local land-use planning is analyzed against the six concerns outlined in Chapter 6, one sees several similarities to those developments which occurred at the higher levels of land-use planning. Several differences are also worthy of note.

The changing role of planners from "form givers" to planners who serve more as "facilitators" has paralleled the development of metropolitan and rural land-use planning. Even the forces which created those changes were very much alike.

In analyzing the role of disciplinary and professional planners one finds that the latter have played a significantly greater role in local land-use planning than in metropolitan or rural regional planning. Many of the physical planners and the majority of those who are responsible for the proliferation of controls have been general planners even though many of these professional planners have had disciplinary training. Physical planners have often had previous training in architecture, engineering, surveying, and landscape architecture, while nonphysical planners tend to come into planning from such backgrounds as political science, sociology, and cultural geography. The role of disciplinary planners has also been important in local land-use planning. Physical plans are often drawn up by disciplinary firms of architects, engineers, and landscape architects. Although many of these firms also employ professional planners, their land-use plans are usually done by interdisciplinary teams. One can also find members of increasing numbers of disciplines entering into local land-use planning of one kind or another. For instance, with the proliferation of regulations and land-use controls, many members of the legal profession have become land-use planners. Similarly, many sociologists found planning work important since the redevelopment movement generated many social problems.

On the role of public versus private planners, a much clearer distinction exists between the roles of these groups in local as opposed to higher levels of planning. It is safe to say that the majority of physical plans have been done by the private sector, while most controls or nonphysical planning have been advanced by the public planners. There are, of course, plenty of exceptions to this general trend.

Single-purpose planning has dominated local land-use planning efforts. However, signs of more comprehensive approaches have been evident. Landscape planning, for instance, has moved considerably toward a more comprehensive approach. The developing growth management approaches can also be characterized as comprehensive planning, although no one local land-use planning effort has as yet attempted to deal with all the issues discussed in Chapter 1.

On the planning processes, we can conclude that the greater part of local land-use planning appears simplistic when compared to metropolitan and rural regional planning. Among all the local land-use planning techniques, perhaps the suitability assessment procedures are the most developed to date. The public participatory process has also improved significantly during recent decades. Signs of major developments in improving the process of local land-use planning, some of which are discussed in the final chapter, are on the horizon.

Finally, one of the greatest deficiencies of local land-use planning at present is that the majority of plans fail to recognize the larger regional context. With the exception of some impact assessment and local waste-water management studies, and a few transportation studies, most of these local plans have been prepared as if for a small isolated island. The major reason for this phenomenon, presented in the previous chapter, is that the imposition of the metropolitan level on rural, regional, or substate level planning is relatively recent. As these regional planning efforts increase this problem will certainly diminish.

PART THREE
WHAT'S NEXT?

CHAPTER 10

FUTURE PROSPECTS IN LAND-USE PLANNING

Forecasting the future is risky even for the expert futurist. However, in spite of the risk of ultimately being proven wrong, some future prospects are set forth here to stimulate much needed debate between land-use planners and all those interested in land uses, the state of the landscape, and the environment.

I attempt to deal with the future in a relatively conservative manner, drawing prospects only from those developments which are evident to us through some degree of testing and implementation of both scientific and technological endeavors. Even if one takes a relatively conservative view of the future, it must be clear that we are indeed on the brink of enormous changes with effects on land use which will equal or perhaps will many times surpass the changes brought about by the late-18th and early-19th century Industrial Revolution. Whether we accept this phenomenon as Toffler's third wave (Toffler, 1980) or call it the cybernetic revolution or something else, it must be clear to intelligent observers that these changes are contextual in nature.

The very same scientific and technological advancement which is expected to create enormous land-use changes can also provide land-use planners with a more optimistic set of prospects. We have the potential to make our future more certain, to increase the number of options available to us and to increase the quality and diversity of our environment.

CHALLENGE OF CHANGE

Of the many future land-use changes expected, some will dominate the coming decades more than others. These dominant changes may be characterized as new issues, the likely effects of new scientific and technological developments, modifications to values and organizations, the decentralization of urban areas, and the increased need to act locally while thinking globally.

Some of the *new issues* which will greatly influence land-use decisions include the development of energy resources both renewable and nonrenewable and the use of water. Both kinds of energy resource development are significant. The development of nonrenewable resources, especially the mining, transporting and storing of coal and oil shale, presents enormous problems such as locating new settlements to house workers, disposing of the overburden and debris, finding sufficient water resources needed for oil-shale processing and transporting coal in slurry pipelines, selecting additional transportation routes for the next generation of giant transmission lines, and siting unwelcome energy facilities.

The development of renewable energy resources presents another set of major challenges to land-use planners. Biomass production may change the character and recreation potentials of many millions of acres of land, presently kept in a natural state, especially in the United States. More intensive biomass production may directly compete with agricultural food production to satisfy our appetite for more energy. Huge windmill farms may be erected on land or in the ocean, hydropower projects may proliferate on rivers and even on smaller brooks and in coastal areas. But even if we harvest energy from the ocean or solar energy from outer space, the land-use implication at the source of energy routes could be enormous, whether they are terminating in a coastal area or an inland region.

Water resources and related issues will determine not only the fate of oil shale and the construction of slurry pipelines, but it may also become the factor limiting the growth or even the maintenance of existing populations of various regions of the world, including the United States. The reality of widespread water contamination, which is only just being acknowledged, may present enormous challenges to land-use planning, whether our lakes are becoming inhospitable to aquatic life due to acid rains or our ground water is being polluted by a great variety of human and industrial wastes. Water quality is becoming one of the most important environmental quality indicators. Wide acceptance of this indicator may have significant effects on land-use decisions.

The challenge of *scientific* and *technological* developments needs several volumes for exhaustive treatment. There are, however two critical aspects of both science and technology which present a continuous challenge to land-use planning. The first is the need for continuous interpretation of scientific knowledge and technological developments pertinent to land-use planning. Planners in the past have failed to take sufficient advantage of readily available scientific findings in such areas as landscape resources, ecology, earthquakes, landslides, flooding or the effect of noise and air pollution on people. Of course, many scientific advances are directly related to technological improvements. Hence the two, science and technology, are inseparable. The challenge to planners is how to interpret systematically and on a continuous basis the pertinent and significant findings to help us to make better and more intelligent land-use decisions.

The second implication of rapid scientific and technological development is the need to make wise choices from among the many new options which science and technology present to us. In the past we, the population of this earth, adopted numerous regrettable options presented by science and technology, including importing plants together with associated non-controllable diseases from one continent to another, obliterating critical coastal and wetland regions by building industries of enormous size and impact over them, spreading our throwaway litter across the landscape, and locating huge nuclear power plants in highly populated regions creating un-precedented risks to millions. Would we have taken all these steps if we had been able to understand their impacts by simulating their potential con-sequences? Perhaps our past decisions would have been very different. The coming decades will be dominated by such sophisticated scientific capa-bilities as gene splicing and such technologies as the designing of intelligent robots, capable of redesigning and rebuilding themselves. The challenge inherent in these developments is far more significant than anything we faced previously.

Past decisions have involved the rejection of certain technologies, such as the supersonic transport airplane. Several states have had the wisdom to legislate for the protection of critical wetlands and the elimination of throw-away bottles. At last we are seriously debating the potential risk of world-wide nuclear power. Future options, however, will present even more challenge to society. Land-use planners should have a major role in simulat-ing the land-use consequences of the coming options developed by science and technology. Just because we can do something it does not mean that we have to!

The *changing values* of people and especially our lack of accurate percep-tion of those values, and our lack of response to them, offer another set of challenges. Land-use planning decisions or just the presentation of planning alternatives have created enormous conflicts, much frustration, and unneces-sary sacrifices for many in the past. To minimize past mistakes, land-use planning must become much more of a learning process. The challenge for planners remains one of getting better information on the complex cause/effect relationship of land-use decisions on people's well-being, on their economic prospects, and on their environment. The second aspect of learn-ing is how to convey the information so that both public and decision makers can comprehend it in order to eliminate or at least to minimize the unnecessary frustrations and misunderstandings about the possible outcomes of a proposed land-use decision.

The *decentralization* of urban areas, which initially was made possible by the use of the automobile, has spread beyond the so-called urban sprawl around large cities. Another phenomenon, as discussed previously, is the migration of an increasing number of people to rural areas during the past decade. We are now witnessing the unprecedented reversal of a trend which dominated previous human history: a continuous growth of cities, a one-way migration from rural areas to cities. This new trend of reversed migration is foreign to the majority of land-use planners, who have been trained and educated to associate urban centers with expressions of the test of civilizations and cultures. Decentralization therefore involves not only the challenge to accommodate this new land-use shift but also a challenge to planners' attitudes. Land-use planners who have trouble accepting this land-use shift will likely spend their time fighting it in place of planning for it.

Since the 1950s, many land-use planners have fought against shopping centers and suburban developments on the outskirts of cities. They were built anyway, most often without sufficient planning and integration. If land-use planners are unable to change their attitude, if they see the future only through the past, decentralization may be among the most significant issues during the coming decades. The obvious challenge is how to maintain the cultural distemic attributes of cities, that are the viability of public places, while accommodating the needs of an increasing number of people who desire to settle in the small communities of rural regions, outside the metropolitan areas.

The *interaction of local and global issues* has already been discussed in Chapter 1. What remains to be emphasized is that the cumulative effects of millions of local actions often have regional and to some degree national and global consequences. If this is true, how can local needs be met in a responsible manner, so as to minimize the negative consequences of our actions? Local land-use planners are wise to adopt the attitude that while they act locally they learn to think globally. The forces of decentralization, the changing organizational mode discussed in Chapter 4, the increased involvement of the public in land-use decision making, all suggest the importance of local planning. But at the same time local planners have to understand that the development of every acre of productive agricultural land decreases that resource base nationally and internationally. The addition of a house on a well-drained soil will increase runoff more than a house on a poorly drained soil. A sanitary landfill site if not adequately sealed may contribute to faraway water pollution. Dispersed land uses or poorly located developments demand unnecessary amounts of oil, gas, or coal from the limited supply of the global nonrenewable resource base. These are just a few of thousands of plausible examples to show the importance of thinking and concern for the larger environmental context within which we make local decisions. Land-use planners have not yet succeeded in responding to this broader concern, especially at the local planning level (Chapters 7–9).

This set of issues and concerns represents only a sampling of those which, in my judgment, need to be debated and confronted during the coming years.

PROSPECTS ON THE HORIZON

The majority of land-use planners would agree that we should be dealing with the emerging issues, that we should incorporate the pertinent scientific findings in planning decisions, that we should better respond to the changing values of the people and that we should make local decisions in the larger regional, national, and even global context. Intellectually we can handle all these challenges. Where we seem to fail is in the technical area. Indeed, we have insufficient data at our disposal in useful form on the emerging issues. For example, the available information on the renewable resources of New England consists of an overly simplified brief atlas (Glidden and High, 1980) which is so general that it is practically useless for substate or local planning considerations. Scientific findings are scattered around in hundreds of publications and the majority of those findings have not yet been interpreted for planning purposes.

In some areas, such as census information, the government provides planners with readily available and accurate data. However, the majority of planners use this data very inefficiently by looking up the appropriate tables in voluminous reports. Just consider the following. An American city planner was quoted recently in a local paper on his finding unusually large growth (98 percent) in the 25 to 34 age group of the city's population during the 1970s. This increase suggested to the planner a possible rise in the local birth rate, especially if the majority of this age group are married, with a significant future impact on local school systems. However, he was not able to determine at that time how many of the young adults are single and how many married. However, he said he was preparing a more detailed analysis, to present to city boards later that year (*Daily Hampshire Gazette*, Northampton, Mass., January 19, 1982, p. 1). Obviously what this planner lacked was a tool which could make the rapid analysis to turn his speculation into a more substantive finding.

Just imagine if a planner could have readily available information on critical issues, scientific and technological data, and knowledge of public perceptions affecting his or her community, in and within the larger context of his region. How would the planner's effectiveness increase, if he or she could produce assessment maps, planning alternatives, and evaluation procedures to sort out the pros and cons among those alternatives? And further-more, what would be the outcome if planners could produce all these within minutes so that the city and town boards would not need to wait another few months before the planner can answer simple questions?

Do we have anything on the horizon which may help planners to bring the needed information more readily to the decision makers? The brief answer is that the same scientific and technological advancement which is revolu-tionizing the world certainly provides planners with better tools to achieve the basic objectives. The prospect is that aided by the latest scientific knowledge (Chapters 2 and 4) and by the advanced high technology (Chapter 3), planners will be able to help to increase the certainty of our well-being by minimizing the negative, unwanted effects of land-use actions; to increase the options; and to increase the quality of life while maintaining and even improving the quality of the environment.

More specifically, the 1970s saw major strides that brought land-use planners to the brink of those opportunities that may provide us with the needed information and improved planning capabilities essential to achieve the basic objectives described above. At least four concurrent and inter-related developments influence land-use planning as of this writing. Each is essential to the kind of advancement needed to meet the challenge of change. They are: the increased availability of research findings in usable forms for planners; the shifting of the distribution of spatial data from map to elec-tronic or digital form; the recent explosion in computer hardware and soft-ware technology; and the increase in activities in technological transfer in recent years. Where any one of these four events is absent, change is non-existent or very unlikely.

Increased Availability of Research Findings

Governmental agencies in the United States and elsewhere have begun to provide planners with interpretive maps or maps which assess soil, water resources, or other spatial phenomena for a variety of land uses. For example, the United States Department of Agriculture, Soil Conservation Service (1966 and 1969) started to provide land suitability assessment maps as early as the 1960s.

Planners have also undertaken extensive research to translate the results of social and natural sciences into a form to allow more accurate assessment of physical and social data (Chapter 9, Figures 37, 38, and 39), (Fabos and Caswell, 1977). This interdisciplinary study of scientists and planners syste-matically converted the latest scientific findings into a series of assessment models, ranging from the assessment of special value resources to natural and human-caused hazards, development suitability, public service resources, and ecological compatibility among land uses and the various natural ecosystems. Similar types of research have proliferated in the developed countries during the past decade.

Social science has made significant advances since the mid-1960s, especially in the area of landscape perception. In a recent state-of-the-art paper, Dr. Ervin Zube and his colleagues (Zube, Still and Taylor: in press) found over 200 research reports in 20 English, Canadian, American, and international journals dealing with various research approaches to determine landscape quality. This state-of-the-art paper provides invaluable pointers in helping planners to incorporate public values in land-use decision making.

Shift of Spatial Data from Maps to Electronic Formats

The lack of spatial data in electronic or digital form has been the primary reason for the delay in the use of high technology by land-use and landscape planners. All planning and research groups who have experimented with computers discovered the high cost of digitizing by hand. The Canadians were the pioneers who contracted with IBM during the mid-1960s to build an automated scanning device for developing a data base for the Canadian Geographic Information System. This first and very costly experiment scanned large areas of Canada at a gross scale. Although the utility of this data base has been questioned by many, this was nonetheless an important beginning (Ferris and Fabos, 1974, p. 25).

Not until the late 1970s did a significant breakthrough occur in the conversion of polygon data into digital form by scanners. Commercial firms now perform scanning of spatial data. In addition, several governmental agencies of the United States have established major programs in scanning spatial data. The United States Geological Survey, for instance, has started to digitize land use, land cover, and topographic data. Similarly, the U.S.D.A. Soil Conservation Service recently started a scanning program which will convert all data on U.S. soils into electronic form.

The most significant development in electronic data acquisition to date is remote sensing. The National Aeronautics and Space Administration (NASA) launched its first earth resource satellite, commonly known as the Landsat system, in 1972. The data obtained from the first three satellites launched during the past decade has had limited application to land-use and landscape planning, since the data resolution is 1.1 acres, too large for most local planning works. NASA launched its fourth earth satellite in 1982. Landsat 4, this newest satellite has a "thematic mapper" capable of producing a spatial resolution of 30 X 30 m (NASA Module U-2 1980), or approximately every one-fifth of an acre is recorded automatically and in digital form every 18 days.

The most significant aspect of the data base obtained from these satellites is the ability of the latest automated multispectral scanner to distinguish 256 values numerically. These values are relayed from space to the earth electronically and hence in appropriate form for computer processing and analysis. Indeed, we are on the verge of a new era which will provide landscape architects not only with an enormous computerized data base, but also with one which is becoming increasingly more accurate. This data accuracy will further increase as Japan and Western European countries enter into space-age data gathering. The French space agency, Centre National d'Etudes Spatiales (CNES), for example, is now developing its own high resolution earth resources satellite, to be launched in early 1984. Its spatial resolution is planned at 10 X 10 m which is approximately 30' X 30'. It appears that we are moving from a data-poor to a data-rich environment in less than a decade. This is indeed a revolutionary phenomenon! This development is the essential foundation for paperless land-use and landscape planning, since this enormous developing data base will be handled electronically by powerful computers.

New Tools for Land-Use Planners

Just two decades ago, while a student at Harvard Graduate School of Design, I spent many hours coloring large maps with prismacolor pencils, the use of which was specified by my professors. In my second year, I was introduced to the magic of magic markers. Such a change appeared to be a great step forward in those days. Today, our most advanced graphic display device at the University of Massachusetts is capable of using a full range of colors. If the user wishes to study or display a portion or detail of the map, he or she types in a simple command and in a second the detail is available at the desired scale. Once this new scale is established, the user, aided by a cursor, can practically fly over the map and see details at any point at this enlarged scale. This machine is only one of many display systems on the market which can be used interactively. In a recent survey, Datapro Research Corporation (1979) describes 66 graphic display devices in great detail.

Such graphic display devices are backed up by other computer hardware systems which are, of course, designed to store, retrieve, and manipulate the enormous quantity of digital data prior to display. Spatial data, when compared with regular numerical statistical data, requires a much greater computer storage and manipulation capacity. For this reason, computer-aided land-use planning was limited in the past to institutions and agencies with access to large computers. With the development of powerful mini-computer and microcomputer hardware systems, however, this dependence on large systems has become history. A favorite quote of computer literature is that a minicomputer purchased for $3,000 in 1980 can do the work of a computer which cost one million dollars a decade ago. In 1970, there was only a handful of giant computer companies selling computer hardware. Last year, the *Harvard Newsletter on Computer Graphics* (Harvard University Laboratory for Computer Graphics, 1980) listed 140 vendors, most of them selling powerful minicomputer and microcomputer systems, many of which are most appropriate for land-use planners.

This new generation of computer hardware is designed for the interactive mode. Dumb terminals are being replaced by the so-called intelligent terminals. Interconnected computer networks also are being developed. These networks are designed to provide users with additional data sources and manipulation capabilities. Indeed, we can accept Sleeper's description of the working woman in Vermont (Chapter 3) as realistic. Her computer may be able to do in minutes all that a team of planners presently do in a day and perhaps much more. The major difference between present-day land-use planners and those of the near future seems to be that much of what is now time-consuming, tedious work will soon be done by the machine. Hence planners of the next decade will be able to spend more of their time on thinking and on creative work.

These new tools of planning would not be useful in themselves without clear instructions. The development of instructions or computer programs, commonly known as computer software, is an essential part of this future tool of land-use planning. As one would expect, the development of computer software capabilities has been as spectacular as that of hardware systems. This phenomenal change can best be illustrated by two publications. A study on computer software systems for landscape planning listed five developing systems in 1974 (Ferris and Fabos, 1974). A recent report entitled "Computer Software for Spatial Data Handling" (Marble, 1980) lists some 800 systems. Among these are almost 100 full geographic information systems. Although these software systems are primarily useful for landscape planning, the development of software for design is also most encouraging. Research in architectural science and engineering is proliferating. Designers of airplanes, automobiles, and many other objects have utilized sophisticated computer systems for more than a decade. Dynamic systems for designing buildings and even houses have also been around for some time. For instance, architects at the University of Sydney developed software which is capable of manipulating over 130 variables or approximately 20 times more than an average human being can do. Aided by this software, an architect can produce a finished design, working drawings, documentation, and cost estimates for approximately $100 in 1980 dollar values (Gero and Dudnik, 1978; Gero and Oguntade, 1978). Since the designer can do all the technical work and cost calculations, 2-D and 3-D presentations, and working drawings by machine, he or she would spend most of the time on aesthetic refinements. More important, at this low cost, architectural services would be affordable to everyone building a house. This high technology, with its computer hardware and software capabilities, already exists to perform land-use planning. It is up to the planning professions to bring these capabilities into use.

Technology Transfer

Programs to transfer this new technology to land-use and landscape planning and design have been under way since the mid-1960s, which also marked the birth of the Harvard University Laboratory for Computer Graphics. Any widespread technology transfer did not start, however, until recently. This current technology transfer takes at least three forms — governmental programs, university and other teaching programs, and training by corporations as part of "turnkey" sales.

Perhaps the most ambitious technology transfer program by a governmental agency is the NASA program. This program has a dual objective: to make potential users aware of the benefits of Landsat data and to assist [state and substate agencies] in becoming self-sufficient users of the technology. According to a recent task force study (ISETAP, 1978, p. VIII) over two-thirds of the states have "ongoing operational Landsat application capabilities...[or are undertaking] demonstration projects." Their awareness programs consist of short seminars, conferences, and workshops. To date, they have exposed their technology to many thousands of people.

Teaching programs to introduce professionals to remote sensing, interactive computer planning, and design systems have been on the increase in recent years. Short courses for professionals have been offered by the American Society of Landscape Architects (ASLA), various planning organizations, and several universities. In New England alone, three institutions, Harvard, Yale, and the University of Massachusetts have ongoing training programs. These courses are designed to help people who have little or no previous experience with computer-aided land-use and landscape planning. Through highly developed, user friendly programs, these people can learn to solve complex planning and design problems with only a few hours of individualized training. For instance, one of our comprehensive programs at the University of Massachusetts, the Interactive Landscape Planning Program (ILPP) can be learned with a couple of hours of hands-on training. During the past 2 years, over 200 people have taken this training in Amherst, Massachusetts and in Melbourne, Australia, and within 2 hours the majority have become proficient in the use of the system. The majority of planning programs today offer an introduction to and applications of the computer. By the end of the decade, computer literacy will be as much a part of the education of land-use planners as are traditional forms of literacy today.

If universities fail to aid in the transfer of this technology, private corporations may well speed up this development. Computer graphic suppliers are not only marketing their hardware but are also usually including in the sale pertinent software packages. The most recent development is the selling of turnkey systems, which are comprehensive package deals including the provision of hardware and software, making the system operational in the office of the buyer, training the personnel, and providing follow-up service. *The 1980 Harvard Directory of Computer Graphic Suppliers* identifies about a dozen vendors who are marketing such turnkey systems. During this decade, we shall see many new firms entering this rapidly growing field.

In summary, these new forces and change agents, or the four essential ingredients necessary to make the changes, are moving into the profession in high gear. Indeed, the use of natural and social science findings by planners is proliferating; the establishment of spatial data bases is well under way; the new tools, both hardware and software, are developing rapidly; and finally, the technology transfer programs have started and are proliferating rapidly.

INTEGRATIVE APPROACHES IN SIGHT

To make our future more certain, to increase our land-use options, and the quality and the diversity of our environment, the developing integrative approaches present hope for land-use planners. Numerous research and testing of new approaches is currently underway, with developing integrated land-use planning models showing promise for significantly improving current land-use planning practices. While a comprehensive summary of these integrative models is beyond the scope of this book, a few examples show how land-use planning could become more democratic, could be combined with other models to make the planning process more comprehensive, and how high technology and especially the developing computerized data management systems could make lower level planning more a part of higher level or larger scale planning.

Interactive Land-Use Suitability Models

Computer-aided suitability assessment as the basis of community planning was discussed in the previous chapter. While the assessment of situations and resources is a useful and essential start to all land-use planning, it is evident that there are numerous plausible alternatives available for planners to achieve any one or a whole set of human objectives. Before the development of computer-aided procedures, planners were limited to the formulation of one or a few alternatives at the most, because of the time factors involved in drawing up land-use plans by hand. But planners have been limited not only to searching for a small number of options, but also they have been able to consider only a few factors used in the formulation of the alternatives and a few criteria in evaluating the alternatives. This latter, or evaluation, process is commonly used in planning for the selection of the most preferred alternatives.

With these limitations, it is no surprise that land-use planners buffered themselves against including more than a few scientific findings, as factors or parameters in the planning process, or were discouraged from adopting more powerful evaluation procedures used, for instance, by transportation and economic planners. The availability of spatial data in electronic format and the developing computer graphic hardware and software technology provide land-use planners with powerful interactive computer graphic tools which were not available until very recently. Now they promise to help in the generation of a great number of alternatives or in the search for many more options, and the computer also can aid the application of more sophisticated evaluation procedures to determine the consequences of the various alternatives.

Two planning and plan evaluation procedures illustrate the use of the integrative approach to land-use suitability issues (Fabos and Gross, 1981, pp. 179–185). Both studies described here are suitable for different planning needs. The first procedure was designed to formulate and evaluate long-range, comprehensive land-use plans against a set of land-use suitability criteria. The second was developed for evaluating the social costs and benefits of incremental growth scenarios and the costs of plans which may include such community goals as preservation of agricultural land or protection of critical resources from development.

Procedure for evaluating the suitability of land-use plans is designed to answer the landscape planning question: what are the spatial implications of future land-use and landscape resource policies? More specifically, this procedure was developed to generate two types of land-use plans, the first a projection of alternatives based on existing land-use policies and procedures, and the second a product of what is called here the "landscape sensitive approach." Using these two extreme approaches, planners can produce many alternative plans between the two extremes. The second part of this procedure is an evaluation of the alternative plans by an interactive computer system to ascertain the long-range environmental costs and benefits, but more importantly to see the spatial overlaps and conflicts among the alternatives when evaluated against a set of landscape planning criteria. Because the computer can generate and evaluate the plans quickly, the system is ideal for participatory planning and conflict resolution.

To illustrate this procedure, the plan formulation using the landscape sensitive approach and the evaluation procedure which is applied here to extreme alternatives is described in greater detail. The plan formulation is based on a computer search procedure which is designed to find areas where desired landscape characteristics occur together. Prior to this planning, planners need to have information on what constitutes desired characteristics: that is, the computer must be able to generate what are commonly called landscape assessment maps, which show the spatial distribution and values of the various landscape characteristics such as agricultural productivity, flood hazard probability, or physical development suitability (Figures 37–39). Using these assessed landscape values, the planner can search for development sites to meet a set of desired criteria or characteristics. If, for instance, a planner would like to find out the availability of land suitable for development so that it would not conflict with any of the critical resource and hazard areas, he or she can simply type into the computer terminal the desired values. The computer can quickly generate the acreage of areas (Table 8), and if desired it can produce a map showing the spatial distribution of the land areas which meet the desired criteria. The hypothetical search example (Table 8) shows this procedure for generating alternative plans or scenarios.

Alternative one, which is called run 1 in the computer language, is based on a maximum set of landscape planning constraints for development. Under this scenario, all valuable or critical resources are protected; the known hazardous areas are avoided; and only land suitable for development is sought out by the machine. When applied, the result shows that this hypothetical community would have only 200 acres which meet all these criteria. A planner would have great difficulty convincing a growing community, for instance, that it has only 200 acres to develop. In run 2, the attainment of objectives of wildlife protection and minimization of physical development costs are lowered, resulting in a total of 1,150 acres meeting the specified criteria (Table 8). Since the computer can make a run quickly, the users can generate many alternatives, each showing clearly what the community would need to give up for development if any one of the alternatives were implemented (Fabos, Greene, and Joyner, 1978, Chapter 8). The key attribute of this procedure is that the user or users interact with the computer. Theoretically it is possible to generate plans which express the values or goals of each interest group, or, for that matter, each member of a community. The second part of this procedure assists in resolving the potential conflicts among the alternatives. This interactive computer system has an evaluation

TABLE 8. *Hypothetical Search for Plan Alternatives*

Objective	Criteria Specification Run 1	Criteria Specification Run 2
Agricultural Productivity	BC	BC
Wildlife Productivity	BC	ABC[1]
Water	BC	BC
Forest Productivity	BCD	BCD
Sand and Gravel	BC	BC
Air Pollution	BC	BC
Noise Pollution	BC	BC
Flooding	BC	BC
Physical Development Suitability	AB	ABC[2]
Topoclimate Development Suitability	AB	AB
Visual Development Suitability	ABC	ABC
Acres Available for Development	200	1150

[1] Lower wildlife objective by trading of A quality areas.
[2] Lower physical development cost objective by developing on less suitable class C quality areas.

Where A = High quality special value resource, e.g., agricultural productivity or high probability hazardous areas, e.g., 50 year flood plain or development suitability.
    B = Medium quality values
    C = Low values
    D = Lowest quality values

procedure which is designed to aid that process.

This part of the procedure was developed from the premise that in the participatory planning process, the conflicts are often perceived by the various interest groups as greater than they are found to be on analysis. If this is actually so, there is a need for a method which can quickly show the areas of agreement and the disagreement among the biased alternatives, and can also map out the areas where the overlaps or agreements and disagreements are found. An evaluation showing great disagreements among the alternatives perhaps calls for a need to develop additional alternatives. If, on the other hand, the evaluation shows large areas where agreement exists among alternatives, that result could be the basis for land-use decisions for these areas, while decisions are delayed for those areas where conflict exists.

This evaluation method was applied to extreme alternatives developed for three townships in Massachusetts. Plan one represented the continuation of existing land-use policies while plan two was based on the "landscape sensitive approach." This finding showed that there were no conflicts on 60 percent of the study area (Figure 44). This finding is perhaps the most significant since it supports our hypothesis that the disagreement we found among the extreme alternatives was significantly less than one would expect. Even if one was to find lesser agreements among alternatives in other applications, this procedure could well serve as a mediator to resolve land-use planning conflicts.

Procedure for evaluating social costs and benefits is developed to aid the decision-making process of incremental development at the community level of land-use planning. This is the second procedure to illustrate a potential of interactive, computer-aided land-use suitability models. Current planning literature makes a distinction between two types of evaluation, the benefit-cost and goal achievement approaches (Hill and Tigal, 1972; Miller, 1975). The procedure described here incorporates both these approaches.

The benefit-cost calculations are based on 12 landscape suitability criteria (Table 8 shows the list of landscape parameters). Resource economists calculated the monetary values of each of the landscape parameters listed, and developed a rationale to composite those values which are additive (Sandhu, 1980). For example, the development of an acre of highly productive agricultural land would be a loss of $2,200 to a Massachusetts community in 1976 dollar values. If this tract of land were also on a 50-year or 2 percent probability flood plain, this development would incur an estimated additional $4,800 loss to the community. If these values were to be taken into consideration by a community, this procedure is capable of rank ordering and spatially displaying all homogeneous land units to estimate the costs of development in terms ranging from no or very little social loss to large losses. The interactive computer program can search for any number of acres (100, 500, 1,000, 3,000 and so on) desired for development, in areas where the social loss is the least as estimated by this calculation method (Figure 45).

The second part of this procedure, and perhaps the more interesting, deals with the social costs of community goals. For instance, using a multi-objective approach, a community may wish to find not only those areas where monetary losses are minimized to the community itself, but also sites which spare all their highly productive agricultural land. This multiobjective approach raises two questions: first, can both be attained and second, at what cost?

The application of this evaluation procedure to the town of Greenfield, Massachusetts showed that the preservation of agricultural land would limit the amount of development areas in Greenfield. For example, if Greenfield wished to allocate for development 3,000 acres from the over 10,000 acres

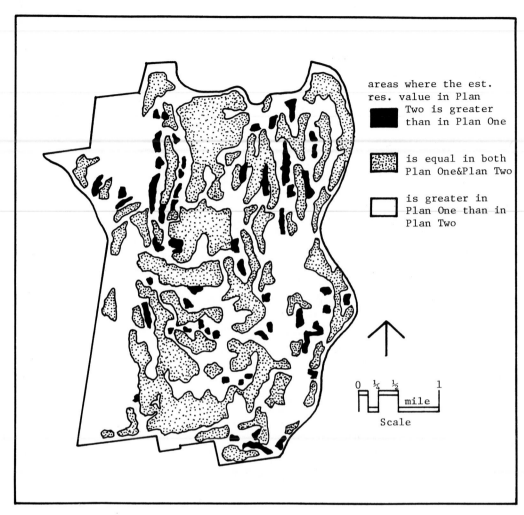

areas where the est.
res. value in Plan
Two is greater
than in Plan One

is equal in both
Plan One&Plan Two

is greater in
Plan One than in
Plan Two

0 ¼ ½   1
                 mile
Scale

FIGURE 44 *Composite economic difference between Plan One and Plan Two for Deerfield, MA. Composite Special Value Resource Economic Difference Between Plan One and Plan Two. The map shown here reflects a spatial subtraction of the resource values in Plan Two from the resource values in Plan One. Where a land use is converted to a use which would incur a greater loss of value in Plan Two than in Plan One, the map shading is the white (about 35 percent of the town). The dotted section depicts where there is no resource value difference between Plan One and Plan Two (about 60 percent of the town). The most dense map shading is where the resource value in Plan Two is greater than in Plan One (about 5 percent of the town).*

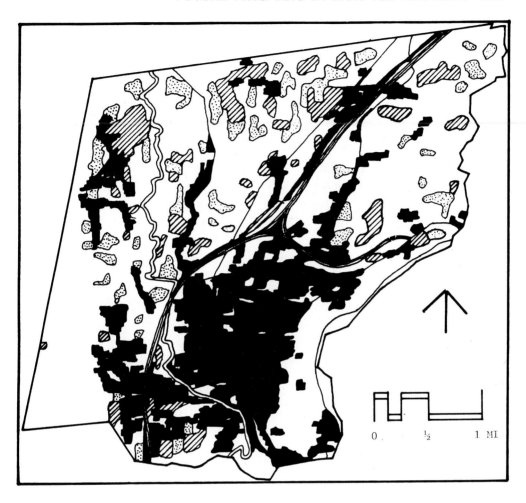

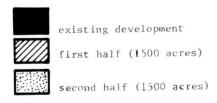

existing development

first half (1500 acres)

second half (1500 acres)

FIGURE 45 *Proposed development on the first 3,000 acres where economic losses for the community are minimized.*

of her undeveloped land, while preserving all her productive agricultural land, the computer found only a total of 2,884 acres (Figure 46).

More specifically, this interactive procedure can be used to estimate the social costs of the attainment of these goals, or any other desired goals. For instance, the preservation of the agricultural land alone would cost the community $3 million in 1976 dollar values, since this measure would force development into areas where social losses would be greater when compared with developing productive agricultural land. Greenfield may still wish to preserve its productive agricultural areas, but aided by this interactive system, the community can make a more informed decision. This type of information could be valuable in the participatory process and would, it is hoped, result in a more intelligent decision.

New Integrative Procedures and Data Base Management Systems

These include some new models which can be integrated with the other system. These models, by taking greater advantage of the computer's capabilities, enable the planner to address increasingly complex planning issues and to develop improved planning and evaluation procedures.

The first group of models which is currently being integrated by planners into the land-use suitability procedures are the Lowry type gravity and potential land-use activity allocation models (Lowry, 1964). The purpose of this family of models is to explain and *predict* the intensity and spatial distribution of land-use activities resulting from various land-use policies.

Recent development suggests that the Lowry type models can constitute the basic component of a comprehensive modeling package which could be used to deal with an entire spectrum of interactions between manmade and natural systems. For this development it would be appropriate to adopt a modular strategy, in which individual environmental subsystems such as air quality, surface water runoff, terrestrial ecosystems, and energy consumption would be added incrementally. Such integrated systems would enable the land-use planner to predict not only changes in the spatial pattern of land-use activities but also the effects of these changes on the environment (Fabos and Gross, 1981; Gross, 1979).

Mathematical programming models are the second group currently being integrated into the system in order to improve it as a planning tool. This type of model, developed and used in various other disciplines such as economics and economic planning, operations research, and industrial management, is being used increasingly to address more difficult but more realistic land-use planning problems.

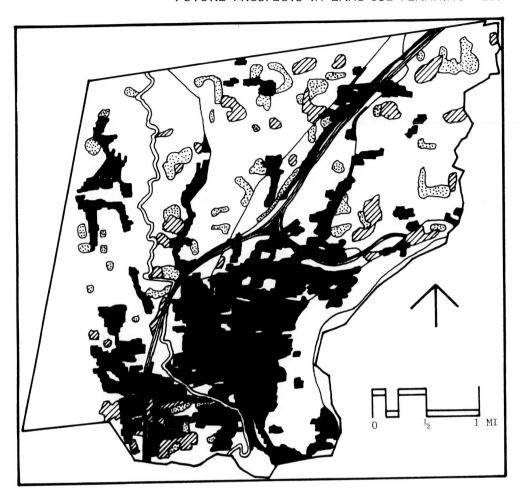

 existing development

first half (1500 acres)

second half (1384 acres)

FIGURE 46 *Proposed development on areas where losses are minimized while agricultural land is preserved.*

The important characteristic of the mathematical programming family of models is its optimization capabilities. In the context of land-use planning this implies that such models can assist in determining the optimal, or preferred, plan among various alternatives. Thus, this type of model, also called a plan-making model, can be regarded as a logically complete synthesis of the three central stages of the planning process: generating alternative plans, predicting their outcome, and choosing the best one (Gross, 1979; and Hopkins, 1975).

Mathematical programming models have been used individually or in combination for various types of planning (Boyce, 1973; Hopkins, 1975 and 1977; and Los, 1975). There are four principal applications in which these models, combined with land resource data systems, have been proposed or tested in land-use planning. The first is where the demand for various land uses is large relative to the available supply of land. The second is where the landscape plan must respond to many, often conflicting, objectives. The third is where the plan has to respond to changes over time. And the fourth is where the suitability of the land to accommodate a given land use is not only a function of the characteristics of the land itself but also its location in relation to other land uses. The location of the land use determines its interactions, or interdependence, with other land uses. These interactions could be culturally related (such as movement of people and flow of goods), or related to a combination of manmade activities and environmental factors such as air pollution dispersion or surface water runoff. Inclusion of any of these factors (supply-demand, multiobjective, time, interdependence) greatly increases the complexity of the landscape planning and evaluation procedure. However, the integration of interactive mathematical programming models will aid in the process by generating plans which consider these factors. The interactive nature of this process must be stressed. Recent developments in mathematical programming indicate that many planning problems are such that the interaction between the decision maker, public participants, and computer is necessary in order to produce improved plans (Smith 1981). Thus the role of the decision maker and the public participants becomes even more critical in the land-use planning procedure.

Data Base Management Systems (DBMS) offer great potential for both handling the massive data base of land-use models discussed above and, perhaps, more importantly, for providing possibilities to integrate the various levels of planning ranging from global to local levels. In Chapters 7–9 the need for hierarchical interaction among the various planning levels was emphasized. It also was pointed out that present practices are falling short in their ability to interpret these levels sufficiently. But now if land-use planners would adopt these powerful computerized data base management systems, which are already being adopted by large corporations and military planners, we would have at last a potential capability for "acting locally while thinking globally." In other words, the new generation of land-use planners will have access to data ranging from national- to local-level information, hence local planners will be able to see the impacts of that level of planning on its larger context and vice versa.

One of the most outstanding developers of the data base management systems is James Martin, a brilliant innovator who has had perhaps the greatest influence on promoting its spread. His most recent book on the subject is entitled *End-User Guide to Data Base* (Martin, 1981). He and his disciples, perhaps more than any other group, are currently spreading its use by offering traveling seminars, publications and professional consulting services in setting up data base management systems for private corporations and public agencies. Forecasters and futurists are also attributing great importance to these developing capabilities during the next two or three decades.

Major computer hardware corporations also are developing their own data base management systems to increase the utility of their computer. For instance, our computer system by Control Data Corporation (CDC), at the University of Massachusetts offers six powerful data base management systems for handling massive data bases for research and management. One of the six systems is called the Query Update. This powerful DBMS is perhaps the most promising among the available systems here for land-use planning. It has a hierarchical framework which enables data entry from national to local level. Equally important, it can be easily updated and it readily permits instant retrieval of data at any level. What land-use planners need to develop is a set of subroutines which can instruct the computers to display the desired information, plans, and evaluation in spatial, graphic forms. Before this book is printed, there are likely to be powerful operational data base management systems capable of spatial display of land-use plans.

In conclusion, the development of interactive computer technology and data base management systems is becoming increasingly useful for land-use planning. Procedures have been developed which have significantly expanded our previous capabilities to assess individual characteristics of the land into the phases of plan formulation and evaluation. These procedures not only incorporate pertinent scientific knowledge into the planning process, but can also be used to generate alternative development plans and to predict the consequences of these various alternatives against a set of land-use and landscape planning criteria. This process is becoming increasingly interactive, allowing the planners, decision makers and other interested parties to participate more immediately and closely with the computerized system, combining human judgment with scientific knowledge. One of the most important

utilities of such interactive systems is in identifying and mediating the conflicts which are major obstacles to orderly land-use planning.

Secondly, this section describes the adaptation and incorporation of a
new generation of dynamic computerized land-use models which not only
evaluate direct consequences of alternative development plans but can also
deal with the more complex issue of interaction among various land uses
in the final determination of wise and humane actions. Both the irony and
the beauty of these startling developments is that scientific technology is
being used not to replace the human mind, but to free the person to use
uniquely human judgments more intelligently in the planning process.

Finally, the development of the new data base management systems
promises to provide planners with a far-reaching and expanded capability.
Indeed we are on the brink of changes which can improve land-use planning
significantly.

THE FUTURE IN CAPSULE

The current revolution in science and technology which has already
created unprecedented land-use changes is also providing land-use planners
with a better understanding of human impacts and with significantly
improved planning tools to deal with this revolution. If planners are able to
utilize the newly acquired knowledge and developing tools, we have a chance
not only to minimize uncertainties resulting from land-use changes but we
should also be able to increase the options which are made available to
people by land-use planning. Land-use planners have an opportunity to
increase the diversity and the quality of our living environment.

If the prospects presented in this chapter are plausible then we can
broaden planning from planning for a single or limited number of issues to
dealing with most or all of the seven issues already discussed (Chapter 1); we
can better integrate the findings of natural and social sciences and the effects
of technology, and hence we can better influence the direction and the form
of the cultural landscape (Chapter 5); we can better integrate the three
broad ranges of planning levels (Chapters 7–9); and finally we can improve
the planning process by making it more responsive to public values and
needs — indeed we can make land-use planning a democratic exercise, a true
learning process for all concerned.

These changes, however, will require a great deal of retraining for practicing land-use planners and will alter the training of future planners. Ever more
people from other and perhaps new disciplines will find the opportunity to
work as land-use planners, as the increasing complexity and changing direc-

tion require a different kind of knowledge and approach. The visionary planner may also return, not as a form giver to large urban areas, but instead to influence decisions the way that successful political leaders or intellectuals with great charisma and wisdom do.

Barney, Gerald D., 1980, The Global 2000 Report to the President of the U.S., Pergamon Press, New York.

Berlyne, D. F., 1963, "Complexity and Incongruity Variables as Determinants of Exploratory Choice and Evaluative Ratings," Canadian Journal of Psychology, XXII, No. 3, p. 274-89.

Birch, Eugenie Ladner, 1980 "Radburn and the American Planning Movement: The Persistance of an Idea," Journal of the American Planning Association, v. 46, no. 4, October.

Bishop, Bruce A., 1972, "An Approach to Evaluating Environmental Social and Economic Factors in Water Resource Planning," Water Resource Bulletin, v. 8, no. 4, August.

Black, J. Thomas, 1978, "Germantown, Maryland: A New Approach to Community Development" in Management Control of Growth, v. IV, Schmidman, Frank, Silverman, Jane A., Young, Rufus C. Jr., eds., The Urban Land Institute, Washington, D.C.

Bosselman, Fred and Callies, David, 1971, The Quiet Revolution in Land Use Control, Council on Environmental Quality, Washington, D.C.

Boyce, David E., Day, Norman D., and McDonald, Chris, 1970, Metropolitan Plan Making: An Analysis of Experience with the Preparation and Evaluation of Alternative Land Use and Transportation Plan, Monograph Series Number Four, Regional Science Research Institute, Philadelphia, PA.

Boyce, D. E., Farhi, A., and Weischedel, R., 1973, "Optimal network problem: a branch-and-bound algorithm," Environment and Planning 5, 519-533.

Boyer, Christine M., 1981, "National Land Use Policy: Instrument and Product of Economic Cycle," de Neufville, Judith, ed., The Land Use Policy Debate in the United States, Plenum Press, New York.

Branch, Melville, 1972, "Reducing Air Pollution through Land Use and Public Facility Planning," in Land Use and the Environment: An Anthology of Reading, Office of Air Programs, E.P.A.

Bryson, Reid A., 1971, "All Other Factors Being Constant...," Theories of Global Climatic Change in Man's Impact on Environment, Detwyler, Thomas R., ed., McGraw Hill Book Company, New York.

Burchell, Robert W., and Listokin, David, 1975, The Environmental Impact Handbook, Center for Urban Policy Research, Rutgers University, New Brunswick, NJ.

Burchell, Robert W. and Sternlieb, George, 1978, Planning Theory in the 1980's: A Search for Future Directions, Center for Urban Policy Research, Rutgers University, New Brunswick, NJ.

Burke, Albert E., 1956, "Influence of Man Upon Nature — The Russian View: A Case Study," in Man's Role in Changing the Face of the Earth, Thomas, William C., Jr., ed., The University of Chicago Press, Chicago, IL.

Cain, Stanley A., 1968, General Ecology, Human Ecology and Conservation, Department of Conservation, Resource Planning and Conservation, University of Michigan.

Centre National d'Etudes Spatiales, 1978, The Earth Observation Test System, G.N.E.S., Paris.

Cerchione, Angela, Rahenkamp, John, Yannacone, Jr., Victor, John, 1981, "Impact Zoning: Alternative to Exclusion in the Suburbs," The Land Use Awakening, Freilich, Robert H., and Jtuhler, A.B.A. Press.

Clawson, Marion, 1971, Suburban Land Conversion in the United States, The Johns Hopkins University Press, Baltimore and London.

Clawson, Marion and Held, Burnell, 1957, The Federal Lands: Their Use and Management, University of Nebraska Press, Lincoln.

Coates, Donald R., 1973, Environmental Geomorphology and Landscape Conservation, Dowden, Hutchinson, and Ross, Inc., Stroudsburg, PA.

Commoner, Barry, 1966, Science and Survival, Viking Press, New York.

————, 1971, The Closing Circle: Nature, Man and Technology, Knopf, New York.

Control Data Corporation, 1980, Cyber 70 Computer Systems, Query Update Version 3 Reference Manual, DMS-170, Graduate Research Center, University of Massachusetts, Amherst, MA.

Council on Environmental Quality, 1972, Environmental Quality, U.S. Government Printing Office, Washington, DC.

Daily Hampshire Gazette, Northampton, Massachusetts, January 19, 1982.

Dansereau, Pierre, 1966, "Ecological Impact and Human Ecology" in Future Environments of North America, Darling, F. F. and Milton, J. P., eds., Natural History Press, Garden City, NY.

Datapro Research Corporation, 1979, "All About Graphic Display Devices" in Graphic I/O, Datapro Research Corporation, Delran, NJ.

Davidoff, Paul, 1978, "The Redistributive Function in Planning: Creating Greater Equity Among Citizens of Communities," in Planning Theory in the 1980's, Burchell and Sternlieb, eds., Center for Urban Policy Research, Rutgers University, New Brunswick, NJ.

Day, H., 1967, "Evaluation of Subjective Complexity, Pleasingness and Interestingness for a Series of Random Polygons Varying in Complexity," Perception and Psychophysics, II., p. 281-86.

Dee, Norbert, and others, 1973, "An Environmental Evaluation System for Water Resource Planning," Water Resources Research, v. 9, no. 3.

Delafons, John, 1969, Land Use Controls in the United States, The MIT Press, Cambridge, MA and London, England. Second edition.

Department of Interior, Bureau of Outdoor Recreation, 1968, New England Heritage: The Connecticut River National Recreation Area Study, U.S. Government Printing Office, Washington, DC.

Detwyler, Thomas R., 1971, Man's Impact on Environment, McGraw-Hill Book Company, NY.

Doxiadis, Constantinos, A., 1966, Between Dystopia and Utopia, Trinity College Press, Hartford, CT.

Eckbo, Dean, Austin, and Williams, Inc., 1970, State of Hawaii Land Use Districts and Regulations Review, Summary report prepared for the State of Hawaii, Land Use Commission by the Consulting Office of Eckbo, Dean, Austin, and Williams, San Francisco, CA.

Eidgenössische Oberaufsicht Über Die Forstpolizei, 1971, Schweizerische Bundeskanzlei.

Einsweiler, Robert C., and others, 1975, "Comparative Description of Selected Municipal Growth Guidance System" in Management and Control of Growth, Scott, Randall W., Brower, David J., and Miner, Dallas D., eds., v. II, The Urban Land Institute, Washington, DC.

Eliot, Charles W., 1902, Landscape Architect, Houghton-Mifflin, Boston, MA.

Emanuel, Manuel, 1975, "Ramapo's Managed Growth Program: After Five Years Experiment," in Management and Control of Growth, Scott, Randall, Brower, David, and Miner, Dallas D., eds., v. III, The Urban Land Institute, Washington, DC.

England, H. N., 1973, "Problems of Irrigated Areas," in Environmental Geomorphology and Landscape Conservation, Coates, Donald R., ed., Dowden, Hutchinson and Ross, Inc., Stoudsburg, PA.

Fabos, Julius Gy., 1973, Model for Landscape Resource Assessment, Research Bulletin No. 602, Agricultural Experiment Station, University of Massachusetts, Amherst, MA.

———, 1979, Planning the Total Landscape: A Guide to Intelligent Land Use, Westview Press, Boulder, CO.

Fabos, Julius Gy., and Caswell, Stephanie J., 1977, Composite Landscape Assessment: Assessment Procedures for Special Resources, Hazards and Development Suitability; Part II of the Metropolitan Landscape Planning Model (METLAND), Research Bulletin 637, Massachusetts Agricultural Experiment Station, College of Food and Natural Resources.

Fabos, Julius Gy., Greene, Christopher M., and Joyner, Spencer A., Jr., 1978, The METLAND Landscape Planning Process: Composite Landscape Assessment, Alternative Plan Formulation and Evaluation: Part 3 of the Metropolitan Landscape Planning Model, Research Bulletin No. 653, Massachusetts Agricultural Experiment Station, Amherst, MA.

Fabos, Julius Gy., and Gross, Meir, 1981, "The Interactive Computer System: A Tool for Participatory Landscape Planning," in The Proceedings of Educational Sessions on Regional Landscape Planning, American Society of Landscape Architects Annual Meeting.

Fabos, Julius Gy., and Joyner, Spencer A., Jr., 1980, "Landscape Plan Formulation and Evaluation," in Landscape Planning no. 7.

Fabos, Julius Gy., Milde, Gordon T., Weinmayr, V. Michael, 1968, Frederick Law Olmsted: Founder of Landscape Architecture in America, University of Massachusetts Press, Amherst, MA.

Fein, Albert, 1972, Frederick Law Olmsted and the American Environmental Tradition, George Braziller, NY.

Ferris, Kimball H., and Fabos, Julius Gy., 1974, The Utility of Computers in Landscape Planning, Research Bulletin No. 617, Massachusetts Agricultural Experiment Station, Amherst, MA.

Flawn, Peter T., 1970, Environmental Geology: Conservation, Land Use Planning and Resource Management, Harper and Row, Publishers, NY.

Ford, Kristina, 1979, Remote Sensing for Planners, Center for Urban Policy Research, Rutgers University, New Brunswick, NJ.

Fuller, Buckminster R., 1973, Earth, Inc., Anchor Press/Doubleday, Garden City, NJ.

Galbraith, John Kenneth, 1958, The Affluent Society, A Mentor Book, The New American Library, Inc., New York and Toronto.

Gero, John S. and Dudnik, Eliot E., 1978, "Uncertainty and the Design of Building Subsystems — A Dynamic Programming Approach," in Building and Environment, v. 13, Program Press Limited, Great Britain.

Gero, J. A., and Oguntade, O. O., 1978, "Fuzzy Set Evaluators," in Architecture, Preliminary Studies, Dept. Arch. Sci., University of Sydney, Computer Report, CR 29.

Giedion, Sigfried, 1967, Space, Time and Architecture, Harvard University Press, Cambridge, MA. Fifth Edition.

Glidden, William T., Jr., and High, Colin, 1980, The New England Energy Atlas, Resource Policy Center, Thayer School of Engineering, Dartmouth College, Hanover, NH.

Glorig, A., 1975, "Audiometric Testing in Industry," in Handbook of Noise Control, Harris, C. M., ed., McGraw-Hill, NY.

Goodman, Robert, 1971, After the Planners, Simon and Schuster, NY.

Gottman, J., 1961, Megalopolis: The Urbanized Northeastern Seaboard of the United States, MIT Press, Cambridge, MA.

Gross, Meir, 1979, The Impact of Transportation and Land Use Policies on Urban Air Quality, Ph.D. Dissertation, University of Pennsylvania, Philadelphia, PA.

Haar, Charles M., 1971, Land-Use Planning: A Casebook on the Use, Misuse, and Reuse of Urban Land, Little Brown and Company, Boston and Toronto.

Harrison, J. F. C., 1969, Robert Owen and the Owenites in Britain and America, Routledge and Kegan Paul.

Harvard University Laboratory for Computer Graphics, 1980, Directory of Computer Graphic Supplies: Hardware, Software, Systems and Services, Harvard University Laboratory for Computer Graphics, Cambridge, MA.

Harwood, Coirbon Crewes, 1977, Using Land to Save Energy, Ballinger Publishing Company, Cambridge, MA.

Heady, Earl O., 1976, "The Agriculture of the U.S." in Scientific American, September.

Healy, Robert G., 1976, Land Use and the States, The Johns Hopkins University Press, Baltimore and London.

Healy, Robert G., and Rosenberg, John S., 1979, Land Use and the States, Second Edition. The Johns Hopkins University Press, Baltimore and London.

Heller, Alfred, 1971, The California Tomorrow Plan, William Kaufmann, Inc., Los Altos, CA.

Hendrix, William G., 1977, An Ecological Sub-model for the Metropolitan Landscape

Planning Model (METLAND), Ph.D. Dissertation, Department of Forestry and Wild-life, University of Massachusetts, Amherst, MA.

Hill, Morris and Tigal, Tzamin, 1972, "Multidimensional Evaluation of Regional Plans Serving Multiple Objectives," Papers and Proceedings of the Regional Science Association, v. 29, p. 139-165.

Hiller, Frederick S., and Lieberman, Gerard J., 1968, Introduction to Operations Research, Holden-Day, Inc., San Francisco, Cambridge, London and Amsterdam.

Hjelmfelt, Allen T., and Cassidy, John J., 1975, Hydrology for Engineers and Planners, Iowa State University Press, Ames, IA.

Hopkins, L. D., 1975, "Optimum seeking methods for design of suburban land use plans." Ph.D. Dissertation, Department of City Planning, University of Pennsylvania, Philadelphia, PA.

———, 1977, "Land use plan design-quadratic assignment and central-facility models," Environment and Planning A 9, p. 625-642.

Hor, J., 1972, Air Pollution, Part I, Marcel Decker, Inc., NY.

Hoskins, W. G., 1955, The Making of the English Landscape, Penguin Books, Harmonds-worth, England.

Howard, Ebenezer, 1965, Second Printing, Garden Cities of To-Morrow, The MIT Press, Cambridge, MA and London, England.

Ise, John, 1967, Our National Park Policy: A Critical History, The Johns Hopkins Press, Baltimore, MD.

ISETAP (Intergovernmental Science, Engineering and Technology Advisory Panel), 1978, State and Local Government Perspectives on a Landsat Information System, Office of Science and Technology Policy, Executive Office of the President.

Iverson, Wayne D., 1975, "Assessing Landscape Resources: A Proposed Model," in Landscape Assessment: Values, Perceptions and Resources, Zube, E., Brush, R., and Fabos, J., eds., Dowden, Hutchinson, and Ross, Inc., Stroudsburg, PA.

Jacobs, Jane, 1961, The Death and Life of Great American Cities, Random House, NY.

Kates, B. R., and Snead, R., 1969, The Human Ecology of Coastal Flood Hazard in Mega-lopolis, University of Chicago, Department of Geography, Research Paper 115, Chicago, IL.

Kemmerer, Donald L., and Jones, Clyde C., 1959, American Economic History, McGraw-Hill Book Company, NY.

Kendig, Lane, Connor, Susan, Byrd, Cranston, and Heyman, Judy, 1980, Performance Zoning, APA Planners Press, Washington, DC.

Krueckeberg, Donald A., 1983, The American Planner: Biographies and Recollections, Methuen, New York and London.

Le Corbusier, 1959, L'Urbanisme des Trois Etablissements Humains, Editions de Minuit, Paris.

———, 1967, La Villa Radieuse, Translated to English by Pamela Knight under the title, The Radiant City, The Orion Press, NY.

Legget, Robert F., 1973, Cities and Geology, McGraw-Hill Book Company, NY.

Leopold, Luna B., 1956, "Land Use and Sediment Yield," in Man's Role in Changing the Face of the Earth, Thomas, William L., ed., The University of Chicago Press, Chicago, IL.

———, 1971, Procedure for Evaluating Environmental Impact, Geological Survey Circular 645, U.S. Geological Survey, Washington, DC.

————, 1974, Water: A Primer, W. H. Freeman and Company, San Francisco, CA.

Lewis, Philip, 1964, "Quality Corridors in Wisconsin," Landscape Architecture Quarterly, January.

Lindsay, John, 1969, The City, W. W. Norton and Company, Inc., NY.

Locke, John, 1690, The Second Treatise on Government.

Logan, Carolyn J., 1982, Winning the Land Use Game, Praeger Publishers, NY.

Los., M., 1975, "Simultaneous optimization of land use and transportation: A synthesis of the quadratic assignment and optimal network problem," Publication 31, Centre de Recherche sur les Transports, Montreal, Quebec.

Lowry, Ira S., 1964, A Model of the Metropolis, The Rand Corporation, RM-4035-RC, Santa Monica, CA.

Lyons, Stephen, 1982, "Census Shows City Grows Younger," Daily Hampshire Gazette, Northampton, MA, January 19.

Mabbutt, J. A., 1968, "Review of Concepts of Land Classification," in Land Evaluation, Stewart, G. A., ed., MacMillan and Company, Australia.

MacConnell, William P., and Garvin, L. E., 1956, "Cover Mapping a State from Aerial Photography," Photogrametric Engineering, September, v. 22, p. 702–707.

McHarg, Ian L., 1969, Design with Nature, The Natural History Press, Garden City, NY.

MacKaye, Benton, 1962 (reprinted), The New Exploration: A Philosophy of Regional Planning, 1928; University of Illinois Press, Urbana, IL.

Maddox, John, 1972, The Doomsday Syndrome: An Attack on Pessimism, McGraw-Hill Book Company, NY.

Mandelker, Daniel R., 1963, Managing Our Urban Environment: Case, Text and Problems, The Bobbs-Merrill Company, Inc.

Marble, D. F. (ed.), 1980, Computer Software for Spatial Data Handling, v. 1, 2 and 3, International Geographical Union, Commission of Geographical Data Sensing and Processing, Ottawa, Ontario, Canada.

Margalef, R., 1971, Perspectives in Ecological Theory, as quoted in Fundamentals of Ecology, Odum, F. P., Third Edition, Saunders, Philadelphia, PA.

Marsh, George Perkins, 1967, (Second Printing), Man and Nature, The Belknap Press of Harvard University Press, Cambridge, MA., originally published in 1864.

Martin, James, 1981, End-User Guide to Data Base, Prentice-Hall, NJ.

Meadows, Donella H., and others, 1972, The Limits to Growth, The New American Library Inc., NY.

Mesarovic, Mihajlo and Pestel, Eduard, 1974, Mankind at the Turning Point, E. P. Dutton and Co., Inc., Reader's Digest Press, NY.

Miller, Donald A., 1975, The Landsat Story, National Aeronautics and Space Administration, Washington, DC.

Moss, Elaine (ed.), 1977, Land Use Controls in the United States, The Dial Press/James Wade, NY.

Mumford, Lewis, 1961, The City in History: Its Origins, Its Transformations and Its Prospects, Harcourt, Brace and World, Inc., NY.

Munsinger, H., and Kessen, W., 1964, "Uncertainty, Structure and Preference," Psychological Monographs: General and Applied, v. 78.

Murray, Bruce H., and Nieman, Bernard J., 1975, "A Landscape Assessment Optimization Procedure for Electric-Energy Corridor Selection," *in* Landscape Assessment: Values, Perceptions and Resources, Dowden, Hutchinson and Ross, Inc., Stroudsburg, PA.

Naisbitt, John, 1982, Megatrends: Ten New Directions Transforming Our Lives, Warner Books, NY.

NASA Module U-2, 1980, The Landsat Story, National Aeronautics and Space Administration, Washington, DC.

National Capital Planning Commission, 1961, A Plan for the Year of 2000, The National Capital Planning Commission, Washington, DC.

Newton, Norman, 1971, The Design of the Land: The Development of Landscape Architecture, The Belknap Press of Harvard University Press, Cambridge, MA.

North Atlantic Regional Water Resources Study Coordinating Committee, 1970, North Atlantic Regional Water Resources Study, Printed by the NAR Water Resources Study Coordinating Committee, U.S. Corps of Engineers, NY.

Novak, Michael, 1970, The Experience of Nothingness, Harper and Row, Publishers, New York, Evanston and London.

Observer in Progressive Architecture, 1965, "Heart of Gruen's Fresno Plan," Progressive Architecture, January.

Odum, Eugene P., 1963, Ecology, Holt, Rinehart and Winston, Inc., NY.

———, 1969, "The Strategy of Eco-system Development," Science 164, April.

Parker, D. C., and Wolff, M. F., 1973, "Remote Sensing," *in* The Surveillant Science: Remote Sensing of the Environment, Holtz, R. K., ed., Houghton Mifflin, Boston, MA.

Patterson, William T., 1979, Land Use Planning: Techniques of Implementation, Van Nostrand Reinhold Company, New York, London, Melbourne.

Perraton, Jean and Baxter, Richard, 1974, Models, Evaluations and Information Systems for Planners, Land Use and Built Form Studies Conference Proceedings No. 1, MTP Construction.

Pettyjohn, W. A., 1972, Water Quality in a Stressed Environment, Burgess Publishing Company, Minneapolis, MN.

Plattner, Rolf M., 1975, "The Regional Landscape Concept for the Basel Region," *in* Landscape Assessment, Zube, Ervin H., Brush, Robert and Fabos, Julius Gy., eds., Dowden, Hutchinson and Ross, Inc., Stroudsburg, PA.

Public Land Law Review Commission, 1970, One Third of the Nation's Land, U.S. Government Printing Office, Washington, DC.

Putman, S. H., 1975, "Urban Land Use and Transportation Models: A State-of-the-Art Summary," Transportation Research, v. 9.

Reiner, Edward N., 1975, "Traditional Zoning: Precursor to Managed Growth," *in* Management and Control of Growth, Scott, Randall W., Brower, David J., and Miner Dallas D., eds., v. I, The Urban Land Institute, Washington, DC.

Research Planning and Design Associates, Inc., 1970, North Atlantic Water Resources Study: Visual and Cultural Environment, North Atlantic Regional Water Resources Study Coordinating Committee, NY, November.

Richman, Hershell J., and Kendig, Lane H., 1981, "Transfer Development Rights—A

Pragmatic View," *in* The Land Use Awakening, Freilich, Robert H., and Stuhler, Eric O., eds., A.B.A. Press.

Sandhu, Harjinder S., 1980, Valuation of Social Benefits of Planned Development: An Application of Metropolitan Landscape Planning Model, Ph.D. Dissertation, Department of Food and Resource Economics, University of Massachusetts, Amherst, MA.

Scheffey, Andrew J. W., 1969, Conservation Commissions in Massachusetts, The Conservation Foundation, Washington, DC.

Schon, Donald A., 1967, Technology and Change: The Impact of Invention and Innovation on American Social Economic Development, Dell Publishing Co., NY.

Service de Presse et d'Information, 1965, France: Town and Environmental Planning, Ambassade de France, NY.

Sheils, Merrill, 1980, "And Man Created The Chip," Newsweek, June 30.

Sleeper, David, July 1980, "Technological Choices Can Be Deceptive," Conservation Foundation Letter, Conservation Foundation, Washington, DC.

Smardon, Richard, 1975, "Assessing Visual-Cultural Values of Inland Wetlands in Massachusetts," *in* Landscape Assessment: Values, Perceptions and Resources, Zube, E., Brush, R., and Fabos, J., eds., Dowden, Hutchinson and Ross, Inc., Stroudsburg, PA.

Smith, James M., 1981, Wicked Design Problems and Interactive Optimization. Presented in the IEEE-Systems, Man and Cybernetics Conference, Atlanta, GA, October 24–27, Unpublished.

Soleri, Paolo, 1971, Visionary Cities: The Arcology of Paolo Soleri, Praeger, NY.

Stalley, Marshall, 1972, Patrick Geddes: Spokesman for Man and the Environment, Rutgers University Press, New Brunswick, NJ.

Starr, Roger, 1976, "Making New York Smaller," The New York Times Magazine, Section 6, November 14.

Stein, Clarence S., 1966, Towards New Towns for America, The MIT Press, Cambridge, MA.

Stern, A. C., 1973, Fundamentals of Air Pollution, Academic Press, NY.

The Stockholm Regional Planning Office, 1968, The 1966 Outline Regional Plan of the Stockholm Area, The Stockholm Regional Planning Office, Sergels, Jorg 12, Stockholm.

Strong, Ann Louise, 1971, Planned Urban Environments, The Johns Hopkins Press, Baltimore and London.

——, 1977, Needed: National Land Use Goals and Standards, Dennis O'Harrow Memorial Lecture, American Society of Planning Officials Conference, April 26.

——, 1981, "Land as a Public Good: An Idea Whose Time has Come Again," *in* The Land Use Policy Debate in the United States, de Neufville, Judith I., ed., Plenum Press, NY.

Terwillinger, R. R., 1963, "Pattern Complexity and Affective Arousal," Perceptual and Motor Skills, XVII, p. 387-395.

Thomas, William A., 1972, Indicators of Environmental Quality, Plenum Press, New York and London.

Toffler, Alvin, 1980, The Third Wave, William Morrow and Company, Inc., NY.

Toll, Seymour I., 1969, Zoned America, Grossman Publishers, NY.

U.S.D.A. Forest Service, 1973, National Forest Landscape Management, v. 1-4, U.S. Government Printing Office, Washington, DC.

U.S. Department of Agriculture, 1973, "Restoring Surface-minded Land" *in* Environmental Geomorphology and Landscape Conservation, Coates, Donald, ed., Dowden, Hutchinson and Ross, Inc., Stroudsburg, PA.

U.S. Department of Agriculture, Soil Conservation Service, 1966, Guide to Making Appraisals of Potential for Outdoor Recreational Developments, Staff Publication, S.C.S., USDA, Hyattsville, MD, June.

U.S. Department of Agriculture, Soil Conservation Service, 1969, Soil Suitability Guide for Land Use Planning in Maine, Miscellaneous Publication No. 667, Agricultural Experiment Station, 77 p., Orono, ME, September.

U.S. Environmental Protection Agency, 1972, Report to the President and Congress on Noise, U.S. Government Printing Office, Washington, DC, February.

U.S.D.I. Bureau of Land Management, 1980, Visual Resource Management Program, U.S. Government Printing Office, Washington, DC.

Vitz, P. C., 1966, "Preference for Different Amounts of Visual Complexity," Behavioral Science, XI, p. 105–114.

Warner, Sam B., 1962, Streetcar Suburbs, Harvard University Press and MIT Press, Cambridge, MA.

Water Resources Council, 1968, The Nation's Water Resources: Summary Report, U.S. Government Printing Office, Washington, DC.

Wohlwill, J. F., 1968, "Amount of Stimulus Exploration and Preference as Differential Function of Stimulus Complexity," Perception Psychophysics, v. 4, n. 5.

Zeidler, Frank P., 1968, A Plan for Wisconsin, State of Wisconsin, Department of Resource Development, Madison, WI.

Zube, Ervin H., and Carlozzi, Carl A., 1966, An Inventory and Interpretation — Selected Resources of the Island of Nantucket, Publication n. 4, Cooperative Extension Service, University of Massachusetts, Amherst, MA.

Zube, Ervin, Brush, Robert, and Fabos, Julius Gy., 1975, Landscape Assessment, Dowden, Hutchinson and Ross, Stroudsburg, PA.

Zube, Ervin H., Sill, James L., and Taylor, Jonathan G., 1982, "Landscape Perception, Application and Theory, Landscape Journal.

Zumbrun, Ronald A., and Hookano, Thomas E., 1981, "No Growth and Related Land Use Legal Problems: An Overview," *in* The Land Use Awakening, Freilich, Robert H., and Stuhler, Eric O., eds., A.B.A. Press.

acid rain, 24
Adirondack Park, 66-67
advocacy planning, 96
agricultural productivity, 168
air pollution, 17, 27, 29, 38, 39, 48
Alaska, 3, 5, 15
Alaskan pipeline, 14
Amazon River (Brazil), 14
Amelia Island, Fla., 163
American Society of Landscape
    Architects (ASLA), 194
American Society of Planning Officials,
    98
Arno River (Italy), 48
articulators, 62, 66, 68, 106
assessment techniques, 168
Australia, 111
automobile, 47, 52, 54, 85

Baltimore metropolitan region, 137
Barney, Gerald, 13, 14, 43
Baroque period, 72, 76, 94, 103, 128,
    152
Basel, Switzerland, 130, 133
Bath, England, 11
Belgium, 143
Beos River (India), 109
Birch, Eugene Ladner, 154
Birkenhead Park (Liverpool, Eng.), 65, 66
Blake, Peter, 68
Bolsheviks, 72
Boston, Mass., 8, 12, 16, 46, 47, 68, 95,
    128-130, 135, 139, 140, 158
Boston Redevelopment Authority, 96
Broadacre City, 93-94
Budapest, Hungary, 52
Bureau of Land Management, 148
Burke, Albert E., 60

California, 5, 46, 68, 172
California Tomorrow, 119
Canada, 111

Carter administration, 5
Catholic Church, 72
census information, 189
Centre National d'Etudes Spatiales
    (CNES), 54, 192
Chicago, Ill., 46, 95
China, 14
Chrysler Corporation, 3, 5, 8
climate, 41
Club of Rome, 108, 125
Coca-Cola, 72
Colorado River, 14
Columbia, Md., 154
Columbia River (Oregon), 61
Commoner, Barry, 107
community planning, 153
complexity, 82
composite assessment, 163
comprehensive planning, 102
computer hardware, 192
computer software, 193
Computer Software for Spatial Data
    Handling, 193
computers, 54-56, 192, 197
Conference on State Parks, 68
Connecticut, 64
Connecticut River, 14, 109
Connecticut River National Recreation
    Area Study, 144-145
conservation commissions, 62
contextual changes, 45
Control Data Corporation (CDC), 205
conversion, 12, 36
corporate model, 74, 77
critical areas, 176
corporate organization, xxii
cultural landscape, 78, 79

Dansereau, Pierre, 22
Data Base Management Systems (DBMS),
    204-206
data manipulation, 6

Davis, Calif., 158
decentralization, 52, 188
Delaware, 143
Des Plaines River (Illinois), 162
desertification, 109
destruction of vegetation, 33
development control devices, 174
— annexation, 174
— capital programming, 175
— cost/benefit, 175
— geographic restraints, 175
— official mapping, 175
— public improvements, 175
— subdivision regulations, 174
— tax and fee systems, 174
development suitability, 140
disciplinary planners, 92, 97, 149
diversity, 82
Doxiadis, Constantinos A., 9, 10

ecological diversity, 82
ecological explosions, 33
ecumenopolis, 10
Eliot, Charles, 6, 16, 49, 50, 130, 140,
    161
Emerald Necklace, 129
enclosure acts, 72
energy resources, 186
English Channel, 110
environmental concerns, 176
environmental movement, 96
Essex County, N.J., 68
exclusionary zoning ordinances, 173

Fein, Albert, 95
Filarete, Antonio, 72, 91
flooding, 17, 38, 48
Florence, Italy, 48
forest protection law (Switzerland), 115
Forester, Jay, 108
France, 114
Fresno, Calif., 157
Fuller, Buckminster, 107

garden city, 93, 154
Geddes, Patrick, 21, 22
General Motors, 72
geographic information systems, 161
Georgetown, Guyana, 47
Germantown, Md., 180
Giedion, Sigfried, 11
Goodman, Robert, 96
Gottman, Jean, 79
Grant, Ulysses, S., 144
green revolution, 109

Greenfield, Mass., 199, 202
Gros Morne National Park (Canada), 144
growth management, 172
growth policy, 11, 172

Harvard Newsletter on Computer
    Graphics, 193
Harvard School of City Planning, 98
Harvard School of Landscape
    Architecture, 98
Harvard University Laboratory for
    Computer Graphics, 194
Haussmann, Georges-Eugène, 128, 130
Hawaii, 118, 119, 121
hazardous areas, 176
hazardous waste, 4
Hendrix, William G., 34, 35
high technology, xxii, 172, 191
Hoover Dam, 46
Howard, Ebenezer, 12, 93
Howard Johnson's, 85
Hubbard, Henry Vincent, 98
Hungary, 84
Hunt, Richard Morris, 95

illegal immigration, 3, 5
immigration, 4
impact assessment, 17, 168
imperialism, 72
incremental changes, 44
India, 109
Industrial Revolution, 9, 72, 114, 115,
    152
industries, declining, 4
industries, sunset, 4
information network, xxii, 76
integrated circuits, 54, 56
Interactive Landscape Planning Program
    (ILPP), 194
international organizations, 107, 108
Israel, 64, 111
Italian Renaissance, 71, 72, 91, 94, 152

Jackson, John Brinckerhoff (J.B.), 49
Jacobs, Jane, xx, 96
Japan, 48
Johnson administration, 6, 69
Johnson, Lady Bird, 69

Kendig, Lane, 180

Lake County, Ill., 180
Landsat, 54, 194
landscape approach, 152, 196
landscape hazards, 38

— natural phenomena, 38
   — earthquakes, 38
   — flooding, 38
   — landslides, 38
— human action, 38, 39
   — air pollution, 38, 39
   — noise pollution, 38, 39
landscape planners, 137, 163, 165, 172
landscape planning, 139, 140, 161, 162
landscape resources, 36
   — biomass production, 37
   — ground water, 37
   — productivity for agriculture, 37
   — surface water, 37
landscape suitability, 162
land-use allocation models, 135, 139, 202
land-use change, 11, 12
land-use characteristics, 39
land-use control, xix, xx, 120, 172–174
land-use density, 11
land-use fit, 10
land-use issues
   — common characteristics, 7
      — generation of uncertainty, 7
      — problem or opportunity, 7
      — supply or demand, 8
      — systematic/conceptual, 8
   — cumulative effects, 5
   — significance of, 5
   — types of, 9
      — decline-related, 13
      — impact-related, 16
      — new-growth related, 9
      — preservation, 15
      — reclamation, 14
      — resource exploitation/utilization,
         14
   — stable population planning, 12
land-use maps, 50
land-use suitability, 196
Le Corbusier, 94
Le Notre, 59, 97
legal devices, xix, 95
Leningrad, 84
Leonardo da Vinci, 48
Leopold, Luna B., 22
level two planning, 125, 127, 140, 146
Lewis, Phil, 117
Lincoln, Abraham, 99
Locke, John, 64, 65, 70, 76
Logue, Edward, 96
London, 6, 29, 72, 97
Louis XIV (Sun King), 59
Love Canal (Niagara Falls, N.Y.), 3, 7, 18,
   63

Lowry type gravity models, 202

MacKaye, Benton, 22, 106
Maddox, John, 107, 109
Marble, Duane, 161
Mariposa Big Tree Groves, 4, 66, 95
Marsh, George Perkins, 21, 24
Martin, James, 205
Massachusetts Open Space Commission,
   116
mathematical modeling, 29, 30, 56, 101,
   125, 135, 202, 204
Mather, Stephen, 68
McHarg, Ian, 137, 139, 161
Meadows, Donella H., 108
Mediterranean Sea, 110
megalopolis, 79
Mercator, 48
metropolitan expansion, 127
Michigan, 85
Millers River (Massachusetts), 14
mission planning, 102
Modesto, Calif., 173
monocultural landscape, 78, 79, 84
multiobjective planning, 102, 130, 146,
   148
multispectral scanner, 54, 56, 192
Mumford, Lewis, 11, 59

Naisbitt, John, 74, 75
Nantucket Island Study, 168
National Aeronautics and Space
   Administration (NASA), 191, 194
National Environmental Policy Act, 168
national land use planning, 111
National Park Service, 66, 68
national parks, 5, 15, 66
natural landscape, 78, 79
natural resource base, 12
natural science, 19, 43
Navajo Indians, 60
Netherlands, 143
networking, 75
New England River Basin Commission,
   139
New Federalism, 74, 77
New Harmony, Ind., 93
New York (City), 11, 95, 133, 172
New York (State), 66
Niagara Falls, 110
noise pollution, 17, 30, 31, 38, 39
North Atlantic Regional Water Resource
   Planning Study, 121, 122, 125, 139
Novak, Michael, 61, 62

Odum, Eugene, 22, 34, 82, 83
off-shore drilling, 44
Olmsted, Frederick Law, Sr., 15, 65, 66,
    95, 98, 125, 128, 130, 161, 162
ordinance survey, 112, 125
organizational capabilities, 58, 70
organizations, 62, 70
Outdoor Recreation Resource Review
    Commission, 68
Owen, Robert, 93

Paris, 46, 114, 128
participatory planning process, 198
Paxton, Joseph, 65
performance zoning, 180
Peter the Great, 60
physical development suitability, 41
physical planners, xx, 152, 158
Pittsburgh, Pa., 29
Plan for the Year 2000, 133, 149
plan formulation, 197
planner
  as catalyst, 58, 96
  as facilitator, 181
  as mediator, xxi, 62, 96
  as synthesizer, xxi, 96
planning hierarchy, 103, 149
  – level one, 103
    – framework planning, 103
    – planning for planning, 103
    – policy planning, 103
    – strategy planning, 103
  – level two, 103
    – meso-scale planning, 103
    – structure planning, 103
  – level three, 103
    – community level planning, 103
    – local level planning, 103
  – level four, 103–104
    – design, 103–104
planning norms or principles, 83
planning process, 100, 101, 149, 198
planning, types of, 102, 149
  – single purpose or mission, 102
  – comprehensive or place, 102
pluralistic society, 71, 77
police power, 69, 120
policy-level planning, 105, 116
population growth, 108
Portland, Ore., 158
preservation movement, 4, 66, 95, 110
preservation
  of cultural heritage, 15
  of nature, 15, 95
preventive planning, 17

private values, 58, 63
professional planners, 92, 98, 149
Public Land Law Review Commission,
    148
public recreation landscapes, 68
public values, 58, 63
Punjab state (India), 109
pyramid model, 71, 77

Quabbin Reservoir (Massachusetts), 6, 14,
    46
quantitative methods, 161
Quincy Market (Boston), 158

Radburn, N.J., 153, 154
Ramapo, N.Y., 179, 180
Ravi River (India), 109
reclamation, 16
Regional Plan Association, 133
Regional Planning Federation of
    Stockholm, 132
remote sensing, 37, 50, 54, 56
resource exploitation, 109
resource utilization, 109, 143
Revere Beach, Mass., 16
Rhode Island, 143
Riverside, Ill., 161, 162
Rockefeller, Nelson A., 94
Rome, Italy, 97
rural areas, development pressures on,
    127
rural planning, 143, 148
Russia, 60, 61

Sacramento, Calif., 176
San Francisco, Calif., 8, 95
Satluy River (India), 109
scenic misfits, 69
Schon, Donald, 74, 75
Schumacher, E. F., 53
scientific knowledge, xxi, 18, 19, 20,
    172, 186, 206
Sforzinda, 72, 91
Sierra Club, 62
Sixtus V, Pope, 97
Sleeper, David, 50, 52, 193
social and environmental land-use
    controls, 176
  – administrative processing and delay,
      177
  – impact zoning, 178
  – land banking, 178
  – numerical restraints, 178
  – one stop permit, 178
  – public acquisition, 177

— transfer of development rights, 177
social concerns, 173
social costs and benefits, 199
societal values, 18, 58, 59
soil erosion, 17
Soleri, Paolo, 94
sources of values, 59
    — articulators, 62
    — environmental/cultural, 60
    — public surveys, 63
    — science and technology, 61
spatial data, 56
Starr, Roger, 53
Staten Island, N.Y., 137
Stockholm, 95, 130
stresses on plant and animal life, human-
    caused, 33
Strong, Ann Louise, 111
subdivision regulations, 5, 174
surveying, 48, 49, 50, 112, 125
Sweden, 110, 132
Switzerland, 111, 114–116

technological change, xxi, 18, 186
technology, 18, 44, 47, 194, 195, 206
3M Company, 74, 82
Three-Mile Island, Pa., 59
threshold, 6
Toffler, Alvin, 52
transporation engineers/planners, 54, 56,
    101, 135
Trustees of Public Reservations, 16, 68
turnkey systems, 195
Twain, Mark, 63

United Nations, 106, 107, 109
United States, 111
U.S. Corps of Engineers, 61, 122
United States Department of Agriculture,
    66, 190
United States Department of the Interior,
    66
U.S. Forest Service, 148
United States Geologic Survey, 50, 191
U.S. Soil Conservation Service, 165, 190,
    191

U.S.S.R., 60, 61
University of Massachusetts, 194, 205
University of Sydney, 193
utopias, 93

value-free planning, 63
Vermont, 120, 121, 127
Vermont Environmental Control Act,
    120
Versailles, 97
Victor Gruen Associates, 157
Vinal Haven Island, Me., 8

waste disposal, 12
water, 25
water pollution, 5, 25–27
water quality, 58
water resource issues, 139, 186
water resource planners/engineers, 54, 56,
    102
Water Resources Council, 121
water shortage, 4
wetlands, 8, 15
White House Conference on Natural
    Beauty, 69
Wisconsin Department of Resource
    Development, 117
Wisconsin Heritage Trail Proposal, 117,
    121, 125
World Trade Center (New York City), 47
Wren, Christopher, 97
Wright, Frank Lloyd, 93, 94

Yale University, 194
Yellowstone National Park, 66, 113, 144
Yosemite Valley, 4, 5, 66, 68, 95

zero population growth, 10, 12, 13
zoning, 11, 91, 95, 172, 173
zoning variations, 173
    — bonus and incentive, 174
    — conditional zoning, 173–174
    — contract zoning, 174
    — flexible zoning, 174
    — performance standard, 174
    — planned unit development, 174
Zube, Ervin, 191

DATE DUE

DEC 1 2 '88			
MAY 2 1992			
DE 20 '93			
GAYLORD			PRINTED IN U.S.A.